DELIA'S
HOW TO COOK

This book is published to accompany the television series
Delia's How To Cook
which was produced for BBC Birmingham by Spire Films Ltd
Series Producer: David Willcock
Directors: John Silver and Philip Bonham Carter
Executive Producers for the BBC: Rod Natkiel and Stephanie Silk

Published by BBC Worldwide Ltd,
Woodlands, 80 Wood Lane, London W12 0TT

First published in 1998
Reprinted 1998 (four times)

ISBN 0 563 38430 1

Edited for BBC Worldwide Ltd by New Crane Publishing Ltd
Printed and bound in Great Britain by Butler & Tanner Ltd, Frome, Somerset
Colour separation by Radstock Reproductions Ltd, Midsomer Norton
Jacket printed by Lawrence Allen Ltd, Weston-super-Mare

DELIA'S
HOW TO COOK

BOOK ONE

Photographs by Miki Duisterhof

For the young cooks of Britain

Book and TV Series Coordinator: Sarah Randell
Production Editor: Eirwen Oxley Green
Editorial Consultant: Susan Fleming
Photography Assistant: Karen Hatch

I would very much like to thank all the people who have helped me produce *How To Cook*. Thank you to Flo Bayley, Miki Duisterhof, Karen Hatch and Caroline Field for design and photography. To Celia Stone, Mary Cox and Pauline Curran for help with testing recipes. To Annabel Elliott, Helen Benfield and Annie Rigg at New Crane Publishing for extra help on testing, Susan Fleming for help on editorial and Linda Dwyer for equipment. To my brilliant television crew, David Willcock, John Silver, Philip Bonham Carter, Vivien Broome, Simon Wilson, Mal Maguire, Andy Bates, Andy Young, Pauline Harlow and Georgina Faulkener. Thanks also to Sara Raeburn, Lesley Drummond and Jeanette Farrier for make-up, hair and clothes.

A huge thank you to my life-saving team of Melanie Grocott, Amanda Clark, Sarah Randell and Eirwen Oxley Green.

Finally, my thanks to Carrs Flour Mills in Cumbria for all their help with the flour section, to the Martelli family in Lari for their help with the pasta section, and to Alberto Camisa, who has helped me throughout the past 30 years.

Conversion tables

All these are approximate conversions, which have either been rounded up or down. In a few recipes it has been necessary to modify them very slightly. Never mix metric and imperial measures in one recipe, stick to one system or the other. All spoon measurements used throughout this book are level unless specified otherwise; all butter is salted unless specified otherwise.

Weights

½ oz	10 g
¾	20
1	25
1½	40
2	50
2½	60
3	75
4	110
4½	125
5	150
6	175
7	200
8	225
9	250
10	275
12	350
1 lb	450
1 lb 8 oz	700
2	900
3	1.35 kg

Volume

2 fl oz	55 ml
3	75
5 (¼ pint)	150
10 (½ pint)	275
1 pint	570
1¼	725
1¾	1 litre
2	1.2
2½	1.5
4	2.25

Dimensions

⅛ inch	3 mm
¼	5 mm
½	1 cm
¾	2
1	2.5
1¼	3
1½	4
1¾	4.5
2	5
2½	6
3	7.5
3½	9
4	10
5	13
5¼	13.5
6	15
6½	16
7	18
7½	19
8	20
9	23
9½	24
10	25.5
11	28
12	30

Oven temperatures

Gas mark	°F	°C
1	275°F	140°C
2	300	150
3	325	170
4	350	180
5	375	190
6	400	200
7	425	220
8	450	230
9	475	240

Contents

My little corner of Suffolk, and (previous page) the writer's tree house at the end of the garden, where How To Cook was written

Introduction

It's now almost 30 years since I first started writing recipes, and 25 since I first started cooking on television. As you would expect, things have changed quite dramatically during this, the last quarter of the 20th century.

In food terms we have moved on into what I would call an era of plenty. Absolutely everything we could possibly want is available. We can now walk into any large supermarket and literally shop for ingredients around the world. We can eat whatever we want when we want. If we don't want to cook at all we can buy ready-prepared meals, vegetables and salads. Every high street has any number of food-to-go outlets – fast food, takeaways, home deliveries, as well as all kinds of restaurants. On top of all that we can simply 'graze' all day on snack foods, crisps and chocolate bars.

It could be said that we're immensely privileged in being so spoilt for choice. Therefore, where on earth does *How To Cook* fit in? Well, it's my personal belief that the opposite could be true – that we may be in danger of losing something very precious, and that is a reverence for simple, natural ingredients and the joy and pleasure they can bring to everyday life. We are not talking about spending masses of time in the kitchen, either. We need to be reminded that, after a hard day, a perfectly made moist, fluffy omelette – which is so easy to make – is not only more satisfying but quicker than the average ready-meal.

One thing we have to come to terms with is that food, perhaps more than any other subject, lends itself to pretentiousness, and the beauty of simplicity can so easily be eclipsed. Yes, we all want to experience the 'highs' of eating on special occasions and celebrations, of eating a meal in a beautiful restaurant cooked by a great chef, but the sensual pleasure of eating belongs to everyday life as well, and it's not always to be found in the vast amounts of mass-produced, easy-cook fast foods that we're subtly persuaded to eat.

I am hoping to achieve two things in *How To Cook*: one is to reintroduce people to the pleasure of basic, staple ingredients, and the second is to provide a first-time cookbook, something that will be a good grounding in the simple basics and provide a springboard for a lifetime of learning – not just in how to cook but in how to experience the sheer joy and pleasure of eating good food every single day.

Delia Smith

1
All about eggs

If you want to learn how to cook, start with eggs. That's my advice. Eggs are, after all, a powerful symbol of something new happening – new life, a new beginning. But there is another reason. Somehow eggs have become an equally negative symbol. When someone says, 'Oh, I can't even boil an egg,' what they are actually saying is, 'I can't cook anything at all.'

It's the amount of air in the pocket at the wide end of the egg – which in turn depends on the egg's freshness – that will determine how best to use the egg

The inner membrane within the shell begins as a taut, stretched skin; with age, however – and the inclusion of more air – this skin slackens

That's why anyone wanting to make a start should begin by understanding eggs. Yes – even how to boil them. By cracking egg cookery (sorry about the pun) and simply knowing how to boil, poach, scramble, make an omelette and so on, you're going to give your cooking confidence a kick-start and ensure you will never go hungry. You'll also be able to offer your friends and loved ones a very quick but pleasurable meal. But that's not all: eggs are a supremely important ingredient in the kitchen, serving the cook in any number of ways. They can thicken soups and sauces, set liquids and baked dishes, they can provide a glorious airy foam to lighten textures and will also, quite miraculously, emulsify oils and butter into a rich smoothness.

What we have to do first and foremost, though, before we even begin cooking, is to try and understand what eggs are and how they work.

Understanding eggs

A hen's egg is, quite simply, a work of art, a masterpiece of design and construction with, it has to be said, brilliant packaging! It is extremely nutritious, filled with life-giving protein, vitamins and minerals. It has a delicate yet tough outer shell which, while providing protection for the growing life inside, is at the same time porous, meaning the air can penetrate and allow the growing chick to breathe.

It's the amount of air inside the egg that the cook needs to be concerned with. If you look at the photograph above left, you'll see the construction of the egg includes a space for the air to collect at the wide end, and it's the amount of air in this space that determines the age and quality of the egg and how best to cook it. In newly laid eggs, the air pocket is hardly there, but as the days or weeks pass, more air gets in and the air pocket grows; at the same time, the moisture content of the egg begins to evaporate. All this affects the composition of the egg, so if you want to cook it perfectly it is vital to determine how old the egg is. Now look at the photograph at the top of the opposite page and see what the egg looks like when it is broken out. What you start off with, on the left, is an egg at its freshest, with a rounded, plump yolk that sits up proudly. The white has a thicker, gelatinous layer that clings all around the yolk, and a thinner outer layer. After a week, on the right, the yolk is flatter and the two separate textures of white are not quite so visible.

Now all is revealed! You can see very clearly why you may have had problems in the past and why an egg needs to be fresh if you want to fry or poach it, because what you will get is a lovely, neat, rounded shape. Alas, a stale egg will spread itself more thinly and what you will end up with if you are frying it is a very thin pancake with a yellow centre. If you put it into water to poach, it would probably disintegrate, with the yolk and white parting company. Separating eggs is yet another hazard if the eggs are too old, because initially the yolk is held inside a fairly tough, transparent membrane, but this weakens with age and so breaks more easily.

So far, so good. But we haven't quite cracked it yet because, just to confuse matters, a very fresh egg isn't always best. Why? Because we have another factor to take into consideration. If we get back to the presence of air, what you will see from the photograph below left is that inside the shell is an inner membrane, a sort of safety net that would have protected the chick if the egg had been fertilised. When the egg is fresh, this is like a taut, stretched skin; then, as more air penetrates the egg, this skin slackens. This explains why, if you hard-boil a really fresh egg, peeling off both the shell and the skin is absolute torture. But if the egg is a few days' or even a week old, the skin will become looser and the egg will peel like a dream.

What all this means is, yes, you can cook perfect eggs every time, as long as you know how old they are.

How to tell how old an egg is

How to tell how old a raw egg is while it is safely tucked away in its shell could seem a bit tricky, but not so. Remember the air pocket? There is a simple test that tells you exactly how much air there is. All you do is place the egg in a tumbler of cold water: if it sinks to a completely horizontal position, it is very fresh; if it tilts up slightly or to a semi-horizontal position, it could be up to a week old; if it floats into a vertical position, then it is stale. The only reason this test would not work is if the egg had a hairline crack, which would allow more air in. That said, 99 per cent of the time the cook can do this simple test and know precisely how the egg will behave. To sum up, the simple guidelines are as follows:

1   For poaching and frying, always use eggs as spanking fresh as you possibly can.

Below, left to right: a very fresh egg will sit horizontally when placed in a glass of water; one that lies semi-horizontally is generally up to a week old; and one that floats in a vertical position is stale

2 For separating egg yolks from whites, use eggs that are as fresh as possible, though up to a week old is fine.

3 For peeled hard-boiled eggs, about a week old or up to a fortnight is okay.

4 For scrambled eggs and omelettes, the fresher the eggs the better, but up to two weeks is fine.

5 For baked dishes, such as quiches or for home baking and so on, eggs more than two weeks old can be used.

6 In my opinion, all eggs should be used within two weeks if at all possible. An extra week is okay, but three weeks is the maximum keeping time.

How to buy and store eggs

Number one on the list here (unless you happen to know the hens) is to buy your eggs from a supplier who has a large turnover. Boxes now (and sometimes the eggs themselves) carry a 'best before' date. What you should know is that this date, provided the egg box is stamped with the lion mark, corresponds precisely to 21 days after laying (not packing), so you are, therefore, able to work out just how fresh your eggs are.

Although it is now being recommended that eggs should be stored in the refrigerator, I never do. The reason for this is that for most cooking purposes, eggs are better used at room temperature. If I kept them in the fridge I would have the hassle of removing them half an hour or so before using them. A cool room or larder is just as good, but if, however, you think your kitchen or store-cupboard is too warm and want to store them in the fridge, you'll need to try and remember to let your eggs come to room temperature before you use them. My answer to the storage problem is to buy eggs in small quantities so I never have to keep them too long anyway.

The very best way to store eggs is to keep them in their own closed, lidded boxes. Because the shells are porous, eggs can absorb the flavours and aromas of other strong foods, so close the boxes and keep them fairly isolated, particularly if you're storing them in the fridge.

There is, however, one glorious exception to this rule. My dear friend and great chef Simon Hopkinson once came to stay in our home. He brought some new-laid eggs in a lidded box, which also contained a fresh black truffle. He arrived on Maundy Thursday, and on Easter Sunday made some soft scrambled eggs, which by now had absorbed all the fragrance and flavour of the truffle. Served with thin shavings of the truffle sprinkled over, I have to say they were the very best Easter eggs I have ever tasted!

What about cholesterol?

Eggs, I am very happy to report, are out of the firing line on the cholesterol front. It is now believed that the real culprits on this one are saturated fat and partially hydrogenated fat, which eggs, thankfully, are low in. There is more good news, too: even if you are on a low-fat diet, eating up to seven eggs a week is okay. Hooray!

The porosity of eggs' shells isn't always a bad thing: here a fresh black truffle is kept with the eggs, which in turn absorb its flavour and fragrance, adding an unexpected dimension to the finished dish

How safe are they?

Poor old eggs; just as they recover from one slur, along comes another. Eggs, as we know, can harbour a bacterium called salmonella. Cases of food poisoning, or even death, from eating eggs are isolated but do occur. Therefore, the only way we can be absolutely certain of not being affected is by only eating eggs that are well cooked, with hard yolks and no trace of softness or runny yolk at all. Ugh!

What we all need to do is consider this very seriously and be individually responsible for making our own decisions. Life, in the end, is full of risks. The only way I can be absolutely sure I won't be involved in a car accident (and statistically this is a far greater risk than eating eggs) is to never ride in a car. But I am personally willing to take that risk – as I am when I eat a soft-boiled egg. So it's a personal decision. As a general practice, though, it is not advisable to serve these to vulnerable groups, such as very young children, pregnant women, the elderly or anyone weakened by serious illness.

Some general egg information

1 Is there any difference between brown and white shells?
   None whatsoever. The colour of the shell is determined by the breed of the hen that laid it. Aesthetically speaking, white denotes a sophisticated kind of purity, while brown is full of rural wholesomeness.

2 Size. Having gone through a couple of decades of numbering eggs, we are now back to size descriptions, which are as follows: very large, large, medium and small. Please note that in this book the eggs used in all recipes are large.

3 The eggs now available on a large scale commercially are as follows: free-range means the hens have continuous daytime access to open-air runs that contain vegetation; barn or perchery means the hens are enclosed but have floor space covered in straw or other materials. Eggs labelled organic are produced in the same way as free-range, but, in this case, the hens' habitat is land that has been certified as free from herbicides and pesticides (as is the land on which their feed has been grown). The remaining eggs are all produced in battery units.

4 There are, of course, other types of eggs. I have included recipes and timings for commercially produced eggs (ie, hens' and quails' eggs), but if you have access to and want to cook other types of eggs (goose, turkey, duck), then allow extra time for size. If you are baking, the best way to measure is by comparing the eggs you are using weight for weight with hens' eggs to give you a guideline. Gulls' eggs are pretty rare and exclusive, but they should be boiled like quails' eggs, peeled, and are traditionally served with a sprinkling of celery salt.

How do you boil eggs?

A pinprick made in the rounded end of an egg will allow steam to escape while it boils, thus avoiding cracking

The answer to this is carefully. Even the simplest of cooking tasks demands a degree of care and attention. But in the end all it involves is first knowing the right way to proceed and then happily being able to boil perfect eggs for the rest of your life without even having to think about it. What we need to do first of all, though, is memorise a few very important rules.

1 Don't ever boil eggs that have come straight from the refrigerator, because very cold eggs plunged straight into hot water are likely to crack.
2 Always use a kitchen timer. Trying to guess the timing or even remembering to look at your watch can be hazardous.
3 Remember the air pocket? During the boiling, pressure can build up and cause cracking. A simple way to deal with this is to make a pinprick in the rounded end of the shell, as left, which will allow the steam to escape.
4 Always use a small saucepan. Eggs with too much space to career about and crash into one another while they cook are, again, likely to crack.
5 Never have the water fast-boiling; a gentle simmer is all they need.
6 Never overboil eggs (you won't if you have a timer). This is the cardinal sin because the yolks will turn black and the texture will be like rubber.
7 If the eggs are very fresh (less than four days old), allow an extra 30 seconds on each timing.

Soft-boiled eggs – method 1

Obviously every single one of us has a personal preference as to precisely how we like our eggs cooked. Over the years I have found a method that is both simple and reliable, and the various timings set out here seem to accommodate all tastes. First of all have a small saucepan filled with enough simmering water to cover the eggs by about ½ inch (1 cm). Then quickly but gently lower the eggs into the water, one at a time, using a tablespoon. Now switch a timer on and give the eggs exactly 1 minute's simmering time. Then remove the pan from the heat, put a lid on it and set the timer again, giving the following timings:

Don't boil eggs in too large a saucepan: the less room they have to move about in the simmering water, the less likely they are to crack

> 6 minutes will produce a soft, fairly liquid yolk and a white that is just set but still quite wobbly
>
> 7 minutes will produce a firmer, more creamy yolk with a white that is completely set

Soft-boiled eggs – method 2

I have found this alternative method also works extremely well. This time you place the eggs in the saucepan, cover them with cold water by about ½ inch (1 cm), place them on a high heat and, as soon as they reach boiling point, reduce the heat to a gentle simmer and give the following timings:

> 3 minutes if you like a really soft-boiled egg
>
> 4 minutes for a white that is just set and a yolk that is creamy
>
> 5 minutes for a white and yolk perfectly set, with only a little bit of squidgy in the centre

Hard-boiled eggs

Some people hate soft-boiled eggs and like to eat them straight from the shell, hard-boiled. All well and good, but if you want to use hard-boiled eggs in a recipe and have to peel them, this can be extremely tricky if the eggs are too fresh. The number one rule, therefore, is to use eggs that are at least five days old from their packing date. The method is as follows: place the eggs in a saucepan and add enough cold water to cover them by about ½ inch (1 cm). Bring the water up to simmering point, put a timer on for 6 minutes if you like a bit of squidgy in the centre, 7 minutes if you want them cooked through. Then, the most important part is to cool them rapidly under cold running water. Let the cold tap run over them for about 1 minute, then leave them in cold water till they're cool enough to handle – about 2 minutes. Once you've mastered the art of boiling eggs you can serve them in a variety of ways, and one of my favourites is in a curry, as in the recipe on the following page.

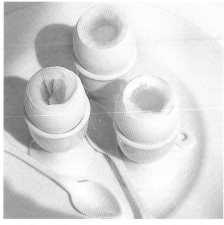

Clockwise from top: a very soft-boiled egg has a liquid yolk and a white that is still wobbly; a soft-boiled egg has a creamy yolk and a white that is just set; in a medium-boiled egg, both the white and yolk are set

Peeling hard-boiled eggs

The best way to do this is to first tap the eggs all over to crack the shells, then hold each egg under a slow trickle of running water as you peel the shell off, starting at the wide end. The water will flush off any bits of shell that cling on. Then back they go into cold water until completely cold. If you don't cool the eggs rapidly they will go on cooking and become overcooked, then you get the black-ring problem.

Quails' eggs

Quails' eggs for boiling should, again, not be too fresh, and these are best cooked by lowering them into simmering water for 5 minutes. Then cool them rapidly and peel them as above.

The distinctive colouring of quails' eggs makes them a beautiful alternative to hens' eggs, and they're just as simple to cook

Egg and Lentil Curry with Coconut and Pickled Lime

This is one of my very favourite store-cupboard recipes. If you always keep a stock of spices and lentils handy and a pack of creamed coconut stashed away in the fridge, you can whip this one up in no time at all. It also happens to be inexpensive and highly suitable for vegetarians.

Serves 2
4 large eggs
3 oz (75 g) green lentils
3 oz (75 g) creamed coconut
1 rounded teaspoon lime pickle
juice and grated zest ½ fresh lime
1 large onion
1 small red chilli (preferably bird eye)
2 fat cloves garlic
1 inch (2.5 cm) piece root ginger
3 cardamom pods, crushed
1 teaspoon cumin seeds
1 teaspoon fennel seeds
1 dessertspoon coriander seeds
2 tablespoons groundnut or other flavourless oil
1 rounded teaspoon turmeric powder
1 teaspoon fenugreek powder
salt

To serve:
5 fl oz (150 ml) rice, cooked (see page 200)
a little extra lime pickle

You will also need a medium frying pan with a lid.

Start off by getting everything prepared and ready to go. First peel the onion, cut it in half and then into thin slices. Next deseed and finely chop the chilli, peel and chop the garlic as well, then measure out the lime pickle and chop that quite finely. Now peel and grate the ginger – you need a good heaped teaspoonful. The creamed coconut should be shredded with a sharp knife and placed in a heatproof measuring jug. At this stage put the kettle on to boil.

Now place the frying pan over a medium heat and, as soon as it gets hot, measure the whole spices (cardamom, cumin, fennel and coriander) straight into it. What they need to do now is dry-roast, and this will take 2-3 minutes. Shake the pan from time to time to toss them around a bit and, as soon as they start to jump, remove them from the heat and tip them straight into a mortar.

Now place the pan back over the heat, turn it up high and add the oil. As soon as it is really hot, add the onions and, keeping the heat highish, let them sizzle and brown and become quite dark at the edges, which will take about 4 minutes. After that, turn the heat back down to medium and add the chilli, ginger, garlic and lime pickle, along with the turmeric and fenugreek. Now crush the roasted spices finely with a pestle, add these to the pan as well, then stir everything together. See to the coconut next: all you need to do here is pour boiling water up to the 1 pint (570 ml) level in the jug containing the coconut, then whisk it all together.

Now stir the lentils in to join the rest of the ingredients, add the grated lime zest and the coconut liquid, stir again and, as soon as it reaches simmering point, turn the heat down. Put the lid on and let the mixture simmer as gently as possible for 45 minutes, stirring it now and then (don't add any salt at this stage).

About 10 minutes before the end of the cooking time, place the eggs in a saucepan of cold water, bring them up to a gentle simmer and time them for 6-7 minutes, depending on how you like them. When they're ready, let the cold tap run on them until they're cool enough to handle. When the sauce is ready, season it well with salt and add the lime juice. Now peel the eggs under cold running water, slice them in half and pop them on top of the sauce, giving everything a couple more minutes' cooking with the lid on. Serve the egg curry with rice, some more lime pickle and perhaps some mango chutney to add a touch of sweetness.

Open-Faced Egg, Chive and Spring Onion Sandwiches

My next-door neighbour Dot always keeps me well supplied with delightful home-made grainy brown rolls. As supper at home on Sundays is almost always a snack meal, we love to eat them warmed, halved and buttered, then spread with one of these yummy egg toppings.

Serves 2
3 small bread rolls, warmed, halved and buttered

For the topping:
3 large eggs, hard-boiled as described on page 17
1 rounded tablespoon fresh snipped chives
4 spring onions, very finely chopped (including most of the green as well)
½ teaspoon butter
1 tablespoon mayonnaise
salt and freshly milled black pepper

To garnish:
1 box fresh cress

As soon as the eggs are cool enough, peel them, discard the shells and place the eggs in a bowl with the rest of the topping ingredients. Now take a large fork and mash like mad until the eggs are thoroughly blended with the rest of the ingredients. Then pile it on to the rolls and sprinkle each one with the cress before serving.

For an egg and bacon topping
Grill six rashers of streaky bacon until crispy, chop four of these into small pieces and add these to the egg mixture (minus the spring onions and chives). Top the rolls with this and garnish with the other two rashers, as in the photograph, right.

For an anchovy and shallot topping
Add six drained and finely chopped anchovies to the egg mixture (minus the spring onions and chives), and add a very finely chopped shallot and a dessertspoon of finely chopped parsley. Pile this on to the rolls and garnish each one with another anchovy fillet wrapped around a black olive, as in the photograph, right.

Opposite, clockwise from top: Open-Faced Egg and Bacon Sandwich; Open-Faced Egg, Chive and Spring Onion Sandwich; Open-Faced Egg, Anchovy and Shallot Sandwich

How to
poach eggs

The key to a well-poached egg is to keep the water at a bare simmer throughout the cooking

Before we begin to talk about how to poach eggs, I think it is appropriate to clear up a few myths and mysteries that surround the whole subject. I met someone recently who said they had been to six leading kitchen shops and not one of them sold an egg poacher. My reaction was, 'What a great leap for mankind.' Egg poachers not only came out of the ark, but they never did the job anyway. What they did was to steam and toughen the eggs, not poach them – and did you ever try to clean one afterwards? The dried-on toughened egg white was always hell to remove.

Then came professional chefs, who passed their exams only if they created a strong whirlpool of simmering water using a whisk and then performed a sort of culinary cabaret act by swirling the poached egg back to its original shell shape. At home we can now relax, throw out our egg poachers and poach eggs simply and easily for four or even six people. The method below is not at all frightening or hazardous, but bear in mind that for successful poaching the eggs have to be really fresh (see page 13). You will need:

    4-6 large, very fresh eggs (under four days old)
    a suitably sized frying pan (according to the number of eggs)
    boiling water from the kettle
    a draining spoon and a folded wodge of kitchen paper

Place the frying pan over a gentle heat and add enough boiling water from the kettle to fill it to 1 inch (2.5 cm). Keep the heat gentle, and very quickly you will see the merest trace of tiny bubbles beginning to form over the base of the pan (above left). Now carefully break the eggs, one at a time, into the water and let them barely simmer, without covering, for just 1 minute. A timer is essential here because you cannot guess how long 1 minute is.

After that, remove the pan from the heat and let the eggs sit calmly and happily in the hot water, this time setting the timer for 10 minutes. This timing will give perfect results for a beautifully translucent, perfectly set white and a soft, creamy yolk. Now remove each egg by lifting it out of the water with the draining spoon and then letting the spoon rest for a few seconds on the kitchen paper, which will absorb the excess water. As you remove the eggs, serve them straight away. (For the toast, see page 83.)

There are now dozens of ways that you can use your new-found skill in egg poaching. For someone on a strict budget (or not), baked beans on toast topped with a poached egg (or two) is one of the world's cheapest but greatest nutritional combinations. If you're not on a budget, wholefood shops sell baked beans that taste almost home-made, in a sauce that does not contain any sugar. More expensive but very good.

Another fast but comforting supper dish is to poach smoked haddock in a frying pan of water. Drain well and keep it warm while you slip a couple of eggs into the same water to poach. Serve the haddock with the eggs on top and buttered chunks of brown Irish soda bread.

Warm Spinach Salad with Poached Eggs, Frizzled Kabanos and Bacon

This is actually a delightful combination of sausage, egg, bacon and mushrooms. Sorry about the chips – but you won't miss them because the salad leaves, crisp, crunchy croutons and the sherry dressing make this much more special.

Serves 2 as a light lunch or supper
4 oz (110 g) ready-washed young leaf
spinach, plus a few sprigs of watercress
4 large, very fresh eggs
3 oz (75 g) smoked kabanos sausage
4 rashers smoked back bacon or
8 streaky rashers
1 small onion, peeled
2 oz (50 g) open mushrooms
2 slices white bread, crusts removed
3 tablespoons extra virgin olive oil
3 tablespoons dry sherry
1½ tablespoons sherry vinegar
freshly milled black pepper

You need to begin this by preparing everything in advance. The onion, mushrooms and bacon rashers need to be finely chopped into ¼ inch (5 mm) pieces; the sausage should also be chopped, but fractionally larger. Then cut the bread into ¼ inch (5 mm) cubes (croutons) and arrange the spinach and watercress on two large plates, removing any large stalky bits first.

Now poach the eggs as described on the previous pages, and, while they're sitting in the hot water, take a medium-sized, heavy-based frying pan and heat 1 tablespoon of the oil in it until it's very hot and gives off a fine haze. Then fry the croutons, tossing them around in the pan, until they're crisp and golden brown – about 1-2 minutes – and after that remove them to drain on some kitchen paper.

Now add the rest of the oil to the pan and, again, let it get really hot before adding the prepared bacon, onion and sausage. Toss them all around, keeping the heat high to make everything brown and toasted at the edges.

After 4 minutes, add the chopped mushrooms and toss these around, still keeping the heat high, for about 2 minutes. Finally, season with freshly milled black pepper, add the sherry and sherry vinegar to the pan, giving it a few seconds to bubble and reduce. Then transfer the eggs to sit on top of the spinach and watercress, pour the contents of the pan over everything and sprinkle the croutons on top.

Eggs Benedict

Can there be anybody who doesn't drool at the thought of Eggs Benedict? Soft, squidgy, lightly toasted bread, really crisp bacon and perfectly poached eggs which, when the yolks burst, drift into a cloud of buttery hollandaise sauce. It's certainly one of the world's great recipes. Although originally it was meant to be served at breakfast or brunch (and still can be), I think it makes a great first course, particularly in winter. A light version of this can be made using Foaming Hollandaise on page 71, which also has the advantage that it can be prepared ahead.

Poach the eggs as described on page 22. When the pancetta is cooked, keep it on a warm plate while you lightly toast the split muffins on both sides. Now butter the muffins and place them on the baking tray, then top each half with two slices of pancetta. Put a poached egg on top of each muffin half and then spoon over the hollandaise, covering the egg (there should be a little over 1 tablespoon of sauce for each egg).

Now flash the Eggs Benedict under the grill for just 25-30 seconds, as close to the heat as possible, but don't take your eyes off them – they need to be tinged golden and no more. This should just glaze the surface of the hollandaise. Serve straight away on hot plates.

Serves 3 for brunch or 6 as a starter
1 quantity Hollandaise Sauce (see page 70)
6 large, very fresh eggs
12 slices pancetta, grilled until crisp
3 English muffins, split in half horizontally
a little butter

You will also need a grill pan and rack and a 10 x 14 inch (25.5 x 35 cm) baking tray.

Pre-heat the grill to its highest setting.

How to
fry eggs

A perfectly fried egg is a glory to behold – crispy edges and a wobbly, pinkish yolk. One of my treasured memories of eating fried eggs is on the beautiful Caribbean island of Barbados, where I have been lucky enough to spend several holidays. For me it's the best place on earth for an early morning dip in the sea, and as you swim and look back at all that beauty, the evocative smell of bacon and eggs cooking is sheer heaven. Afterwards, at breakfast, there's always a happy, smiling Bajan wielding an old, blackened frying pan, enquiring how you like your eggs fried.

When considering a recipe for fried eggs, this is the pertinent question – how *do* you like them? It's very personal, but my own method, below, can be adjusted to suit most tastes. So here goes.

You will need:

2 large, very fresh eggs
1 dessertspoon of fat left from frying bacon (or groundnut or grapeseed oil)
1 small heavy-based frying pan
1 slotted kitchen slice
some kitchen paper

First place the pan over a high heat and, as soon as the fat or oil is really hot (with a faint shimmer on the surface), carefully break the eggs into the pan. Let them settle for about 30 seconds, then turn the heat down to medium and carry on cooking them, tilting the pan and basting the eggs with the hot fat so that the tops of the eggs can be lightly cooked, too. After about 1 minute the eggs will be ready, so remove the pan from the heat, then lift the eggs out with the slice. Let them rest on the kitchen paper for a couple of seconds before putting them on a plate, then lightly blot up any excess fat with kitchen paper and eat them as soon as possible.

This method will provide a fried egg with a slightly crispy, frilly edge; the white will be set and the yolk soft and runny. If you prefer not to have the crispy edge, use a medium heat from the beginning and, if you like your eggs more cooked, give them a little longer.
Note: If you would like to fry your eggs in butter, then you need to use a gentler heat and give them a bit longer so the butter doesn't brown too much.

Basting the egg while cooking, top, will help it to cook evenly, resulting in a perfectly fried egg: crispy edges and a wobbly pinkish yolk, above

For fried eggs and bacon, fry the eggs as above but fry the bacon first. To do this, make a few nicks with a pair of scissors along the fat edge of some back bacon (this stops it frilling while it's cooking), then add a tiny spot of groundnut oil (about a teaspoon) to a fairly hot frying pan and fry the rashers until they are crisp and golden. Transfer them to a warm plate, blotting them with kitchen paper, and keep them warm while you fry the eggs in the fat left from the bacon.

Corned-Beef Hash with Fried Eggs

I love New York and, in particular, New York delis, where I always order a hot pastrami sandwich on rye bread and my husband always orders corned-beef hash with a fried egg. Although we don't have the same type of corned beef here, our humble, modest tinned version makes a mean old hash and, what's more, at an amazing price. A great meal made with incredible ease for under £1 a head!

Start this off by cutting the corned beef in half lengthways, then, using a sharp knife, cut each half into four ½ inch (1 cm) pieces. Now chop these into ½ inch (1 cm) dice, then scoop them all up into a bowl. Combine the Worcestershire sauce and mustard in a cup and pour this all over the beef, mixing it around to distribute it evenly.

Now peel and halve the onion, cut the halves into thin slices and then cut these in half. The potatoes need to be washed and cut into ½ inch (1 cm) cubes, leaving the skin on, then place the cubes in a saucepan. Pour enough boiling water from the kettle to almost cover them, then add salt and a lid and simmer for just 5 minutes before draining them in a colander and then covering with a clean tea cloth to absorb the steam.

Now heat 2 tablespoons of the oil in the frying pan and, when it's smoking hot, add the sliced onions and toss them around in the oil to brown for about 3 minutes altogether, keeping the heat high, as they need to be very well browned at the edges.

After that, push all the onions to the edge of the pan and, still keeping the heat very high, add the potatoes and toss these around, too, because they also need to be quite brown. Add a little more oil here if necessary. Now add some seasoning, then, using a pan slice, keep turning the potatoes and onions over to hit the heat. After about 6 minutes, add the beef and continue to toss everything around to allow the beef to heat through (about 3 minutes).

After that, turn the heat down to its lowest setting and, in the smaller frying pan, fry the eggs as described left. Serve the hash divided between the two warm plates with an egg on top of each and don't forget to have plenty of tomato ketchup on the table.

Note: There's now a tomato ketchup available in wholefood shops that does not contain sugar and has a real tomato flavour.

Serves 2

7 oz (200 g) tinned corned beef
2 large, very fresh eggs
2 tablespoons Worcestershire sauce
1 rounded teaspoon grain mustard
1 large onion
10 oz (275 g) Desirée or King Edward potatoes
2-3 tablespoons groundnut or other flavourless oil
salt and freshly milled black pepper

You will also need a heavy-based frying pan approximately 8 inches (20 cm) in diameter, a slightly smaller frying pan for the eggs and two plates placed in a warming oven.

Chorizo Hash with Peppers and Paprika

This, if you like, is a more sophisticated version of the previous recipe, with red peppers as well as onion and potato. It's brilliant, but only worth making if you get genuine Spanish chorizo made in Spain, available at deli counters and specialist food shops – the English 'made in Surbiton'-type clones are not at all what they should be.

First the onion needs to be peeled, sliced in half and then each half sliced as thinly as possible so you end up with little half-moon shapes. Next halve and deseed the red pepper, slice it, then chop it into ½ inch (1 cm) pieces. After that, peel the skin off the chorizo sausage and cut into pieces roughly the same size as the pepper.

The potatoes need to be washed and cut into ½ inch (1 cm) cubes, leaving the skin on. Then place them in a saucepan and pour enough boiling water from the kettle to almost cover them, then add salt and a lid and simmer for just 5 minutes before draining them in a colander and covering with a clean tea cloth to absorb the steam.

Next heat 2 tablespoons of the oil in the frying pan and, when it's fairly hot, add the onion, pepper and garlic and cook for about 6 minutes, until softened and tinged brown at the edges. Then push these to the side of the pan, add the chorizo and, keeping the heat fairly high, cook for about 2 minutes, again, till nicely browned at the edges. Next, add the paprika and stir everything together, then remove the whole lot to a plate. Now add the last tablespoon of oil to the pan and, still keeping the heat high, add the potatoes and seasoning. Toss them around in the hot pan for about 3 minutes, keeping them moving, until they begin to crisp and brown at the edges, then return the chorizo, onion and pepper to the pan and, using a pan slice, keep turning the mixture over. Carry on cooking the whole thing for 5-6 minutes, until it's all really brown and crispy. Then turn the heat down to its lowest setting and, in the other pan, fry the eggs as described on page 28. Serve the hash divided between the two warmed plates with an egg on top of each, as shown on page 29, and have plenty of tomato ketchup on the table.

Serves 2

5 oz (150 g) chorizo sausage
1 small red pepper
1 rounded teaspoon hot paprika
1 medium onion
10 oz (275 g) Desirée or King Edward potatoes
3 tablespoons olive oil
1 fat clove garlic, peeled and crushed
2 large, very fresh eggs
salt and freshly milled black pepper

You will also need a heavy-based frying pan approximately 8 inches (20 cm) in diameter, a slightly smaller frying pan for the eggs and two plates placed in a warming oven.

How to make softly scrambled eggs

Add the beaten eggs to the butter in the pan and scramble until three-quarters of the egg is a creamy mass. Off the heat, add the rest of the butter and finish scrambling

I learnt how to make scrambled eggs for the very first time by following a recipe by the famous French chef Auguste Escoffier, and I still think his is the best version of all. However, during the past 20 years, since the first *Cookery Course* was published, there has been an enormous move away from butter, which in some ways is right because at one stage we were all far too heavy-handed with it, and it sometimes obscured the delicate flavour of fresh vegetables and so on. But let's never forget what a beautiful ingredient butter is and what a great affinity it has with eggs. For this reason I am sticking with Escoffier on scrambled eggs.

To begin with, there's only one rule, and that is not to have the heat too high; if you do, the eggs will become flaky and dry. The trick is to remove the pan from the heat while there's still some liquid egg left, then this will disappear into a creamy mass as you serve the eggs and take them to the table.

Scrambled Eggs for One

For more people, just multiply the ingredients accordingly. The method remains the same, but more eggs will obviously take longer to cook.

2 large eggs
½ oz (10 g) butter
salt and freshly milled black pepper

First of all, break the eggs into a small bowl and use a fork to lightly blend the yolks into the whites, whisking gently. Add a good seasoning of salt and freshly milled black pepper.

Now take a small, heavy-based saucepan and place it over a medium heat. Add half the butter to the pan and swirl it around so that the base and about 1 inch (2.5 cm) of the sides of the pan are moistened with it. Then, when the butter has melted and is just beginning to foam, pour in the beaten eggs. Using a wooden fork or a wooden spoon with a point, start stirring briskly using backwards and forwards movements all through the liquid egg, getting into the corners of the pan to prevent it from sticking. Don't, whatever you do, turn the heat up: just be patient and keep on scrambling away until you calculate that three-quarters of the egg is now a creamy, solid mass and a quarter is still liquid.

At this point, remove the pan from the heat, add the rest of the butter and continue scrambling with the fork or spoon. The eggs will carry on cooking in the heat from the pan. As soon as there is no liquid egg left, serve the scrambled eggs absolutely immediately. The secret of success is removing the pan at the right stage, because overcooking makes the eggs dry and flaky. Once you've mastered the art of allowing them to finish cooking off the heat, you will never have a problem. If you like you can add a little double cream or crème fraîche as well as the butter. Either way, soft clouds of perfectly scrambled eggs are one of life's special joys. Serve on buttered toast or bagels.

Slimmers' Scrambled Eggs

This recipe is devised for people on a diet or for those who have to cut down on fat. Nevertheless, it's extremely good, and on diet days I like to spread it on to sesame Ryvitas. I like it best made with Quark, which is a skimmed-milk soft cheese, but it also works well with cottage cheese.

Serves 1

2 large eggs
1 tablespoon milk
1 heaped dessertspoon Quark or cottage cheese
1 tablespoon fresh snipped chives
salt and freshly milled black pepper

You will also need a small non-stick saucepan and a wooden fork.

Begin by beating the eggs in a bowl, together with a good seasoning of salt and pepper. Now place the saucepan over a gentle heat, then add the milk to moisten the pan, whirling it around the edges. Add the eggs and, using a wooden fork or pointed wooden spoon, briskly stir backwards and forwards through the liquid egg. Keep on scrambling until three-quarters of the egg is a creamy, solid mass and a quarter is still liquid. Now add the Quark or cottage cheese and chives and continue to scramble, then remove the pan from the heat and continue scrambling until no liquid egg is left.

Scrambled Eggs with Smoked Salmon and Brioche

This has to be one of the most sublime combinations: soft, creamy scrambled eggs, together with the subtle, smoky flavour of the salmon. Some restaurants serve the scrambled eggs topped with slices of smoked salmon, but what a waste: soaking strips of salmon in cream and incorporating them into the scrambled eggs is in another league altogether.

Serves 2

4 large eggs
4½ oz (125 g) traditional smoked salmon trimmings
4 tablespoons single cream
2 all-butter brioche buns
½ oz (10 g) butter
salt and freshly milled black pepper

To garnish:
a little fresh dill

The salmon needs to be chopped fairly small for this, so if you're using offcuts you might still need to chop some of the larger pieces. I say chop here, but very often I use scissors. Either way, place all the salmon pieces in a small bowl, pour in the cream, give it all a good stir, cover the bowl and leave it aside for 30 minutes.

When you are ready to make the scrambled eggs, pre-heat the grill to its highest setting. Slice the top off each brioche, then carefully scoop out and discard half the bread from inside, then place each one, alongside its lid, under the grill, and lightly toast on both sides.

Now melt the butter in a medium-sized saucepan over a very gentle heat. While it's melting, break the eggs into a bowl and beat them lightly with a fork, seasoning with a little salt and freshly milled black pepper. When the butter has melted and begins to foam, swirl it around the edges of the pan, then pour in the beaten eggs. Increase the heat slightly and, using a wooden fork or a wooden spoon with a point, stir continuously backwards and forwards, getting right into the corners of the pan.

As soon as the eggs begin to solidify – after about 1 minute – and when you have about 50 per cent solid and the rest still liquid, quickly add the salmon and cream, then keep on stirring like mad until almost all the liquid has gone, which will take 3-4 minutes. Then remove the pan from the heat and continue stirring until the eggs become a soft, creamy mass. Taste to check the seasoning and spoon into the toasted brioche buns. Top with a little dill, replace the lids and serve immediately.

Gratin of Eggs with Peppers and Chorizo

This is a variation on oeufs sur le plat, and the name means, literally, eggs cooked on a plate, and a plate can indeed be used, provided it's heatproof. Best, though, are shallow gratin dishes measuring 6 inches (15 cm) in diameter, which have enough space for one or two eggs. This recipe has a Basque element, as the eggs are baked on a base of onions, garlic, peppers and chorizo sausage. The whole thing is topped with bubbling cheese, and it makes a perfect lunch or supper dish, taking hardly any time to prepare.

Begin by preparing all the ingredients. Remove the skin from the chorizo and slice it into ¼ inch (5 mm) rounds. The onion needs to be peeled, sliced in half and then each half sliced as thinly as possible so you end up with little half-moon shapes. Remove the stalk from the pepper and then halve it, scooping out the seeds. Slice it first into quarters and then each quarter into thin slices. The tomatoes need to be skinned, so pour boiling water over them, leave for 30 seconds, then drain and slip off their skins. Slice each tomato in half, squeeze each half gently to remove the seeds, then chop the flesh into small cubes. Peel and finely chop the garlic.

Next take a large, heavy-based frying pan, place it over a high heat and add the olive oil. When the oil is really hot, brown the chorizo pieces, tossing and turning them around until they turn slightly brown at the edges. Using a slotted spoon, transfer the chorizo from the pan to a plate. Next add the onion and pepper to the pan and toss these around, keeping the heat high, until they're nicely tinged brown at the edges and softened, which will take 5-10 minutes. Now add the tomatoes and garlic and cook for 1 minute more, then return the chorizo to join the rest of the ingredients. Finally, give everything a good mix and season with salt and freshly milled black pepper.

Then remove the pan from the heat and divide the mixture between the two gratin dishes. Carefully break two eggs side by side on top of the mixture in each dish, season them, then sprinkle them with the grated cheese. Place the dishes on the baking sheet on the top shelf of the oven to cook for 12-15 minutes (or a little longer, depending on how you like your eggs). I think this needs some quite robust red wine and some warm crusty baguette served alongside.

Serves 2
4 large eggs
1 small red or green pepper
3 oz (75 g) chorizo sausage
1 medium onion
3 medium tomatoes
1 fat clove garlic
1 tablespoon olive oil
2 oz (50 g) Gruyère, grated
salt and freshly milled black pepper

You will also need two round, 6 inch (15 cm) diameter gratin dishes moistened with a few drops of olive oil, and a baking sheet measuring 14 x 11 inches (35 x 28 cm).

Pre-heat the oven to gas mark 4, 350°F (180°C).

Eggs en Cocotte

This is another special way of cooking and serving eggs. The classic French name for this type of egg dish is oeufs en cocotte, and it is named after the dishes in which the eggs are cooked, which are called ramekins and look like mini soufflé dishes with enough space for baking one egg. The following recipe will give you the basic method of baking eggs in ramekins, including several variations.

First boil some water. Break an egg into each ramekin, season, then put a knob of butter on top of each yolk. Place the dishes in the baking tin, then pop it on the centre shelf of the oven and pour enough boiling water into the tin to come halfway up the sides of the dishes. Now let the eggs bake for 15 minutes if you like them soft and runny, or 18 minutes if you like them more set. Either way, bear in mind that they go on cooking in the dishes as they leave the oven and reach the table.

There are several variations, too. Instead of a knob of butter, pour in a tablespoon of double cream, soured cream, crème fraîche or, for a lower-fat version, Greek yoghurt works superbly. In addition, you could sprinkle a dessertspoon of grated cheese on top of the cream. Other ingredients that can be included under the egg are lightly cooked asparagus tips or cooked, chopped leeks. You could also use chopped smoked salmon or lightly cooked flakes of smoked haddock.

Serves 2 as a starter
2 large, fresh eggs
about 1 oz (25 g) butter
salt and freshly milled black pepper

You will also need two ramekins with a 3 inch (7.5 cm) diameter, 1½ inches (4 cm) deep, well buttered, and a baking tin measuring 11 x 8 inches (28 x 20 cm), 2 inches (5 cm) deep.

Pre-heat the oven to gas mark 4, 350°F (180°C).

Eggs en Cocotte with Morel or Porcini Mushrooms

I love to make this with dried morels, which are available from specialist food shops, but dried porcini will also be excellent.

Serves 4 as a starter

4 large, very fresh eggs
½ oz (10 g) dried morels or porcini
5 fl oz (150 ml) boiling water
3 shallots, peeled and finely chopped
4 oz (110 g) dark-gilled flat mushrooms, roughly chopped
¼ whole nutmeg, grated
1 oz (25g) butter
3 rounded tablespoons crème fraîche, half-fat crème fraîche or Greek yoghurt
salt and freshly milled black pepper

You will also need four ramekins with a base diameter of 3 inches (7.5 cm), 1½ inches (4 cm) deep, well buttered, and a baking tin measuring 11 x 8 inches (28 x 20 cm), 2 inches (5 cm) deep.

Start by soaking the morels or porcini about 30 minutes ahead of time. Place them in a bowl with the boiling water and leave them aside to soak. After that, strain them in a sieve and squeeze them to get rid of any surplus water. (You can reserve the soaking water, which can be frozen and is great for soups and sauces.) Set aside 4 pieces of the morels or porcini and put the rest in a food processor, along with the shallots, flat mushrooms, nutmeg and salt and freshly milled black pepper. Process until finely chopped.

Heat the butter in a small saucepan. When it starts to foam, add the chopped mushroom mixture and, keeping the heat low, let it cook very gently, without a lid, for 25-30 minutes; the idea is that any excess liquid will evaporate and leave a lovely, dark, concentrated mixture.

All this can be prepared in advance, but when you're ready to cook the eggs, start by pre-heating the oven to gas mark 4, 350°F (180°C) and boil a kettle. Gently re-heat the mixture and, stirring in 1 rounded tablespoon of the crème fraîche or yoghurt, divide it between the ramekins, making a small indentation where the egg will be placed. Now break an egg into each one and season. Stir the rest of the crème fraîche or yoghurt around to loosen it, divide between the dishes, then spread it gently over the eggs using the back of the spoon or a small palette knife. Place a piece of the reserved morels or porcini on top of each ramekin, then place the ramekins in the baking tin, pop the tin on the centre shelf of the oven and add enough boiling water to the tin to come halfway up the sides of the dishes. Bake for 15-18 minutes. These are lovely served with slices of wholemeal bread and butter.

2

The art of the omelette

'Egg may be dressed in a multiplicity of ways but seldom more relished in any form than in a well made, expeditiously served omelette.'
(Eliza Acton)

So says Eliza, and things have not changed. She has said everything I want to say. If I can teach you how to master the 'well made, expeditiously served omelette' then I will have served you well, because you'll never be short of one of life's simplest, quickest and most pleasant dishes.

However, the art of the omelette begins not, as you might think, in the kitchen but in the high street. 'First catch your frying pan' is the optimum expression here. In all my years of attempting to teach cooking, buying the right frying pan has always been a tricky business. Yes, I was there when the non-stick revolution arrived in the shops, and the number of miserable, peeling, scratched and worn non-stick pans that have passed through my kitchen since is legion.

The problem is that there are strict rules, and the rules have to be obeyed: thou shalt never place the pan over direct heat without anything in it; thou shalt never turn the heat higher than medium; thou shalt never, ever use metal utensils. My problem with non-stick is that I *can't* stick to the rules. I like to heat the pan before I put the butter in; I can't sear a steak unless the pan is scorching hot, and I simply cannot make an omelette without a metal spoon. Then, having made a glorious, open-faced flat omelette to be served in wedges, I'm not allowed to use a sharp knife to cut it.

Yes, I know there are special non-metal tools, but wood simply sticks to the food, and plastic is not for people with busy lives who leave it in the pan when the phone rings and then find it's melted down into the food. I am not against non-stick if carefully handled – it is a useful piece of equipment – it's just that I am not careful enough.

My last warning is beware of the 'I'm only here for my looks' brigade. Stainless steel never was a good conductor of heat, and pans made only of stainless steel, however good they look, are to be avoided.

There I'll rest my case, but the good news is that after years of testing omelette pans I have discovered a little gem: the humble, unglamorous but utterly reliable British-made, heavy gauge aluminium pan. Yes, I know red lights are flashing, 'What about the safety of aluminium?' I have done my homework and discovered that, like most health scares, this was unproven. Extensive tests have concluded that aluminium is perfectly safe for all cooking, except for very acidic fruits and vegetables, such as plums, tomatoes and rhubarb, where the acid can attack the metal. This type of pan is also one of the cheapest quality pans on the market and, if you season it properly, it becomes virtually non-stick and will serve you for a lifetime of happy omelette-making.

Size is crucial

First of all, the size of the pan is vital: too small and the omelette will be thick, spongy and difficult to fold; too large and the eggs will spread out like a thin pancake and become dry and tough. When you buy a pan, take a tape measure and measure the base (not the top), because that's where the cooking happens. I have found the pan recommended above best for either a two- or three-egg omelette, which is average for a folded omelette. The base measures 6 inches (15 cm) in diameter. Pans with an 8 inch (20 cm) base are suitable for tortillas or open-faced omelettes.

How to season a new frying pan

Please, please don't forget to do this. All you do is fill the base of the pan with about ½ inch (1 cm) of any old cooking oil (something lurking in the back of the cupboard, past its use-by date would be ideal). Make sure the sides are well oiled, then heat up the oil in the pan and, when it is simmering hot, turn the heat down to its lowest setting and leave it there for eight hours, or even longer. The best frying pan is a well-used one, so what this is doing is pre-empting all that use. Should you make only omelettes in this pan? No, you can use the pan for any kind of frying; in fact, the more you use it the better it will be. After use, wash it in mildly soapy hot water with a dish cloth. Dry it and then rub a little oil round the inside surface.

Making a folded omelette

Before you begin, have everything ready: bowl, eggs, omelette pan, fork, tablespoon, salt and pepper, butter and oil. Put the plates in a warm oven.

1 *Eggs*
   One omelette will serve one person and, because it is so quick to make, it's not worth cooking a large one for two. So, according to how hungry you are, use two or three large eggs per person. Just break the eggs carefully into a bowl, add a seasoning of salt and freshly milled black pepper, then gently combine the yolks and whites with a fork – don't overbeat them, combine is the word you need to think of here. Under-rather than overbeating the eggs seems to make a fluffier omelette.

2 *Oil or butter?*
   You can use either, but remember that butter burns very easily on a high heat. Some oil will prevent this from happening so, if you like a buttery flavour, I would recommend that you use half a teaspoon of each. For extra butteriness or creaminess you could add a teaspoon of melted butter or double cream to the eggs in the bowl.

3 *Heat*
   Heat is a vital element in omelette-making because the essence of success is speed. Begin by turning the heat to medium, place the pan over the heat and let it get quite hot (about half a minute). Now add the butter and oil and, as soon as it melts, swiftly swirl it round, tilting the pan so that the base and the sides get coated. Turn the heat up to its highest setting now – when I first demonstrated this on television I remember saying, 'hot as you dare', and that still stands.

4 *Cooking the omelette*
   When the butter is foaming, pour the eggs into the pan, tilting it to and fro to spread the eggs evenly over the base. Then leave it on the heat without moving it for a count of five.

5 *Working with a spoon*
   After 5 seconds a bubbly frill will appear round the edge. Now you can tilt the pan to 45° and, using a tablespoon, draw the edge of the omelette

When making an omelette, begin by heating the oil or butter on as high a heat as you dare; next, pour the eggs into the pan, tilting it so they cover the base; using a spoon, start to draw the edge of the omelette into the middle so the liquid egg runs into the space, continuing until almost all the liquid egg has cooked into the centre. The liquid egg will flow into and fill the space. Now tip the pan the other way and do the same thing. Keep tilting it backwards and forwards, pulling the edges in with the spoon and allowing the liquid egg to travel into the space left – all this will take only half a minute. Soon there will be just a small amount of liquid left, just on the surface, so now is the time to start folding. Tilt the pan again and flip one side of the omelette into the centre, then fold again. Take the pan to the warm plate, and the last fold will be when you tip the omelette out on to the plate.

6 Remember, an omelette will go on cooking, even on the plate, so serve it immediately. For this reason it is important to have some liquid egg left before you start folding, but if you have left too much, leave it to set on the plate before eating. The perfect omelette is one just tinged with gold on the surface and very soft and squidgy on the inside.

Omelettes with fillings

Now you have mastered the art of a plain omelette you can begin to think about fillings.

Fontina, Gruyère (pictured) and Taleggio make a great melted-cheese omelette, particularly with the addition of ham

To make a *straightforward cheese omelette*, add 1½ oz (40 g) of grated mature Cheddar to the egg mixture and sprinkle some Parmesan over the finished omelette before it goes to the table.

For a *blue cheese and onion omelette*, add 1½ oz (40 g) of grated Stilton, Roquefort or Gorgonzola, plus 2 finely chopped spring onions, to the egg mixture, then cook as described.

For a *melted-cheese omelette*, first pre-heat the grill, then take 2 oz (50 g) of a good melting cheese, such as Fontina, Gruyère or Taleggio, slice it thinly, lay the slices all over the omelette at the stage where it is almost set but still liquid (you could also add some ham now if you like), then flash the omelette pan under the pre-heated grill to melt the cheese quickly. Then turn it out as described earlier and this will produce a melted cheese centre that oozes out when you take your first forkful.

For a *Swiss omelette*, pre-heat the grill and add ½ oz (10 g) of grated Gruyère to the egg mixture. Have ready another ½ oz (10 g) of grated Gruyère mixed with 1 tablespoon of double cream. After folding and turning out the omelette, spoon this mixture over the folded omelette and flash it under the hot grill to form a cheesy, creamy glaze. Not good for the waistline but…

On a diet? Yes, you can still have a *cheese omelette*. Grated Parmesan (Parmigiano Reggiano) has a wonderful flavour and not too high a fat content. Just ½ oz (10 g) – half in the egg mixture and half sprinkled over the top after turning out – will set you back only 39 calories and 2.8g of fat.

For a *mushroom omelette* for one person use 4 oz (110 g) of chopped mushrooms. Very gently stew them, uncovered, in 1 teaspoon of oil or butter for 20 minutes, until all the excess moisture has evaporated and the flavour is concentrated. Scatter them over the omelette before folding.

For a *fines herbes omelette*, combine 1 tablespoon of chopped parsley and 1 tablespoon of fresh snipped chives (or any herb combination you choose). Stir the herbs into the mixed eggs 30 minutes before making the omelette to allow the flavours to develop.

For a *smoked salmon omelette*, soak 2 oz (50 g) of smoked salmon trimmings in 1 tablespoon of cream or milk for 30 minutes, then add this to the egg mixture before making the omelette.

Open-Faced Flat Omelettes

While the French folded omelette described earlier is probably the ultimate 'fast food' in the home, it does make certain demands on the cook in that it all has to happen fairly swiftly, which is great for one or two people but not so easy when you're doing a kind of production line for four or more. The open-faced omelette, on the other hand, gives you time to play with. Here, the whole thing is much more laid back – you can even pop one on the stove to cook while you sip an aperitif and chat, and then serve even six people with absolute ease.

Tortilla (Spanish Omelette)

I sometimes marvel how it is that three basic, very inexpensive ingredients – eggs, onions and potatoes – can be transformed into something so utterly sublime. Yet it's simply the way the Spanish make their omelettes. A Spanish omelette, or tortilla, is not better than a French one, and it certainly takes longer to make, but in this age of complicated, overstated, fussy food, it's a joy to know that simplicity can still win the day. A well-made tortilla served with a salad and a bottle of wine can give two or more people a luxury meal at any time and at a very low cost.

Serves 2-3
5 large eggs
1 medium onion, about 4 oz (110 g)
10 oz (275 g) small Desirée potatoes
3 tablespoons olive oil
salt and freshly milled black pepper

First some points to note. The size of the frying pan is important: a base measurement of 8 inches (20 cm) diameter is about right for two to three people. If using a larger pan for more people, it should not be too heavy because you need to turn the omelette out using both hands. Use a non-stick pan if you don't have a well-seasoned frying pan. An enormous asset here is a flat saucepan lid or large plate that fits the pan.

Tortilla can be served as a main course or, because it is good served cold, it makes excellent picnic food cut into wedges and wrapped in clingfilm. In Spain they serve it as tapas, cut into small cubes and speared with cocktail sticks – lovely with chilled amontillado sherry. The Spanish also serve tortilla sandwiched between chunks of crusty bread – sounds yummy but very fattening!

First of all, peel and cut the onion in half, then thinly slice each half and separate the layers into half-moon shapes. Now thinly pare the potatoes using a potato peeler and slice them into thin rounds – you have to work pretty quickly here because you don't want the slices to brown. When they are sliced, rub them in a clean tea cloth to get them as dry as possible.

Next, heat 2 tablespoons of the olive oil in the frying pan and, when it's smoking hot, add the potatoes and onions. Toss them around in the oil to get a good coating, then turn the heat right down to its lowest setting, add a generous sprinkling of salt and pepper, put a lid on the frying pan and let the onions and potatoes cook gently for 20 minutes, or until tender. Turn them over halfway through and shake the pan from time to time, as they are not supposed to brown very much but just gently stew in the oil.

Potatoes and onions are cooked until they are gently stewed; every now and then the edge is drawn in gently with a palette knife, giving the tortilla a rounded edge

Meanwhile, break the eggs into a large bowl and, using a fork, whisk them lightly – it's important not to overbeat them. Finally, add some seasoning. When the onions and potatoes are cooked, quickly transfer them to the eggs in the bowl.

Put the frying pan back on the heat, add the rest of the oil and turn the heat back up to medium. Then mix the potato and eggs thoroughly before pouring the whole lot into the frying pan and turning the heat down to its lowest setting immediately. Now forget all about French omelettes and be patient, because it's going to take 20-25 minutes to cook slowly, uncovered. Every now and then draw the edge in gently with a palette knife, as this will give it a lovely rounded edge. When there is virtually no liquid egg left on the surface of the omelette, place a flat lid or plate over the pan, invert it, turning the pan over, and put it back on the heat and use the palette knife to gently ease the omelette back in. Give it about 2 minutes more, then turn the heat off and leave it for a further 5 minutes to settle. It should then be cooked through but still moist in the centre. Serve hot or cold, cut in wedges, with a salad and a glass of Rioja – it's brilliant.

How to make an Italian frittata

This is Italy's version of an open-face omelette, and while the tortilla is golden brown, the frittata is cooked even more slowly and should not be too coloured on the outside. The Italian word here is *lentamente* – very slowly; the eggs cook through gradually and the finished omelette should be very moist. For this reason it is better not turned over but rather quickly flashed under a hot grill so that the top only just sets. It then has to be served immediately, otherwise it goes on cooking and loses its soft creaminess.

Melted Cheese Frittata with Four Kinds of Mushroom

Serves 4
8 large eggs
4 oz (110 g) Fontina or Gruyère
12 oz (350 g) mixed mushrooms
(3 oz/75 g of each)
1 tablespoon olive oil
salt and freshly milled black pepper

You will also need a 10 inch (25 cm) frying pan and the oven pre-heated to its lowest setting.

I like to use Fontina cheese for this, but Gruyère is also a good melting cheese, so you could use that instead. The mushrooms can be whatever is available, though I love the contrasting textures and colours of a mixture of oyster, shiitake, black dark-gilled mushrooms and the vibrant pied de mouton. However, none of this is vital: if you use only one type of mushroom it will still be extremely good.

First of all chop the mushrooms into roughly 1 inch (2.5 cm) chunks – it's going to look an enormous quantity at this stage, but they will lose approximately half their volume in the initial cooking. Now heat a teaspoon of the olive oil in a frying pan and, when it's hot, throw in the mushrooms and toss them around by shaking the pan. Don't worry that there is so little oil, because the mushrooms give off masses of juice once the heat gets to them. Season with salt and pepper, then turn the heat down to very low and just let the mushrooms cook gently, uncovered, so that all the juice evaporates and the flavour of the mushrooms becomes more concentrated. Leave them like that for 30 minutes, stirring them around once or twice.

While they are cooking, cut two-thirds of the cheese into ¼ inch (5 mm) cubes and grate the other third on the coarse blade of the grater. After that, break the eggs into a large bowl, whisk lightly with a fork and season well with salt and pepper. Then add three-quarters of the cooked mushrooms to the eggs, together with the cubed cheese. Place the rest of the mushrooms in a bowl covered with foil and keep them warm in the oven.

Now wipe the pan clean with some kitchen paper and put it back on a medium heat, add the rest of the olive oil and, when it's hot, swirl it around the pan. Turn the heat down to its lowest setting and pour the egg mixture into the pan, scattering the grated cheese all over the surface. Now all you have to do is leave it alone and put a timer on for 15 minutes.

When 15 minutes have passed, turn the grill on to its highest setting and see how the omelette is cooking – it will probably take about 20 minutes in total to cook, but there should still be about 10 per cent of liquid egg left on the top. At that stage transfer the pan to the grill – not too close – and cook briefly to allow the liquid egg to set. This will take 20-30 seconds. Scatter the remaining cooked mushrooms over the top of the frittata and cut it into four wedges. Transfer the wedges to warm plates and serve immediately, because the egg will continue cooking even though the frittata is no longer in contact with the heat. I like to serve this with two salads – a plain, green-lettuce salad and a tomato and basil salad.

The initial quantity of mushrooms for this frittata will seem like an awful lot to begin with, but they will lose about half their volume during the initial cooking

A Soufflé Omelette with Three Cheeses and Chives

Though making a soufflé proper can be a stressful experience, particularly if you've had no practice, making a soufflé omelette is a doddle. It takes no more than five minutes and honestly tastes every bit as good as the oven-baked variety. This one has three cheeses, but you can make it with just one, or even four if you happen to have them hanging around. I've included this in the omelette section, but if you are unsure of beating up the egg whites, read the notes in the next chapter on page 56.

Serves 1
3 large eggs
1 oz (25 g) mature Cheddar,
finely grated
1 oz (25 g) Parmesan (Parmigiano
Reggiano), finely grated
1 oz (25 g) Gruyère, finely grated
1 heaped tablespoon finely
snipped chives
½ oz (10 g) butter
salt and freshly milled black pepper

You will also need a medium
solid-based frying pan with a base
diameter of 7 inches (18 cm).

Pre-heat the grill to its highest setting
for 10 minutes and have a warm
plate ready.

First separate the eggs – yolks into a small bowl and whites into a squeaky-clean large bowl; it helps if you separate the whites singly into a cup first before adding them to the bowl, then if one breaks, it won't ruin the rest. Now beat the egg yolks with a fork, seasoning well with salt and pepper. Next put the pan on to a low heat to warm through.

While that's happening, whisk the egg whites with either an electric hand whisk or a balloon whisk, until they form soft peaks. Next add the butter to the pan and turn the heat up. Then, using a large metal spoon, quickly fold the egg yolks into the egg whites, adding the Cheddar, half the Parmesan and the chives at the same time.

Then, when the butter is foaming, pile the whole lot into the pan and give it a good hefty shake to even it out. Now let the omelette cook for 1 minute exactly. Then slide a palette knife round the edges to loosen it, sprinkle the grated Gruyère all over the surface and whack the omelette under the grill, about 4 inches (10 cm) from the heat. Let it cook for 1 more minute, until the cheese is melted and tinged golden. Next, remove the pan from the heat, then slide the palette knife round the edge again. Take the pan to the warmed plate, then ease one half of the omelette over the other and tilt the whole lot out on to the plate. Scatter the rest of the Parmesan all over and serve immediately.

Note: If you want to make this omelette for two, that's okay if you double everything. Just use a 9 or 10 inch (23 or 25.5 cm) diameter pan and give each stage more time, then divide the omelette into two.

3

Separate ways with eggs

For me, the talent of the egg as an ingredient seems infinite. It could be thought of as rather humdrum and everyday, but when closely examined, the humble egg becomes an absolute star turn in the kitchen. Though we've already discovered its potential for providing endless combinations of delightful and nutritious meals that can be made in moments, in addition, eggs are essential for making batters, baking puddings and cakes and for setting the fillings of tarts and quiches.

For now, though, I want to introduce you to yet another dimension of egg cookery, namely what happens when you separate the yolk from the white. While, as whole eggs, they can make puddings, batters, cakes and so on, once separated, they move on to being two quite unique and essential components in cooking.

If you want to separate the yolk from the white of an egg, the egg has to be as fresh as possible. The protective membrane that encloses the yolk weakens with age and breaks more easily, and this can cause problems, because if even one speck of yolk gets into the white, it won't be suitable for whisking. So with eggs as fresh as possible there's much less chance of that happening.

How to separate eggs

To separate yolks from whites, all you do is hold the egg over one bowl and have another bowl beside it. Crack the egg on the side of the bowl, round about its centre, then, using both hands, break it into two halves, one in each hand. Now slip the yolk back and forth from one half-shell to the other, tilting it as you do so and letting the white trickle down into the bowl while you hang on to the yolk. When there is no white left in the shells, pop the yolk into the other bowl.

Leftover whites and yolks

One query that often comes up in your letters is what I do with leftover whites if I'm only using yolks, and vice versa. The good news here is that eggs freeze very well, so pack them in small containers and don't forget to label them with the amount – trying to guess how many egg whites you have is not a good idea.

Egg whites

In the *Complete Cookery Course* I wrote: 'The secret of beating egg whites is knowing when to stop.' Twenty years and many more egg whites under my belt, I would add another proviso: you also need to know when *not* to stop.

I have to say in all honesty that getting whisked egg whites precisely right is an acquired skill, no doubt about it. But all skills can be acquired, and it does help if, a) someone (hopefully me) explains it properly so you know precisely what you're supposed to do and why, and, b) you are prepared to practise enough, because nothing beats experience.

So let's begin with egg whites.

Egg whites whipped to the soft-peak stage

... and to the stiff-peak stage

Egg whites

What happens when you whisk egg whites?

First of all, the most important ingredient is not the egg white but the air, because the whisked egg white is going to provide aeration for soufflés, meringues, cakes and the like. In whisking them, what you're actually doing is incorporating air, and as you do so, the original volume of the egg white can actually be increased by up to eight times.

As you whisk in the air, tiny air bubbles are formed. It might help to think of what happens when you blow up balloons here: too little air and the balloon will not be buoyant and bouncy, too much air and it will burst and the air will be lost. Therefore the cook has to whisk to precisely the right degree and then stop: too little and the egg white will be flabby, too much and the bubbles will burst, releasing the precious air (and it will still be flabby!).

When do you stop?

Knowing the right moment to stop is tricky, and all the cook can do is follow the tried and trusted guidelines, namely, to stop when you reach the stage at which the egg white stands up in well-defined peaks. If the egg white is for a cake, mousse or soufflé, where it has to be folded into other ingredients, the peaks should be soft (so that when you lift the whisk the peaks drop slightly); if it is for a meringue, where sugar is going to be incorporated, it should stand up in stiff peaks. In this book I will always indicate whether stiff or soft peaks are called for (see the photographs on page 55).

Grease: the enemy

The one thing that will prevent egg whites from reaching their full-blown potential is even the tiniest presence of grease. That's why the merest trace of egg yolk in the white means you are done for. But I'm afraid that's not all: you also have to be scrupulously careful about the bowl and whisk, which must also be grease-free. So always wash them in mild soapy water, rinse in very hot water, then dry them with an absolutely clean tea cloth. Just to make quite sure, run a slice of lemon round the whisk and the bowl.

Which equipment?

A balloon whisk is said by chefs to be the best, but it is too much like hard work for me. If you're young and more energetic, by all means go for it. A free-standing mixer or processor may be used, but I have always felt that the whites are not exposed to enough air this way. Others disagree, and you might find it best for you. An electric hand whisk is my personal favourite, as I can feel and see everything and the motor actually does all the work for me.

How to whisk egg whites

Before you begin, make sure that the mixing bowl is as large as you can get, which means as much air as possible can circulate around the egg whites as you whisk them.

Separate the eggs one at a time, placing each white in a cup or small bowl before adding it to the beating bowl. This means that if an accident occurs with, say, the third egg, and you break the yolk, the other two are safe. Switch the whisk on to a slow speed first of all and begin whisking for about 2 minutes, until everything has become bubbly (this timing will be right for two to three egg whites; you'll need slightly more time for four, five or six). After that, switch to a medium speed for a further minute, then whisk at the highest speed and continue whisking through the soft-peak stage until stiff peaks are formed.

Fear not

Always remember that a cake, or even a soufflé, with less or more air in it will not be a disaster. If the egg whites are not quite right, the finished dish will still taste good. If you're cooking with natural, fresh ingredients, who cares what it looks like? It's bound to taste good. I have often got egg whites wrong but still enjoyed the not-quite-so-puffy pavlova. Of course, we should always endeavour to get things right, but cooking, like life, isn't always perfect.

How to make meringue

I think one of the best ways to start practising whisking egg whites is to make meringues.

Meringue must be the most popular egg-white recipe of all, whipped with fine sugar into tall, stiff, shining peaks, then very lightly baked so that the surface is crisp and the centre is soft and chewy. The tricky bit is whisking the egg whites (see the method above), but the way it is cooked is important, too. My own method of baking has stood the test of time and, provided your oven temperature is correct, it will never let you down. The secret, I think, is allowing the meringue to remain in the closed oven after the heat is turned off so that it partly bakes and then slowly dries out.

Egg whites, whipped with sugar into stiff, glossy peaks, are the basis of all meringues

Petits Monts Blancs

When I first worked in a restaurant kitchen in the early 1960s, this recipe was on the menu and I became totally addicted to the sweetened chestnut purée. Chestnut has an amazing affinity with meringue and whipped cream, but in this modern version I have replaced the cream with Mascarpone and fromage frais; this way you get the flavour and creamy richness of the Mascarpone but lightened by the fromage frais.

Serves 8
For the meringues:
2 large egg whites
4 oz (110 g) white caster sugar

For the topping:
9 oz (250 g) Mascarpone
7 fl oz (200 ml) 8 per cent fat fromage frais
1 rounded dessertspoon caster sugar
1 teaspoon vanilla extract

To finish:
2 x 250g tins crème de marrons de l'Ardèche (sweetened chestnut purée), chilled
a little icing sugar

You will also need a 16 x 12 inch (40 x 30 cm) baking sheet lined with silicone paper (parchment).

Pre-heat the oven to gas mark 2, 300°F (150°C).

To make the meringues, place the egg whites in a large bowl and, using an electric hand whisk on a low speed, begin whisking. Continue for about 2 minutes, until the whites are foamy, then switch the speed to medium and carry on whisking for 1 more minute. Now turn the speed to high and continue whisking until the egg whites reach the stiff-peak stage. Next, whisk the sugar in on fast speed, a little at a time (about a dessertspoon), until you have a stiff and glossy mixture.

Now all you do is spoon 8 heaped dessertspoons of the mixture on to the prepared baking sheet, spacing them evenly. Then, using the back of the spoon or a small palette knife, hollow out the centres. Don't worry if they are not all the same shape – random and rocky is how I would describe them (see the photograph below left). Next, pop them on the centre shelf of the oven, immediately reduce the heat to gas mark 1, 275°F (140°C) and leave them for 30 minutes. After that, turn the oven off and leave the meringues to dry out in the warmth of the oven until it is completely cold (usually about 4 hours) or overnight. The meringues will store well in a tin or polythene box, and will even freeze extremely well.

To assemble the Monts Blancs, spoon equal quantities of the crème de marrons into each meringue, whisk the topping ingredients together and spoon equal amounts on top of the chestnut purée. A light dusting of icing sugar is good for a snowcapped-mountain image.

Meringue nests before cooking…

and afterwards

Meringues with Passion Fruit

This is a variation of the Petits Monts Blancs recipe on the previous page, and all you need is the same amount of meringue and Mascarpone filling, together with 6 passion fruit and a little icing sugar.

To assemble the 8 meringues, spoon the seeds from half a passion fruit into the bottom of each meringue nest. Then, mix the seeds from the other two passion fruit into the Mascarpone mixture. Spoon this mixture on top of the nests, dust with icing sugar and serve.

Meringues with Summer Fruit

The two previous meringue fillings are perfect for the winter months, but in the summer soft fruit make the perfect filling, as their sharp acidity contrasts beautifully with the sweetness of the meringue. For 8 meringue nests, use the same quantity of Mascarpone cream as for the Petits Monts Blancs, together with 1 lb (450 g) of strawberries, raspberries or, my favourite, a mixture of redcurrants, raspberries and strawberries. Then dust the fruit with icing sugar before serving. Nice made with a sauce of puréed fresh raspberries sweetened with a little icing sugar.

Egg yolks

The yolks of eggs fulfil three main functions in cooking. One is turning liquids into solids, as in a baked custard or quiche. The second is as a thickening agent for liquids. What happens here is that when the yolks are whisked into liquids over heat, the thickening agent in the yolk gets distributed to make a smooth, thick sauce or soup. They are also a powerful emulsifier that can bind and thicken oil- or butter-based sauces such as mayonnaise or hollandaise.

How to handle egg yolks

The problem the cook has when dealing with egg yolks is that if they are not treated carefully, and in the right way, they can 'split', or curdle, a mixture. In parting company with the whites they have lost some of their stability, as egg whites are great stabilisers. This often causes problems and stress for beginners, but there is some good news here. Over the years I have spent cooking and developing recipes and trying to help busy people cook at home without undue stress, I have developed various ways of using egg yolks in all the traditional recipes without the worry of curdling and spoiling a recipe. On this subject, I have to part company with the purists. I'm perfectly aware that there are people who simply don't mind standing over things for ages, nurturing them along and whisking till the cows come home (as my Welsh grandmother would say), but not me – I don't want to be confined to the kitchen, missing out on a conversation.

Therefore, I am here to tell you that you need never be afraid to use egg yolks in a custard. If you add just a small amount of cornflour there will never be any danger of it curdling, and even if it looks guilty of it, it will soon whip back to an amazing smoothness, because that tiny amount of cornflour will stabilise the eggs.

No more whisking!

If you do exactly the same making lemon curd, sabayon sauce or zabaglione, it will mean (as with custard) that the time you spend carefully whisking will be 2 minutes instead of 20. So here's an end to boring whisking sessions over bowls of barely simmering water, because life is short enough as it is! Similarly, I have discovered that when trying to make a lighter version of hollandaise sauce (for health reasons – not quite so much butter), adding whisked egg whites not only makes it go twice as far but also stabilises it perfectly. This means no last-minute fuss, that you can make it two days ahead if you want to re-heat it, and you can even freeze it so that if you only want a small amount, you can have some tucked away.

Traditional English Custard

This is the ultimate custard, perhaps <u>the</u> traditional British sauce. I offer it here as it has been made down the centuries – with thick double cream, but you can, if you wish, modify this extravagance by using single cream or creamy whole milk. These last two might be better if the custard is for pouring, but for a trifle for a special occasion I recommend going the whole hog! It's now fashionable to split a vanilla pod and incorporate the seeds into the sauce – this reduces the time it needs to infuse in the hot cream. But I can also recommend pure vanilla extract, which is a wonderful store-cupboard stand-by.

Serves 6-8
1 vanilla pod
1 pint (570 ml) double cream
6 large egg yolks
1 dessertspoon cornflour
2 oz (50 g) golden caster sugar

Begin by splitting the vanilla pod lengthways and using the end of a teaspoon to scoop out the seeds. Then place the pod and the seeds in a small saucepan, along with the cream. Now place the pan over a gentle heat and heat it to just below simmering point. While the cream is heating, whisk the egg yolks, cornflour and sugar together in a medium bowl using a balloon whisk. Next remove the vanilla pod from the hot cream. Then, whisking the egg mixture all the time with one hand, gradually pour the hot cream into the bowl. When it's all in, immediately return the whole lot back to the saucepan using a rubber spatula. Now back it goes on to the same gentle heat as you continue whisking until the custard is thick and smooth, which will happen as soon as it reaches simmering point. If you do overheat it and it looks grainy, don't worry, just transfer it to a jug or bowl and continue to whisk until it becomes smooth again. Pour the custard into a jug or bowl, cover the surface with clingfilm and leave to cool. To serve it warm later, remove the clingfilm and sit the bowl over a pan of barely simmering water.

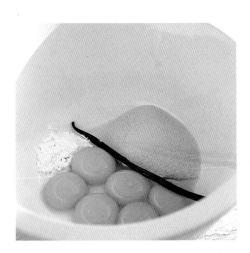

The very finest ingredients make a truly indulgent traditional English custard

Though the vanilla pod is removed from the cream, its distinctive seeds remain

Whisking the custard over a low heat ensures a smooth, creamy finish

Butterscotch and Banana Trifle with Madeira

There are endless variations on the trifle theme, and this is the latest Delia version. It's wickedly rich and quite wonderful – not for an everyday event, but perfect sometimes for those really special days. The best way to measure the syrup is to first weigh the saucepan on its own, keep it on the scales, then add a 5 oz (150 g) weight and pour the syrup straight in.

Serves 6-8
3 medium bananas
5 fl oz (150 ml) Madeira
8 trifle sponges

For the butterscotch sauce:
5 oz (150 g) golden syrup
2 oz (50 g) butter
3 oz (75 g) soft brown sugar
2 oz (50 g) golden granulated sugar
5 fl oz (150 ml) double cream
a few drops vanilla extract

For the topping:
1 quantity Traditional English Custard
(see page 62)
2 oz (50 g) pecan nuts
10 fl oz (275 ml) double cream

You will also need a 3 pint (1.75 litre)
glass trifle bowl.

First of all make the butterscotch sauce, and to do this place the golden syrup, butter and sugars in a small saucepan. Then place over a gentle heat and allow to slowly melt and dissolve, giving it a stir from time to time, which will take 5-7 minutes. Let it continue to cook for about 5 minutes, then gradually stir in the double cream and vanilla extract until well combined. After that, let it cool. While it's cooling, make the custard.

To assemble the trifle, begin by first of all splitting the trifle sponges in half lengthways, spread each half with butterscotch sauce, then re-form them into sandwiches. Cut each one across into three and arrange the pieces in the base of the glass bowl. Now make a few stabs in the sponges with a sharp knife and carefully pour the Madeira all over them, distributing it as evenly as you can. Then set aside to allow the sponges to soak it all up – about 20 minutes.

Now peel and slice the bananas into chunks about ¼ inch (5 mm) thick, scatter these all around the sponges, then pour the remaining butterscotch sauce as evenly as possible all over. Pour the custard in next, then cover the bowl with clingfilm and let the whole lot chill in the fridge to firm up.

Meanwhile, pre-heat the grill, line the grill pan with foil and toast the pecan nuts carefully for about 4 minutes, watching them all the time, as they burn easily. After that, whip the double cream to the floppy stage, spread it all over the trifle, scatter the toasted nuts on top, re-cover and chill till needed.

Note: This is best made the day you want to serve it. I used to scatter the nuts on just before serving, but forgot them so many times that I now put them on directly after the cream.

Hot Lemon
Curd Soufflés

Serves 4
For the soufflés:
3 large eggs
grated zest and juice 1 medium lemon
(2 tablespoons juice)
2 oz (50 g) golden caster sugar and
1 dessertspoon golden caster sugar

For the quick-method lemon curd:
grated zest and juice 1 small lemon
1 large egg
1½ oz (40 g) golden caster sugar
1 oz (25 g) cold unsalted butter, cut
into small cubes
1 teaspoon cornflour

To serve:
a little sifted icing sugar

You will also need four ramekins with
a base diameter of 2½ inches (6 cm),
a top diameter of 3 inches (7.5 cm),
2 inches (5 cm) deep, lightly buttered,
and a small, solid baking sheet.

Pre-heat the oven to gas mark 3,
325°F (170°C).

On the television series I called these 'everlasting', and yes, it's true, because unlike traditional soufflés, they never collapse. They will shrink down when they come out of the oven, but they will still be light and soufflé-like 15 minutes later. And just to prove my point, the soufflé in the small picture was actually a day old – not brimming up over the edge, but still a soufflé: soft and squidgy and very lemony. The quick lemon curd rounds the whole thing off into my favourite lemon recipe to date.

First of all make the lemon curd by lightly whisking the egg in a medium-sized saucepan, then add the rest of the lemon curd ingredients and place the saucepan over a medium heat. Now whisk continuously using a balloon whisk until the mixture thickens; this won't take long – about 3 minutes in all. Next, lower the heat to its minimum setting and let the curd gently simmer for 1 further minute, continuing to whisk. After that, remove it from the heat and divide the curd between the bases of the ramekins. (This can all be done well in advance, but cover and leave at room temperature.)

When you're ready to make the soufflés, separate the eggs, putting the yolks into a medium-sized bowl and the whites into a spanking-clean larger one. Now, using an electric hand whisk, whisk the whites to the stiff-peak stage, which will take 4-5 minutes – start on a slow speed, gradually increasing to medium and then high. Then add the dessertspoon of caster sugar and whisk on a high speed for 30 seconds more. Next add the zest and lemon juice and the remaining 2 oz (50 g) of sugar to the yolks and mix them together briefly. Now take a tablespoon of the whites and fold them into the yolks to loosen the mixture, then fold the rest of the whites in using a light cutting and folding movement so as not to lose the precious air. Spoon the mixture into the prepared ramekins, piling it high like a pyramid, then run a finger round the inside rim of each one.

Next place them on the baking sheet and put this in the oven on the centre shelf for 15-17 minutes or until the tops are golden. Then remove them and let them settle for about 5 minutes to allow the lemon curd to cool. They will sink a little, but that's normal. Just before serving, place them on smaller plates and give them a light dusting of icing sugar.

Twice-Baked Roquefort Soufflés

The obvious advantage of twice-baked soufflés is that they can be done and dusted the day before you need them. Then they rise up again like a dream, with a brilliantly light texture and flavour.

Serves 6
6 oz (175 g) Roquefort
8 fl oz (225 ml) milk
¼ inch (5 mm) onion slice
1 bay leaf
grating of nutmeg
6 whole black peppercorns
1½ oz (40 g) butter
1½ oz (40 g) plain flour
4 large eggs, separated
5 fl oz (150 ml) double cream
salt and freshly milled black pepper

To garnish:
6 sprigs watercress

You will also need six ramekins with a 3 inch (7.5 cm) diameter, 1½ inches (4 cm) deep, lightly buttered, an 11 x 8 x 2 inch (28 x 20 x 5 cm) baking tin, and a 14 x 10 inch (35 x 25.5 cm) baking tray.

Pre-heat the oven to gas mark 4, 350°F (180°C).

Begin by heating the milk, onion, bay leaf, nutmeg and peppercorns in a medium-sized saucepan till it reaches simmering point, then strain the milk into a jug, discarding the rest now. Rinse out the saucepan, then melt the butter in it. Add the flour and stir to a smooth, glossy paste, and cook this for 3 minutes, still stirring, until it turns a pale straw colour. Then gradually add the strained milk, whisking all the time, until the sauce is thick and cleanly leaves the sides of the pan. Then season lightly and cook the sauce on the gentlest heat possible for 2 minutes, stirring now and then.

Next remove the pan from the heat and let it cool slightly, then beat in the egg yolks one at a time. Now crumble 4 oz (110 g) of the cheese into the mixture and stir until most of it has melted – don't worry if some cheese is still visible. Put a kettle on to boil and, in a spanking-clean large bowl, whisk the egg whites to the soft-peak stage, then fold a spoonful of egg white into the cheese sauce to loosen it. Now fold the sauce into the egg white using a large metal spoon and a cutting and folding motion.

Divide the mixture equally between the ramekins. Put them in the baking tin, place it on the centre shelf of the oven, then pour about ½ inch (1 cm) of boiling water into the tin. Bake the soufflés for 20 minutes, then transfer them to a cooling rack (using a fish slice) so they don't continue cooking. Don't worry if they sink a little as they cool, because they will rise up again in the second cooking.

When they are almost cold, run a small palette knife around the edge of each ramekin and carefully turn the soufflés out on to the palm of your hand, then place them the right way up on a lightly greased, shallow baking tray. They can now be stored in the fridge for up to 24 hours, lightly covered with clingfilm.

When you are ready to re-heat the soufflés, pre-heat the oven to gas mark 4, 350°F (180°C) and remove the soufflés from the fridge so they can return to room temperature. Dice the remaining Roquefort into ¼ inch (5 mm) pieces and sprinkle it on top of the soufflés, then place them in the oven, on the shelf above centre, for 30 minutes.

Then, 2 or 3 minutes before serving, spoon a tablespoon of cream over each soufflé and return them to the oven while you seat your guests. Serve the soufflés immediately on warm plates and garnish each with a sprig of watercress.

Hollandaise Sauce

This great classic butter sauce from France can be tricky if it gets too much heat, so great care is in order here. However, since the advent of blenders and processors, the risk is not as large as it used to be with hand whisking over hot water. It has to be said that a blender is best, but a processor works well, too. My own problem has always been how to keep it warm, as I always like to make it in advance, and overheating will make it curdle. There are two possible answers for this: either use a wide-necked Thermos flask rinsed with boiling water, or to make a lighter, more stable version, see right.

Serves 4
2 large egg yolks (reserve the whites if you want to make Foaming Hollandaise)
1 dessertspoon lemon juice
1 dessertspoon white wine vinegar
4 oz (110 g) butter
salt and freshly milled black pepper

Begin by placing the egg yolks in a small bowl and season them with a pinch of salt and pepper. Then place them in a food processor or blender and blend them thoroughly for about 1 minute. After that, heat the lemon juice and white wine vinegar in a small saucepan until the mixture starts to bubble and simmer. Switch the processor or blender on again and pour the hot liquid on to the egg yolks in a slow, steady stream. After that, switch the processor or blender off.

Now, using the same saucepan, melt the butter over a gentle heat, being very careful not to let it brown. When the butter is foaming, switch the processor or blender on once more and pour in the butter in a thin, slow, steady trickle; the slower you add it the better. (If it helps you to use a jug and not pour from the saucepan, warm a jug with boiling water, discard the boiling water and then pour the butter mixture into that first.) When all the butter has been incorporated, wipe around the sides of the processor bowl or blender with a spatula to incorporate all the sauce, then give the sauce one more quick burst and you should end up with a lovely, smooth, thick, buttery sauce.

Once the egg yolks are blended, add the hot lemon juice and white wine vinegar to the processor in a slow, steady stream

Next, melt the butter in the same pan used for the lemon juice and vinegar and add it in a thin, even trickle

When the butter has been incorporated you will end up with a beautifully smooth, thick Hollandaise Sauce

Foaming Hollandaise

Foaming Hollandaise

I tend nearly always to make this one now. What happens here is that the 2 reserved egg whites are whisked to soft peaks and folded into the sauce as soon as it's made. The advantages are legion: firstly it lightens the sauce, so not quite so many calories, and you get a greater volume, so it goes further. It will never curdle because the egg whites stabilise the whole thing, which means you can happily keep it warm in a bowl fitted over simmering water. That's not all: you can also re-heat it in the same way, which means you can make it the day before. Finally, it will even freeze, which means that anything left over can be stored for a rainy day.

Either version of this supremely wonderful sauce can be used for serving with asparagus or artichokes, or with any kind of grilled or poached fish. And served with Eggs Benedict (see page 27), it's a positive star.

4
Rediscovering bread

'Wherefore do ye spend money on that which is not bread?' When the late Elizabeth David was struggling to find the words to introduce her masterpiece *English Bread And Yeast Cookery*, these words, spoken by the prophet Isaiah in 600 BC, said all she wanted to say about the state of commercially made British bread. That was over 20 years ago, and I am here to say that not a lot has changed. It is a sad fact that whilst there has been some improvement, 'that which is not bread' is still what a vast number of people consume.

Small high street and village bakers struggle to produce quality, but it gets harder and harder as they can't possibly compete on price with the larger commercial factories, who can always undercut price for quality. Thus in buying cheaper bread we may well be richer by the money saved, but in truth we are infinitely poorer because, if you think about it, few people could deny that having really good bread on a daily basis would instantly and inexpensively improve the quality of life.

Instead, the majority choose the dull option; perhaps it's because we don't value ourselves enough to feel we deserve the best – who knows? All I know is that 'that which is not bread', ie, the average packed and sliced loaf (although there are, of course, exceptions), compared with what bread should be, is extremely dull and poor quality; a flat, pappy, tasteless kind of blotting paper. Take a close look at a slice: it will be slightly damp and clammy; if you squeeze it in your hands it will emerge looking like an elongated piece of rough dough with the indentations of your fingers all along it. Do you really want to consume it?

It's a kind of downward spiral of 'how low can you go?' Millers mill their flour to provide for larger factories that bake mass-produced bread. Retailers sell it, then large retailers get involved in price wars. Something has to give in order to cut prices, so quality is what has to give. The factory can't afford to provide quality if the retailer can't afford to pay for it, because he has to keep his prices competitive. So quality cutting goes back to the factory, then to the miller and even the farmer. And what do we get?

I once heard modern bread given a sort of job description by a flour miller, who said that it was merely required to be a carrier. Isn't that a sad statement? In other words, it's what goes in or on the bread that's more important. If I can achieve anything at all in this whole *How To Cook* project it will be to persuade the younger generation to make and taste some real bread, just so they know what it's really like.

That which *is* bread

That which *is* bread is both astoundingly simple (after all, the main ingredients are merely flour and water), but at the same time gloriously luxurious because of its rarity. It's a strange paradox – here we are, a nation that spends a fortune on food and restaurants (you could say on the 'food experience'), yet give anyone at all a slice of real home-made bread and you might as well be giving them the moon. When we were filming the bread programme for the television series that accompanies this book, absolutely everyone was drooling, so enthusiastic and so appreciative, and forever wanting just one more slice. So why is it that home-made bread has so much going for it?

I would put flavour as number one on the list – the real, pure, natural flavour of the wheat, which is somewhat enhanced and intensified by the yeast, which also adds its own subtle flavour. Number two on my list would be texture: in a white loaf this is very soft, aerated and silky fine. Number three is the crust, which is very crisp and crunchy but at the same time light, and a well-baked crust is always fairly dark as this darkness creates extra flavour. Freshly baked white bread and good butter is one of the simplest pleasures in life. I love eating it with soft-boiled eggs (see page 16).

Wholemeal bread

This is not as delicate as white bread, but has other charms. Here we have all the flavour of whole, ripe wheat berries crushed so the germ and the bran are present. It therefore has a more gutsy and robust flavour. It also has a crisp and crunchy crust on the outside and is moist and mealy within.

But how can busy people find time to make bread?

I'm afraid it's a myth that breadmaking takes time. True, the bread itself needs its own time, but it will take only about 6-10 minutes of your *actual* time. I have come to the conclusion that it takes me less time than travelling to a really good baker and back. It is also a myth that breadmaking is difficult. One of the joys of making bread is that it needs so few ingredients; in fact, for a straightforward loaf, only four are required.

1 Flour

What the cook needs to know is that there are three types of wheat grain – hard, medium and soft, and the flour they yield will contain something called gluten. In order not to get too technical, gluten can be described as something like chewing gum. Soft grains produce ordinary chewing gum, which will stick somewhat, but hard grains produce something more like bubble gum, which means air can be incorporated and the gluten will stretch and expand into bubbles. Thus, when it comes to baking pastry, biscuits or cakes, what you need are very light-textured, soft grains containing the chewing-gum variety, but in bread, when the action of the yeast needs to rise the dough, you need hard wheat – the bubble-gum variety.

In our country plain flour is always made from soft grains, so this is the one for cakes, pastry and so on, whilst the one labelled strong flour, which has a high gluten content, is the one needed for most types of bread, although for something like a pizza dough, where you don't need the dough to rise as much, a soft ordinary plain flour is, I think, better. So just think chewing gum or bubble gum and you've got your gluten sorted.

Flour milling What happens here is the wheat grains are crushed and ground either between traditional milling stones or modern automatic rollers, but it's the human skill of the miller – not the method – that determines the quality of the flour. A grain of wheat is made up of three components: the protective layers of outer casing called bran, the white starchy endosperm, and the germ, which contains oils, vitamins and protein.

Flours and meals Originally the whole wheat berries were ground into the flour, which, more correctly, should be called meal, hence whole-meal. Flour is the fine white powdery part that has had the bran layers and germ removed. Wholefood enthusiasts will say that white flour, having much of the goodness removed, is a refined produce and not a so-called healthy, whole one.

However, in my opinion we need both types, and thankfully the so-called healthy brown era, with its heavy brown pastries, cakes, pizzas et al has thankfully moved on and given way to a more balanced view on what is or isn't healthy. So now both can be enjoyed equally and combined at times in certain recipes to give the required flavour and texture.

Top row, from left: grains of durum wheat, hard wheat and English soft wheat
Second row: whole meal
Third row: fine semolina and medium semolina
Fourth row: plain white flour, wheatgerm and bran

Self-raising flour This is simply a term used to describe soft flour to which raising agents have been added by the manufacturer.

Semolina This word comes from the Italian, meaning semi milled, and it is, as you can see in the photograph, not ground to fine flour, meaning the grains are coarser. Semolina is what is used for traditionally made pasta – milled from hard wheat grain to a texture specified by the pasta maker so that the finished product will be rough-textured to enable the sauce to cling sufficiently (see page 216). Semolina, from softer wheat, has also played a part in British cuisine, where it has been used in puddings and cakes, and durum semolina gives a lovely texture to shortbread but is now sadly not widely available.

2 Liquid

This is usually water, though milk and buttermilk are sometimes used. The water should always be hand-hot, meaning you can hold your finger in it without discomfort. If the water is too hot it will kill the yeast.

3 Yeast

For beginners this is now blissfully simple, because it's powdered into something called easy-blend dried: no mixing, no waiting for frothy heads and so on. All you do is sprinkle it in with the flour, and that's all. Don't forget to inspect the date stamps, though, because if it's too old it won't do its work.

4 Salt

Salt is an important ingredient in bread, but don't use too much as it slows down the rising. But if you like a little more than I have included in my recipes, then allow a little extra rising time.

Kneading

There are two schools of thought on this: one is 'what a bore', because 3 minutes is a long time in a busy life. Alternatively, some people find the whole operation extremely therapeutic. I am in both camps here: resentful if I'm short of time, but it also has to be said that kneading and daydreaming are a pleasant occupation if time permits.

Kneading in a processor

On busy days it's all perfectly simple. If you use a processor with a dough hook attached, the whole thing – mixing and kneading – really is very little trouble.

How to knead dough

For bread dough that has to be kneaded, simply place it on a flat work surface then stretch it away from you, using the heel of one hand to push from the middle and the clenched knuckles of your other hand to pull the other half of the dough towards you (both hands should move simultaneously to stretch out the dough). Then lift the edges over and back to the middle. Give it a quarter turn and repeat the process. It soon becomes a rather rhythmic operation, and the dough will then start to become very elastic. What happens here is you begin to feel the magic – the dough literally begins to spring into life as you push it away and it defiantly springs back to challenge you. When it's become very smooth, springy and begins to appear blistery on the surface, which takes about 3 minutes, it's then ready to rise.

Rising

We don't need to go into the science of breadmaking, but when flour, water and yeast are introduced to each other, let's say something magical occurs, and the mixture (which started out being a heavy lump of dough), if given the correct amount of time, will stretch and expand to twice its original volume. This process can be speeded up if the dough is put in a warm place, but the longer you leave it to rise naturally at room temperature, the better the bread. I now prefer to just leave it to rise naturally. One point, though: bread will also rise at a cold temperature, so if it's more convenient, pop it in the lowest part of the fridge and let it rise overnight, ready to bake in the morning.

Bread dough, which starts off as a heavy lump, stretches over time and expands to twice its original volume

Once the dough has risen, the air is knocked out – just use your fist – and then left to rise again, this time in its tin

What is knocking back and proving?

White bread dough is better if it has a second rise, as this gives a more even texture. So now what happens is you punch, or knock out, all the air using your fist, shape the dough, place it in a tin and give it a second rise, which will be much quicker. The word 'prove' refers to this second rise, because you're actually testing, or proving, that the yeast is still (we hope) alive and kicking.

Bread tins and cooling trays

Good old-fashioned bread tins with pleated corners are thankfully still available (see the photograph on page 72) in 2 lb/900 g (7¼ x 4½ x 3½ inches/ 18.5 x 11.5 x 9 cm) and 1 lb/450 g (6 x 3¾ x 2¾ inches/15 x 9.5 x 7 cm) sizes. Grease them well with butter first. Then, when the bread is cooked, it's most important to remove it from the tin to cool on a wire cooling tray. If you leave it in the tin or place it on a flat surface, it will become steamy and soggy. A cooling tray allows the air to circulate and ensures the crust stays crisp and crunchy.

Is it cooked?

The way to test this is to turn the loaf out, holding it in a cloth, then give the underneath a sharp tap with your knuckles: if it's cooked it will sound hollow and not dense. Remember, it's always better to overbake rather than underbake bread. Because I like an extra crunchy crust, I always put the loaf back in the oven without its tin for 5-10 minutes to crisp up the underneath and sides, so if you do this it will ensure the loaf is cooked through.

Once this second rising, or 'proving', is done, the loaf is ready to be baked in the pre-heated oven

To test whether the loaf is cooked, hold it in a cloth and tap the underneath with your knuckles — it should sound hollow

Plain and Simple White Bread

A good, old-fashioned, English, white, crusty loaf, soft inside and lightly textured, is still hard to beat – it's my own favourite for soldiers to go with softly boiled eggs, and the next day or the day after it always makes divine toast. Made either by hand or with the help of a food processor, it couldn't be easier, and the pleasure of eating it is difficult to match.

Makes 1 large or 2 small loaves
1 lb 8 oz (700 g) strong white bread flour, plus a little extra for the top of the bread
1 tablespoon salt, or less, according to taste
1 teaspoon easy-blend dried yeast
1 teaspoon golden caster sugar
about 15 fl oz (425 ml) hand-hot water

You will also need two 1 lb (450 g) loaf tins or one 2 lb (900 g) loaf tin, well buttered.

Pre-heat the oven to its lowest setting.

Begin by warming the flour in the oven for about 10 minutes, then turn the oven off. Sift the flour, salt, yeast and sugar into a bowl, make a well in the centre of the mixture, then add the water. Now mix to a dough, starting off with a wooden spoon and using your hands in the final stages of mixing, adding a spot more water if there are any dry bits. Wipe the bowl clean with the dough and transfer it to a flat work surface (you may not need to flour this). Knead the dough for 3 minutes or until it develops a sheen and blisters under the surface (it should also be springy and elastic). You can now either return the dough to the mixing bowl or transfer it to a clean bowl; either way, cover it with clingfilm that has been lightly oiled on the side that is facing the dough. Leave it until it looks as though it has doubled in bulk, which will be about 2 hours at room temperature.

After that, knock the air out, then knead again for 2 minutes. Now divide the dough in half, pat each piece out to an oblong, then fold one end into the centre and the other in on top. Put each one into a buttered tin, sprinkle each with a dusting of flour, then place them side by side in an oiled polythene bag until the dough rises above the tops of the tins – this time about an hour at room temperature. Alternatively, place all the dough in the one tin. Meanwhile, pre-heat the oven to gas mark 8, 450°F (230°C).

Bake the loaves on the centre shelf for 30-40 minutes, or 35-45 minutes for the large loaf, until they sound hollow when their bases are tapped. Now return them, out of their tins, upside-down to the oven to crisp the base and side crust for about 5 minutes, then cool on a wire rack.

White bread using the processor

Although making bread as above is not hard, it can be even easier if you make the whole thing in a processor. To do this you fit the dough hook on to the processor (some also have a special bowl), then all you do is sift the dry ingredients into the bowl, put the lid on and switch it on to a low speed or the one recommended in the manufacturer's handbook for use of the dough hook. Now pour the water through the feeding tube, then leave the processor to 'knead' the dough for about 3 minutes – but don't go away, because the machine can sometimes stick and slide about. Then transfer the dough to a clean bowl and cover it with clingfilm that has been lightly oiled on the side facing the dough. Leave it until it looks as though it has doubled in bulk – about 2 hours at room temperature. You can now return the dough to the food processor and let it 'knead' it again for 1 minute, still at a low speed. Then simply continue to make the loaves as above.

Quick and Easy Wholemeal Loaf

The poet Pam Ayres once said, when describing her home-made wholemeal bread, that it was like 'biting into a cornfield', and that's it – the very best description I've ever come across. A crisp, crunchy crust and then all the flavour of the wholewheat grain – take a bite, close your eyes and you'll know just what she meant. Then, when you've grasped how easy wholemeal bread is to make, you'll probably never stop making it. The recipe here is adapted from Doris Grant's famous loaf in her book Your Daily Bread, for which I continue to give thanks.

Makes 1 large or 2 small loaves
1 lb 4 oz (570 g) 100 per cent organically produced wholewheat flour, plus a little extra for the top of the bread
2 teaspoons salt
1 teaspoon soft light brown sugar
2 teaspoons easy-blend dried yeast
about 14 fl oz (400 ml) hand-hot water

You will also need either a 2 lb (900 g) loaf tin or two 1 lb (450 g) loaf tins, well buttered.

Pre-heat the oven to its lowest setting.

Begin by warming the flour slightly in the oven for about 10 minutes, then turn the oven off for now. Next, tip the warm flour into a large mixing bowl and all you do is simply sprinkle on the salt, sugar and easy-blend yeast, mix these together thoroughly, make a well in the centre and pour in the hand-hot water. Then take a wooden spoon and begin to mix the warm liquid into the flour gradually to form a dough: the exact amount of water you'll need will depend on the flour. Finish off by mixing with your hands until you have a smooth dough that leaves the bowl clean – there should be no bits of flour or dough remaining on the sides of the bowl and, unlike pastry, it is better to have too much water than too little.

Now transfer the dough to a flat surface and stretch it out into an oblong, then fold one edge into the centre and the other over that. Now fit the dough into the tin, pressing it firmly all round the edges so that the top will already be slightly rounded. Next, sprinkle the surface with a generous dusting of flour, then cover the tin with a damp, clean tea cloth and leave to rise in a warm place for 30-40 minutes or at room temperature for about an hour. If you're making two loaves, divide the dough in half before following the steps above and folding it into the two tins.

Meanwhile, pre-heat the oven to gas mark 6, 400°F (200°C). When the dough has risen to the top of the bread tin or tins, bake the bread for 40 minutes for the 2 lb (900 g) loaf tin or 30 minutes for the 1 lb (450 g) loaf tins. When the bread is cooked, turn it out on to a cloth to protect your hands – it will sound hollow when rapped underneath with your knuckles. Then return the bread, out of its tin, upside-down to the oven for a further 5-10 minutes to crisp the base and sides. Cool the bread on a wire rack, and never put it away or freeze it until it is absolutely cold.

Toast

A friend of mine invented the term 'wangy', a very accurate word to describe what 90 per cent of the world's catering establishments call toast. It's a good word because we're all absolutely familiar with what it's saying – cold, leathery, bendy little triangles that arrive at breakfast when you are asked, 'Would you like some toast?'

So I've been thinking, as this is a basic cookery course, why not give the world the definitive recipe for perfect toast? To begin with, I am not a disciple of automatic toasters. The ones I've experienced all seem to be a bit hit and miss, and if you're rather inept at slicing bread (like me), then they're not very helpful at all because if the bread is slightly wonky, a) it probably won't go in the toaster at all, and, b) if it does, one bit ends up not being toasted at all while the other bit is giving off nasty black smoke signals!

1   The key to slicing bread is to use gentle, rapid sawing movements with the knife and not to push down too hard on the loaf. For toast, cut the bread into slices of about ½ inch (1 cm) thickness. The crusts can be on or off, depending on how you like them.
2   Pre-heat the grill for at least 10 minutes before making the toast, turning it to its highest setting.
3   Place the bread on the grill rack and position the tray 2 inches (5 cm) from the heat source.
4   Allow the bread to toast on both sides to your own preferred degree of pale or dark golden brown.
5   While that is happening, keep an eye on it and don't wander far away.
6   When the toast is done, remove it immediately to a toast rack. Why a toast rack? Because they are a brilliant invention. Freshly made toast contains steam, and if you place it in a vertical position, in which the air is allowed to circulate, the steam escapes and the toast becomes crisp and crunchy. Putting it straight on to a plate means the steam is trapped underneath, making it damp and soggy. If you don't possess a toast rack you really ought to invest in a modest one. Failing that, stand your slices of toast up against a jar or something similar for about 1 minute before serving.
7   Always eat toast as soon as possible after that, and never make it ahead of time.
8   Never ever wrap it in a napkin or cover it (the cardinal sin of the catering trade), because the steam gets trapped and the toast gets soggy.
9   Always use good bread, because the better the bread, the better the toast. It is also preferable if the bread is a couple of days old.

A toast rack is absolutely necessary if you want to avoid soggy toast; failing that, prop the slices up against a jar for a minute or so before serving

Goats' Cheese, Onion and Potato Bread with Thyme

Don't make this if you are on a diet – it's so wonderful that it's impossible to stop eating it. It's also great for a packed lunch or journey because you've got the bread and cheese all in one. It must also be the quickest, easiest home-made bread on record.

Makes 1 loaf, to serve 4-6
1 x 4 oz (110 g) round firm goats' cheese
4 spring onions, finely sliced
1 medium red potato weighing approximately 6 oz (175 g)
1 rounded teaspoon chopped thyme leaves, plus a few small sprigs
6 oz (175 g) self-raising flour, plus a little extra for the top of the loaf
1 teaspoon salt
⅛ teaspoon or generous pinch of cayenne pepper
1 large egg
2 tablespoons milk
1 heaped teaspoon grain mustard

You will also need a small, solid baking sheet, very well greased.

Pre-heat the oven to gas mark 5, 375°F (190°C).

Start off by taking your sharpest knife, then pare the rind from the cheese and cut it into ½ inch (1 cm) cubes. Then sift the flour, salt and cayenne into a big, roomy mixing bowl, holding the sieve up high to give the flour a good airing. Then thinly pare off the potato skin using a potato peeler and grate the potato straight into the flour using the coarse side of the grater. Then add the spring onions, chopped thyme and two-thirds of the cheese. Now take a palette knife and blend everything together thoroughly.

After that, beat the egg gently with the milk and mustard, then pour the mixture into the bowl, just bringing it all together to a loose, rough dough, still using the palette knife. Next transfer it on to the baking sheet and pat it gently into a 6 inch (15 cm) rough round. Now lightly press the rest of the cheese over the surface, dust with a little flour and scatter the small sprigs of thyme over.

Bake the bread on the middle shelf of the oven for 45-50 minutes or until golden brown. Then remove it to a cooling rack and serve it still slightly warm if possible (but I have to say it's still divine a day later, warmed through in the oven).

Feta Cheese, Potato and Rosemary Bread

This is a delicious variation on the recipe above, using a different cheese and a different herb. Simply substitute the goats' cheese for the same amount of cubed Feta cheese, a quarter of a red onion, peeled and finely chopped, instead of the spring onions, and use rosemary instead of thyme. Before baking, scatter over a quarter of an onion, sliced into half-moon shapes, along with some small sprigs of rosemary and a few halved olives.

Goats' Cheese, Onion and Potato Bread with Thyme, right; Feta Cheese, Potato and Rosemary Bread, left

Parsnip, Parmesan and Sage Bread

In this loaf the potatoes in the previous recipe are replaced with parsnips – a great alternative. I love to serve this with the Curried Parsnip and Apple Soup from the Winter Collection, as it extends the parsnip flavour, but it's also good with tomato or any other soup, or for a snack with crisp apples and celery and a soft, ripe, creamy cheese such as Brie, Camembert or Dolcelatte.

Makes 1 loaf, to serve 4-6
6 oz (175 g) parsnips (peeled weight)
2 oz (50 g) Parmesan (Parmigiano Reggiano), cut into ¼ inch (5 mm) cubes
1 rounded tablespoon chopped fresh sage
8 oz (225 g) self-raising flour
1½ teaspoons salt
2 large eggs, lightly beaten
1 tablespoon milk

For the topping:
1 oz (25 g) Parmesan (Parmigiano Reggiano) shavings
a few whole small sage leaves
a little extra flour for dusting
1 teaspoon olive oil

You will also need a small, solid baking sheet, very well greased.

Pre-heat the oven to gas mark 5, 375°F (190°C).

First of all sift the flour and salt into a large, roomy bowl. Then put a grater in the bowl and coarsely grate the parsnips into the flour, then toss them around. After that, add the cubes of Parmesan and chopped sage and toss that in. Now lightly beat the eggs and milk together, then add this to the bowl a little at a time, mixing evenly with a palette knife. What you should end up with is a rough, rather loose, sticky dough, so don't worry what it looks like at this stage. Transfer this to the baking sheet and pat it gently into a 6 inch (15 cm) rough round, then make a cross with the blunt side of a knife. Now scatter the Parmesan shavings over the surface, followed by a sprinkling of flour. Finally, spoon the olive oil into a dish, dip each sage leaf in the oil and scatter them over the bread. Now it should go into the oven on a high shelf to bake for 45-50 minutes, by which time it will be golden and crusty. It then needs to go on a wire rack, then either serve it still warm or re-heat it later.

Irish Oatmeal Soda Bread

This is the real thing – proper Irish bread. As it bakes in the oven and the aroma reaches you, close your eyes, picture the beauty of the Irish landscape and dream you're there. It's heaven just spread generously with butter and good jam, or, now that we can buy good Irish cheeses, a chunk of Cashel Blue or Milleens with this bread, as well as a glass of Murphy's, will give you a little taste of that wonderful country, even though you're not there.

This could not be easier. Begin by placing the dry ingredients in a large, roomy bowl, mix to combine, then beat the egg and buttermilk together and add them to the dry ingredients. Start mixing, first with a fork, then finish off with your hands to form a smooth dough. All you do now is transfer the dough to the loaf tin and level the top. Alternatively, shape into a round about 6 inches (15 cm) across and make a deep cut across it three times, but don't cut all the way through. Sprinkle with flour and bake in the centre of the oven for 50-60 minutes, then turn it straight out on to a wire rack to cool. This is best eaten fresh, but fear not, because the next day or the day after, it makes wonderful toast.

Makes 1 loaf, to serve 4-6
6 oz (175 g) wholemeal flour
2 oz (50 g) plain flour
2 oz (50 g) pinhead oatmeal
1 oz (25 g) wheatgerm
1 teaspoon bicarbonate of soda
1½ teaspoons salt
1 teaspoon sugar
1 large egg
10 fl oz (275 ml) buttermilk
a little extra flour for dusting

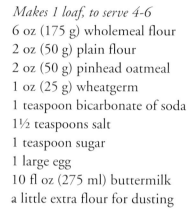

You will also need a 1 lb (450 g) loaf tin, well greased.

Pre-heat the oven to gas mark 5, 375°F (190°C).

Cornmeal and Mixed-Seed Bread

This is another very quick and easy loaf, but with lots of varying textures. And don't worry if the sunflower seeds turn green during baking – it actually looks very attractive.

Makes 1 small loaf

5 oz (150 g) polenta (cornmeal)
6 oz (175 g) strong white bread flour
1 rounded teaspoon salt
1 teaspoon bicarbonate of soda
1 oz (25 g) pumpkin seeds
1 oz (25 g) sunflower seeds
1 oz (25 g) poppy seeds, reserving 1 teaspoon for the top of the loaf
1 oz (25 g) pinhead oatmeal
1 rounded teaspoon golden caster sugar
1 large egg
10 fl oz (275 ml) buttermilk

You will also need a 1 lb (450 g) loaf tin, lightly oiled.

Pre-heat the oven to gas mark 5, 375°F (190°C).

Begin by sifting the flour, salt and bicarbonate of soda together into a large bowl, then add the polenta, all the seeds, the oatmeal and caster sugar and give everything a good mixing. Next, whisk the egg and buttermilk together, add this to the bowl and gradually stir with a wooden spoon until the mixture forms a soft and slack dough. Now just transfer the dough to the prepared loaf tin, scatter the reserved poppy seeds over and bake the loaf on the middle shelf of the oven for 50-60 minutes. The loaf is cooked when after you've turned it out it sounds hollow when you tap the underneath with your knuckles. Return it to the oven upside-down, without its tin, for 5 minutes to give it a final 'crunch', then cool it on a wire rack.

Crostini Lazio

Italian in origin, crostini are 'little crusts'. In France they are called croutons, but both are little rounds or squares of bread brushed with olive oil or butter, and sometimes crushed garlic, then baked in the oven.

For the crostini, drizzle the olive oil over the baking tray, add the garlic, then, using your hands, spread the oil and garlic over the surface of the baking tray. Now place the bread on top of the oil and turn them over so that both sides are lightly coated. Now bake them in the oven for 10-15 minutes, until crisp and crunchy, but put a timer on, as they soon overbake.

For the topping, just peel the rind off the goats' cheese using a sharp knife, then cut the cheese into four pieces. Next place all the ingredients, including the reserved oil, into a liquidiser or processor and blend until the mixture is smooth. If making this ahead, cover and chill in the refrigerator till needed, then remove it half an hour before serving and spread it on top of the crostini, topped with a caper berry (if using). Don't assemble them until the last minute, though, or the bread loses some of its crispness.

Makes 12, to serve 4-6
For the crostini:
1 small, thin French stick cut into 12 slices about 1 inch (2.5 cm) thick, or 3 slices from a thick sliced loaf, cut into quarters
3 tablespoons olive oil
1 fat clove garlic, peeled and crushed

For the topping:
4 oz (110 g) firm goats' cheese
4 oz (110 g) tuna in oil – the best quality you can buy – drained, reserving 1 tablespoon of the oil
1 tablespoon salted capers or capers in vinegar, thoroughly rinsed and drained
1 tablespoon finely grated Parmesan (Parmigiano Reggiano)
1 dessertspoon lemon juice

To garnish:
12 caper berries (optional)

You will also need a baking tray measuring 14 x 10 inches (35 x 25.5 cm).

Pre-heat the oven to gas mark 4, 350°F (180°C).

Bruschetta

Bruschetta is a very special type of toasted bread, pronounced brusketta. When I first tasted the real thing in Tuscany, it was one of the most memorable eating experiences of my life. Italian country bread is toasted on both sides over hot, fragrant coals, then slashes are made along the surface of each piece of bread, which is then rubbed with an open clove of garlic. After that, peppery Italian extra virgin olive oil is poured over quite generously so that it runs into the bread, making little pools all around the base of the plate. The pleasure and joy in its utter simplicity are indescribable.

Given that few of us have hot coals handy (though don't forget bruschetta during the barbecue season), the next best thing is a cast-iron ridged griddle or, failing that, an ordinary domestic grill.

First pre-heat the ridged griddle over a high heat for about 10 minutes. When it's really hot, place the slices of bread – on the diagonal – and grill them for about 1 minute on each side, until they're golden and crisp and have charred strips across each side. (Alternatively, toast them under a conventional grill.) Then, as they are ready, take a sharp knife and quickly make about three little slashes across each one, rub the garlic in and drizzle about half a tablespoon of olive oil over each one. Serve straight away, sprinkled with a little rock salt.

Makes 12, to serve 4-6
1 ciabatta loaf, cut in 12 thin slices
1 clove garlic, peeled and rubbed in a little salt
about 6 tablespoons extra virgin olive oil
rock salt

You will also need a cast-iron ridged griddle.

Bruschetta with Tomato and Basil

Good bread, good olive oil – what more could you want? Just two things: very red, ripe plum tomatoes and basil leaves. It's perhaps the best bruschetta of all, and perfect for serving with drinks before a meal instead of serving a starter.

Prepare the tomatoes before toasting the bread. All you do is place them in a bowl, pour boiling water over them and leave for exactly 1 minute before draining them and slipping off the skins (protect your hands with a cloth if they are too hot). Then chop them finely.

When the bruschetta are made (as above), top with the tomatoes and basil leaves, season with salt and freshly milled black pepper and sprinkle a few more drops of olive oil over before serving. It's hard to believe that something so simple can be so wonderful.

Makes 12, to serve 4-6
6 red, ripe plum tomatoes
a few torn basil leaves
a few drops extra virgin olive oil
rock salt and freshly milled black pepper

Bruschetta with Tomato and Basil

Croque Monsieur

Serves 1
2 large slices good-quality white
bread, buttered
2 oz (50 g) Gruyère, finely grated
2-3 slices smoked cooked ham, Parma
ham or wafer-thin ham
½ oz (10 g) butter, melted
1 dessertspoon finely grated Parmesan
(Parmigiano Reggiano)
salt and freshly milled black pepper

Pre-heat the grill to its highest setting.

This is my version of the toasted cheese and ham sandwich of café society fame, and just thinking about it and imagining atmospheric, crowded pavement cafés makes me long to be in Paris and eat it there. But, that not being possible, it's one of the nicest snack meals for one that I know.

This could not be simpler. On one slice of the buttered bread, spread half the grated Gruyère, then cover that with the slices of ham, folding them if need be to fit the size of the bread. Now sprinkle the rest of the Gruyère on top of the ham, season, then press the other slice of bread on top of that and press it down very firmly. You can at this stage cut off the crusts, but I think they add extra crunchiness. Now brush half the melted butter on the top side of the sandwich, sprinkle it with half the Parmesan and press it in. Now transfer the sandwich to the grill pan and grill it for about 2 minutes, 2 inches (5 cm) from the heat. When it's golden brown, turn it over, brush the other side with the remaining melted butter, sprinkle the rest of the Parmesan all over and grill for another 2 minutes. Then remove it from the grill, cut it into quarters and eat it while it's still crunchy.

Toasted Cheese and Chilli Relish Sandwich

This is the vegetarian version of Croque Monsieur. You can use the ready-made relish normally served with burgers, or my own home-made version on page 188.

Serves 1
2 large slices good-quality white bread,
buttered
2 heaped teaspoons tomato chilli relish
2 oz (50 g) Gruyère, finely grated
½ small onion, peeled and sliced
into thin rings
½ oz (10 g) butter, melted
1 oz (25 g) Parmesan (Parmigiano
Reggiano), finely grated
salt and freshly milled black pepper

Pre-heat the grill to its highest setting.

Start off by spreading both slices of bread with a heaped teaspoon of relish each. Now sprinkle the Gruyère on one of the slices, then sprinkle the onion rings over, season with salt and pepper and then place the other piece of bread on top.

Next, brush the top of the sandwich with half the melted butter and sprinkle over half the Parmesan, lightly pressing it down. Then place the sandwich on the grill rack and grill it 2 inches (5 cm) from the heat until the top of the sandwich is golden brown – about 2 minutes. Then turn the sandwich over and brush the top with the rest of the melted butter and Parmesan, then return the sandwich to the grill for another 2 minutes. Finally, cut it into quarters and eat it pretty quickly.

Croque Monsieur

Basic Pizza Dough

Pizza dough is made in almost the same way as the white bread on page 80 – by hand or using a food processor, except that you add olive oil and a little sugar to the flour mixture and there isn't a second rising. You might consider making double the quantity and freezing half to make another pizza at a later stage. Just pop the dough, after knocking out the air, into a polythene bag, seal and freeze.

Makes a 10 inch (25.5 cm) base pizza – serves 2
6 oz (175 g) plain white soft flour (see page 75)
1 teaspoon salt
1 teaspoon easy-blend dried yeast
½ teaspoon golden caster sugar
1 tablespoon olive oil
4 fl oz (120 ml) hand-hot water

To roll out:
2-3 tablespoons cornmeal (polenta)

You will also need a pizza stone or solid baking sheet measuring 14 x 11 inches (35 x 28 cm).

Pre-heat the oven to its lowest setting.

Left to right: once the dough has doubled in bulk, remove the clingfilm; now tip the dough on to the work surface and knock out the air; finally, knead briefly using the cornmeal and shape into a ball

Begin by warming the flour slightly in the oven for about 10 minutes, then turn the oven off. Sift the flour, salt, yeast and sugar into a bowl and make a well in the centre of the mixture, then add the olive oil and pour in the water. Now mix to a dough, starting off with a wooden spoon and using your hands in the final stages of mixing. Wipe the bowl clean with the dough, adding a spot more water if there are any dry bits left, and transfer it to a flat work surface (there shouldn't be any need to flour this). Knead the dough for 3 minutes or until it develops a sheen and blisters under the surface (it should also be springy and elastic). You can now either leave the dough on the surface covered by the upturned bowl or transfer the dough to a clean bowl and cover it with clingfilm that has been lightly oiled on the side that is facing the dough. Leave it until it looks as though it has doubled in bulk, which will be about an hour at room temperature.

Having made the dough and left it to rise, pre-heat the oven to gas mark 8, 450°F (230°C), along with the pizza stone or baking sheet. The next stage is to tip the dough back on to a work surface that has been sprinkled generously with cornmeal to prevent it from sticking. Knock all the air out of the dough and knead it for a couple of seconds to begin shaping it into a ball. Then dust your rolling pin with cornmeal and roll the dough out to a circle that is approximately 10 inches (25.5 cm) in diameter. Then finish stretching it out with your hands, working from the centre and using the flat of your fingers to push the dough out; it doesn't need to be a perfect round, but you want it to be a fairly thin-based pizza, with slightly raised edges. Now you can top the pizza with one of the toppings that follow.

Quattro Formaggio (Four Cheese) Pizza

This is the classic version of one of the most wonderful combinations of bread and cheese imaginable. You can, of course, vary the cheeses, but the ones I've chosen here are a truly magical combination.

First make the pizza base as described opposite. Then, using a thick oven glove, very carefully lift the baking sheet or pizza stone out of the oven and sprinkle it with cornmeal. Now carefully lift the pizza dough on to the stone or baking sheet and quickly arrange teaspoonfuls of Ricotta here and there all over. After that, scatter the Mozzarella and Gorgonzola pieces in-between and, finally, scatter the Parmesan over. Bake the whole thing on a high shelf for 10-12 minutes, until the crust is golden brown and the cheese is bubbling. You can lift the edge up slightly to check that the underneath is crisp and brown. Carefully remove the baking sheet or pizza stone from the oven, again using a thick oven glove, and serve the pizza on hot plates straight away.

Sufficient for a 10 inch (25.5 cm) base pizza – serves 2
1 basic pizza base (see opposite)
2½ oz (60 g) Ricotta
2 oz (50 g) Mozzarella, cut into 1 inch (2.5 cm) slices
2 oz (50 g) Gorgonzola Piccante, cut into 1 inch (2.5 cm) slices
1 oz (25 g) Parmesan (Parmigiano Reggiano), grated
a little cornmeal (polenta) for dusting

Four Seasons Pizza

*Sufficient for a 10 inch (25.5 cm)
base pizza – serves 2*
1 basic pizza base (see page 94)
1 heaped tablespoon sun-dried
tomato paste
3 oz (75 g) Parma ham (about 4 slices)
5 oz (150 g) Mozzarella, cubed
4 oz (110 g) small tomatoes, thinly
sliced (approximately 3 tomatoes)
2 oz (50 g) small open mushrooms,
thinly sliced
1 rounded tablespoon salted capers or
capers in vinegar, rinsed and drained
8 pitted black olives, halved
4 anchovy fillets, drained and split in
half lengthways
a few basil leaves, dipped in oil and
torn, plus a few extra leaves to garnish
2 tablespoons olive oil

*Originally the toppings were placed on this pizza in four sections,
representing each season, but because this pizza serves two, it's better
to distribute them around more evenly.*

Begin by making the pizza base as described on page 94, then spread the
sun-dried tomato paste up to the edges of the pizza dough. Carefully lift it
on to the hot baking sheet or pizza stone, then first lay the slices of Parma
ham over, folding them, then simply scatter the cubes of Mozzarella, the
tomatoes, mushrooms, capers and olives all over. Finally, decorate with the
anchovy fillets in a criss-cross pattern and the basil leaves. Now drizzle the
olive oil over and bake on a high shelf for 10-12 minutes, until the crust is
golden brown, then scatter the whole basil leaves over before serving.

*Four Seasons Pizza; uncooked, above,
and cooked, right*

Puttanesca Pizza

Puttanesca has always been one of my favourite pasta sauces – strong and gutsy, with lots of flavour – then one inspired day I decided to try it on a pizza base instead. The result is brilliant, with the added charm of pools of Mozzarella and crusty bread.

First make the pizza base as described on page 94. For the sauce, heat the oil in a medium saucepan, then add the garlic and chilli and cook briefly until the garlic is pale gold. Then add all the other sauce ingredients, stir and season with a little pepper – but no salt because of the anchovies. Turn the heat to low and let the sauce simmer very gently without a lid for 40 minutes, by which time it will have reduced to a lovely, thick mass with very little liquid left. Spread the filling over the pizza base, taking it up to the raised edge, then carefully lift it on to the hot baking sheet or pizza stone. Now scatter the Mozzarella over, then dip the basil leaves in the olive oil and place them here and there on top. Bake the pizza on a high shelf for 10-12 minutes, until the crust is golden brown and crusty. Use an oven glove to remove it from the oven, then garnish with the extra basil.

Sufficient for a 10 inch (25.5 cm) base pizza – serves 2
1 basic pizza base (see page 94)

For the sauce:
1 tablespoon olive oil
1 clove garlic, peeled and finely chopped
½ red chilli, deseeded and finely chopped
1 heaped teaspoon chopped fresh basil
8 oz (225 g) fresh tomatoes, skinned and chopped
1 oz (25 g) anchovies, drained and cut in half lengthways
3 oz (75 g) black olives, pitted and chopped small
1 dessertspoon salted capers or capers in vinegar, rinsed and drained
freshly milled black pepper

For the topping:
5 oz (150 g) Mozzarella, cut into 1 inch (2.5 cm) slices
a few small whole fresh basil leaves, plus a few extra to garnish
a little olive oil

Puttanesca Pizza; cooked, left, and uncooked, above

97

Steamed Panettone Pudding with Eliza Acton's Hot Punch Sauce

Yes, this is a bread recipe. Panettone is an Italian fruit bread that's sold here mostly in the autumn and around Christmas time in beautifully designed boxes with carrying ribbons. If you would like a light but quite delectable alternative to Christmas pudding, this is it. I've tried making it in advance, freezing and then re-heating it, and it works beautifully. But don't confine it to Christmas, as it's a truly great steamed pudding to serve at any time, particularly with Eliza's extremely alcoholic citrus sauce.

Serves 6
For the steamed panettone pudding:
3 x 100 g panettone cakes or the same amount from a 500 g panettone cake
6 oz (175 g) dried mixed fruit, soaked in 3 tablespoons rum overnight
2 oz (50 g) whole almonds with their skins left on
2 oz (50 g) candied peel, finely chopped
grated zest 1 orange
grated zest 2 lemons
2 oz (50 g) molasses sugar
10 fl oz (275 ml) milk
5 fl oz (150 ml) double cream
3 large eggs

For Eliza Acton's hot punch sauce:
1 large orange
1 lemon
4 oz (110 g) caster sugar
10 fl oz (275 ml) water
1 oz (25 g) plain flour
2 oz (50 g) unsalted butter, softened
2 tablespoons rum
2 tablespoons brandy
6 fl oz (175 ml) medium sherry

You will also need a 2 pint (1.2 litre) pudding basin, well buttered, and either a double pan steamer or a large saucepan with a fan steamer and a tight-fitting lid, and some foil and string.

You need to begin this by soaking the dried mixed fruit in the rum overnight. The next day, toast the almonds. To do this, pre-heat the grill to its highest setting for 10 minutes, then place the almonds on some foil and toast them under the grill for 2-3 minutes, but don't go away, as they will burn very quickly. When they look nicely toasted and browned on one side, turn them all over and toast the other side, then remove them from the grill and leave them aside to cool.

Next, cut the panettone into 1 inch (2.5 cm) chunks and place them in a large mixing bowl, along with the candied peel, orange and lemon zests and the soaked dried mixed fruit and any drops of rum that didn't get soaked up. Now chop the almonds into thin slivers and add these. Now give it all a really good stir to distribute everything evenly.

Then, in another bowl, whisk together the sugar, milk, cream and eggs and pour this all over the panettone, giving everything another good mix. Now pour the mixture into the buttered pudding basin and press everything down to pack it in. Now cover the top of the pudding with a double sheet of foil measuring about 10 inches (25.5 cm) square and tie it securely with the string round the top of the basin, then make a string handle by taking a length of string over the top of the pudding basin and attaching it to each side – this will help you lift the pudding into the steamer. Now boil a kettle and pour the boiling water into the saucepan, about half-full, place it on a medium heat and, when it comes back to the boil, fit the steamer over the top.

Now pop the pudding in, put the lid on and steam the pudding for exactly 2 hours. After 1 hour, check the water level in the saucepan and, if necessary, top it up with boiling water. If you are using a fan steamer, put in enough water to just reach the steamer, and you'll need to top it up two or three times.

Meanwhile, make the hot punch sauce. First prepare the orange and lemon zests, and to do this it's best to use a potato peeler and pare off the outer zest, leaving the white pith behind. What you need is four strips of each zest measuring approximately 2 x 1 inch (5 x 2.5 cm). Then, using a sharp knife, cut the strips into very thin, needle-like shreds. Now pop these into a medium-sized saucepan, along with the sugar and water, bring everything up to a slow simmer and let it simmer as gently as possible for 15 minutes.

While that is happening, squeeze the juice from the orange and lemon, and in a separate bowl, mix the flour and butter together to form a paste.

When the 15 minutes is up, add the orange and lemon juice, along with the rum, brandy and sherry, and bring it all back up to a gentle heat. Now add the paste to the liquid in small, peanut-sized pieces, whisking as you add them, until they have dissolved and the sauce has thickened. Serve the sauce hot in a warmed serving jug, and if you make it in advance, re-heat it gently without letting it come to the boil.

To serve the pudding, remove the foil and string and let it stand for 5-10 minutes, then slide a palette knife all round to loosen it and turn it out on to a warmed plate. Pour some of the hot punch sauce over the pudding and carry it to the table, with the rest of the sauce in a jug to hand round separately.

5

First steps in pastry

If you can't make pastry, or don't even know how to start, the very first thing you need to do is forgive yourself and not feel guilty – please understand it isn't because you're inadequate or not born to such things, it's probably because no one's ever actually taught you how. In the age we now live in, cooking skills are rarely learnt from watching mother, because working mothers have little time for home baking. So now we have to think differently. But teaching is essential: someone had to teach you to swim, ride a bike or drive a car, things that are now second nature to you.

With pastry it is precisely the same: someone (hopefully me) has to show you how, then, with a bit of practice, pastry-making will also become automatic, something you do without having to think about it.

What I want to do here is show you how to make two basic types of pastry, and, if you master these, you can have a lifetime of happy pastry cooking without having to worry.

What is pastry?

Originally pastry was an inedible paste used to seal in juices and aromas, but there must have been a time when some clever person thought, 'What a waste,' added some fat and made it deliciously edible in its own right, so that now the pastry crust itself is every bit as important as what it encases or surrounds.

But what should it be like? What are the constituents of a really good pastry crust? Firstly it should be crisp, but the word that has been adopted to describe perfect pastry is 'short' (meaning meltingly light). It should also be well baked and offer a character and flavour in its own right so that it complements whatever it is partnering.

I have a theory about how to make good pastry at home, and that's to keep it simple. Professional pâtissiers have years of training and great skills, and we can all be dazzled by what they can produce. The trouble is that if we have busy lives, we can't do the same at home, so we should enjoy their expertise whenever we can. But at home, learn to master simple pastry well. It's also important not to fall into the trap of some chefs by adding too much fat, because sometimes the pastry gets so rich that it begins to compete with and not complement the filling.

The case for shortcrust

Not fashionable, not clever, not over-rich, but for my money the humble shortcrust is one of the best pastries of all. What it provides is a light, crisp, melting crust, which has all the important flavours of the wheat – all that you imagine home-made pastry to be. It is made, quite simply, from flour, fat and water, with nothing else added. But a well-made, thinly rolled shortcrust provides a discreet 'melt in the mouth' presence, a perfect backdrop to the richness, intensity or even delicacy of filling and ingredients. But first let's take a look at what is needed to make a good pastry.

Ingredients

Flour

This should always be plain and made from soft wheat (ie, not strong bread flour). Note the date stamp when you buy it and be careful of how long you store it: flour can lurk in the back of cupboards long after its shelf life has ended, and I have found that stale flour does not make the best pastry. In my opinion, self-raising flour does not make good shortcrust, and neither does 100 per cent wholemeal – witness those stodgy 'brown' creations that are offered in the name of healthy eating. A mixture of half wholemeal and half soft plain flour, however, does work well and gives a nutty flavour.

Fat

The type you use is your choice, and can depend on whether or not you are a vegetarian or have anything against animal fats. Whipped vegetable fats and margarines can be used, but after years of cooking and side-by-side tests and tastings, my opinion is that, in most cases, the very best flavour and texture I've obtained with shortcrust pastry is when equal quantities of lard and butter are used. Generally speaking, the amount of fat in shortcrust is half the amount of flour: thus for 4 oz (110 g) of flour you use 2 oz (50 g) of fat. People sometimes add more fat because they think this will produce a 'shorter' texture; I do not agree with this and feel the result is actually heavier and too rich and fatty.

Fat temperature is the single most important rule to remember. Fat should be at room temperature and soft enough for a knife to make an indentation straight through it in a second. This is because it needs to be incorporated into the flour as quickly as possible – if it's too cold, you will have to rub it in for twice as long, making the fat oily with the warmth of your hands and the pastry difficult to roll out. One tip here: leave a note on the fridge the night before you want to make the pastry saying, 'Don't forget to remove fat!'

But help! I forgot! Don't worry – so do we all, but don't panic. Put the cold fat, cut into lumps, in a processor, together with the flour, and process with the pulse button till you have a crumbly mixture (see page 106).

Salt

I've changed my mind on this over the years and now think that pastry, like bread, needs some salt, even if it is to be used in sweet dishes.

Keep cool

This means you yourself, psychologically, as well, because keeping things as cold as possible is important. If the fat, as I mentioned earlier, becomes oily because the rubbing takes longer and everything is too warm, what happens is it coats more flour grains than it should. This means the flour is unable to absorb enough water and the pastry will crumble and be difficult to roll out. I always make pastry by an open window, as a bit of a draught coming in seems to keep things nicely cool.

Liquid

In shortcrust pastry don't use milk or egg – just add plain water, and leave the tap running to get the water as cold as possible. Remember, too, that exact amounts can never be specified in recipes, because the amount of water that flour absorbs varies. Start with about 1 tablespoon, sprinkling it evenly all round, then add more little by little. Too much water will make the pastry stick and too difficult to roll out, and when it's baked it will be hard; too little water, on the other hand, will also make rolling out a problem, and the cooked result will be too crumbly. However, don't be afraid – if you follow the precise directions given below and on page 106, it's easy to get just the right amount.

Air

Believe it or not, air is the most important ingredient in pastry. So, rule number one is to sift the flour into the bowl, holding the sieve as high up as possible, so that the flour gets a really good airing before you begin.

Rubbing in

Once the flour is sifted into the bowl, add the fat, cut into smallish lumps, then take a knife and begin to cut the fat into the flour. Go on doing this until it looks fairly evenly blended, then begin to rub the fat into the flour using only your fingertips and being as light and gentle as possible. Being light with your fingers is not a special gift, it's just a conscious decision, a signal the brain gives to the fingertips, and then a bit of concentration.

As you lightly rub the fat into the flour, lift it up high and let it fall back down into the bowl, which again means that air is being incorporated all the time, and air is what makes pastry light. Speed is also what's needed here, so don't start daydreaming and go on rubbing all day, but just long enough to make the mixture crumbly with a few odd lumps here and there.

Adding the water and mixing

Sprinkle 1 tablespoon of cold water in, then, with a knife, start bringing the dough together, cutting and turning and using the knife to begin to make it cling together. Then discard the knife and, finally, bring it all together with your fingertips. When enough liquid is added, all the bits of flour and fat should be incorporated and the pastry should leave the bowl completely clean. If this hasn't happened, then add a spot more water (sometimes it really only needs your fingers dipped into water once or twice to bring it together).

Processing pastry

I have found it impossible to make shortcrust pastry in a processor alone, as you can't gauge how much water the pastry needs without feeling it. But it is possible to process the flour and fat in a processor, and the advantage is that you can take the fat straight out of the fridge. Be careful not to over-process: just 1-2 minutes on a low speed is enough. Then tip it into a bowl and add the water as described earlier.

Resting

All pastries must be rested before rolling out. If you're in a hurry, this can seem like an awful bore, but I promise you resting the pastry will, in fact, save you more time in the end. Why does it need to be rested? Flour contains something called gluten (see page 75), and gluten reacts to water in a way which – if it's given time – makes the dough more elastic in texture, so that when you come to roll out the pastry, this elasticity makes the dough roll out like a dream. Without this resting time rolling can be a nightmare, because the pastry won't have enough stretch so it will break and crack. So, as the pastry is made, place it in a polythene bag and leave it in the fridge for 30 minutes.

Surface

A flat surface is all you need to roll out – a pastry board is not absolutely necessary – a scrubbed kitchen top will do. If, however, you want to go on making pastry, you might like to invest in a piece of granite or marble. It is expensive and very heavy, but it will last a lifetime and can be purchased from a stonemason or marble supplier. The ideal size is approximately 18 x 18 inches (46 x 46 cm).

Rolling out

Rolling out, as I've said, is easy if the pastry has been rested. Use a rolling pin that is absolutely straight – handles can get in the way if you want to roll out large quantities. Place the dough on a lightly floured surface and place the pin, also dusted with flour, in the centre of it, then place the flat of your hands lightly on each end of the pin and begin to roll, re-dusting the pin and surface lightly with flour if you need to stop the pastry from sticking.

If you want to roll it out to a round, give it quarter turns as it expands and, provided you roll backwards and forwards, it will roll out into a round shape. Don't be tempted to roll from side to side, unless for some reason you want to roll out a map of the UK! If you can concentrate on only going backwards and forwards, you will end up with a better rounded shape. If you want an oblong, just knock the sides gently with the rolling pin to keep it in shape; if you want a square, give quarter turns – as for a round – and then square it up using the rolling pin to knock the edges into shape.

Storing pastry

Making pastry in advance is perfectly alright – it will keep for up to three days in a polythene bag in the fridge, but don't forget to remove it and let it come back to room temperature before rolling it out. Raw pastry also freezes extremely well for up to three months.

Basic Shortcrust Pastry

4 oz (110 g) plain flour, plus a little extra for dusting
pinch of salt
1 oz (25 g) softened lard
1 oz (25 g) softened butter
a little cold water

Begin by sifting the flour and pinch of salt into a large bowl, holding the sieve as high as possible, so that they get a really good airing before you begin. Now add the lard and butter, cut into smallish lumps, then take a knife and begin to cut the fat into the flour. Go on doing this until it looks fairly evenly blended, then begin to rub the fat into the flour using your fingertips only and being as light as possible. As you gently rub the fat into the flour, lift it up high and let it fall back into the bowl, which again means that all the time air is being incorporated, but do this just long enough to make the mixture crumbly with a few odd lumps here and there.

Now sprinkle 1 tablespoon of water in, then, with a knife, start bringing the dough together, using the knife to make it cling. Then discard the knife and, finally, bring it together with your fingertips. When enough liquid is added, the pastry should leave the bowl fairly clean. If this hasn't happened, then add a spot more water. Now place the pastry in a polythene bag and leave it in the refrigerator for 30 minutes to rest.

Note: This will make 6 oz (175 g) finished weight of pastry, which will be enough to line a 7 or 8 inch (18 or 20 cm) flan or quiche tin.

Begin by sifting the flour and salt into a large bowl, then add the soft fat; if the fat is too cold, it won't rub in effectively

Starting with a knife, cut the fat into the flour, then lightly rub it in with your fingertips until the mixture looks crumbly

Add the liquid by sprinkling it all over the mixture, then use a knife again to start bringing the dough together

The final stage is to bring the pastry together with your hands, adding a little more liquid if necessary

How to line the flan tin

Once the pastry is rolled out to the correct size, place the rolling pin in the centre, fold the pastry over and lift it on to the pin. Then transfer it to the flan tin, laying it down evenly and carefully. Now, using your hands, gently press the pastry into the tin to line the base and sides. (If, while you were lifting the pastry, you found it stretched, don't worry – as you line the tin, ease the stretchiness back, especially round the edges.) When you've pressed it all round with your fingers, try to ease the pastry that is sticking up above the edges back down, so what you're in fact doing is reinforcing the edge, because if it gets stretched too much, it will shrink during cooking. When you've lined the tin, trim off any excess around the edges with a knife, but press the edges again so you have ¼ inch (5 mm) above the edges of the tin.

Pre-baking

Forget about baking beans – it's really all too much bother. Provided you've lined the tin correctly, as above, all you now need to do is prick the base all over with a fork, as this will release any trapped air, which is what causes the centre to rise up. Then brush the base and sides all over with beaten egg, which will provide a sort of waterproof coating so that the pastry stays beautifully crisp even after the filling has gone in. Normally this small amount of beaten egg can be taken from the egg used for the filling in the recipe.

The oven

This needs to be pre-heated and, at the same time, you should pre-heat a good, solid baking sheet on the centre shelf. Then pop the pastry case in to pre-bake for 20-25 minutes or until the pastry is turning golden brown. It's a good idea to have a peep halfway through – if the pastry is bubbling up a bit, just prick it with a fork and press it back down again with your hands.

To remove the flan tin, place the tart on a tin or jar, loosen the pastry all round with a small knife or skewer and ease it down

Now pop the pastry in a polythene bag and refrigerate for 30 minutes, which will make rolling it out far less trouble

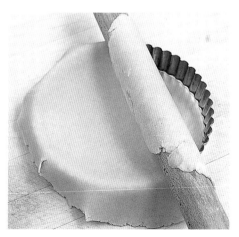

Once rolled out, transfer the pastry to the tin by rolling it over the pin, then gently ease it into the tin using your hands

Finally, prick the base all over with a fork to release any trapped air, then brush the base and sides with the beaten egg

Leek and Goats' Cheese Tart

This is what I call a wobbly tart – creamy and soft-centred. Leeks and goats' cheese have turned out to be a wonderful combination, and the addition of goats' cheese to the pastry gives it a nice edge.

Serves 6 as a starter or 4 as a main course
For the pastry:
1 oz (25 g) firm goats' cheese (rindless)
4 oz (110 g) plain flour, plus a little extra for dusting
pinch of salt
1 oz (25 g) softened lard
1 oz (25 g) softened butter
a little cold water

For the filling:
1 lb 6 oz (625 g) leeks, ie, 12 oz (350 g) trimmed weight (see instructions in the method)
6 oz (175 g) firm goats' cheese (rindless)
½ oz (10 g) butter
3 large eggs, beaten
7 fl oz (200 ml) crème fraîche or double cream
4 spring onions, trimmed and finely sliced, including the green parts
salt and freshly milled black pepper

You will also need a 7½ inch (19 cm) diameter fluted quiche tin with a removable base, 1¼ inches (3 cm) deep, very lightly buttered, and a small, solid baking sheet.

First sift the flour with the pinch of salt into a large bowl, holding the sieve up high to give it a good airing. Then add the lard and butter and, using only your fingertips, lightly rub the fat into the flour, again lifting the mixture up high all the time. When everything is crumbly, coarsely grate the goats' cheese in and then sprinkle in some cold water – about 1 tablespoon. Start to mix the pastry with a knife and then finish off with your hands, adding a few more drops of water, till you have a smooth dough that will leave the bowl clean. Then pop the pastry into a polythene bag and let it rest in the refrigerator for 30 minutes. Meanwhile, pre-heat the oven to gas mark 5, 375°F (190°C) and pop the baking sheet in to pre-heat on the centre shelf.

Now prepare the leeks. First take the tough green ends off and throw them out, then make a vertical split about halfway down the centre of each one

and clean them by running them under the cold-water tap while you fan out the layers – this will rid them of any hidden dust and grit. Then slice them in half lengthways and chop into ½ inch (1 cm) slices.

Next, in a medium-sized frying pan, melt the butter over a gentle heat and add the leeks and some salt. Give it all a good stir and let them cook gently, without a lid, for 10-15 minutes or until the juice runs out of them. Then you need to transfer them to a sieve set over a bowl to drain off the excess juice. Place a saucer with a weight on top of them to press out every last drop.

By this time the pastry will have rested, so remove it from the fridge and roll it out into a circle on a lightly floured surface. As you roll, give it quarter turns to keep the round shape and roll it as thinly as possible. Now transfer it, rolling it over the pin, to the tin. Press it lightly and firmly over the base and sides of the tin, easing any overlapping pastry back down to the sides, as it is important not to stretch it. Now trim the edges and press the pastry up about ¼ inch (5 mm) above the rim of the tin all round, then prick the base all over with a fork. After that, paint some of the beaten egg for the filling over the base and sides. Now place the tin on the baking sheet and bake for 20-25 minutes or until the pastry is crisp and golden. Check halfway through the cooking time to make sure that the pastry isn't rising up in the centre. If it is, just prick it a couple of times and press it back down with your hands.

Leek and Goats' Cheese Tart; cooked, above, and uncooked, left

While the pastry case is pre-baking, crumble the goats' cheese with your hands, then gently combine it with the leeks in the sieve. Now, in a jug, mix the beaten eggs with the crème fraîche or double cream, seasoning with just a little salt (there is some already in the leeks) and a good grinding of freshly milled black pepper. As soon as the pastry case is ready, remove it from the oven, arrange the leeks and cheese all over the base and then sprinkle the spring onions over the top. Now gradually pour half the cream and egg mixture in to join them, then put the tart back on the baking sheet with the oven shelf half pulled out, then slowly pour in the rest of the mixture. Gently slide the shelf back in and bake the tart for 30-35 minutes, until it's firm in the centre and the surface has turned a lovely golden brown. Next, remove it from the oven and allow it to settle for 10 minutes before serving. This 10 minutes is important as it will be much easier to cut into portions. The best way to remove the tart from the tin is to ease the edges from the sides of the tin with a small knife, then place it on an upturned jar or tin, which will allow you to carefully ease the sides away. Next slide a palette knife or wide fish slice underneath and ease the tart on to a plate or board ready to serve, or simply cut it into portions straight from the tin base.

Smoked Fish Tart with a Parmesan Crust

This tart is not as wobbly as the previous one, as it has a substantial amount of filling. The various smoked flavours of the fish are quite sensational partnered with the hint of piquancy in the gherkins and capers.

Serves 6-8 as a starter or 4-6 as a main course
For the pastry:
1 oz (25 g) finely grated Parmesan (Parmigiano Reggiano)
4 oz (110 g) plain flour, plus a little extra for dusting
pinch of salt
1 oz (25 g) softened lard
1 oz (25 g) softened butter
a little cold water

For the filling:
8 oz (225 g) undyed smoked haddock (skinned raw weight)
4 oz (110 g) kipper fillet (skinned raw weight)
9 oz (250 g) smoked salmon trimmings
2 fl oz (55 ml) milk
1 bay leaf
pinch of ground mace
2 large eggs, plus 2 egg yolks
a little ground nutmeg
7 fl oz (200 ml) crème fraîche or double cream
1 dessertspoon salted capers or capers in vinegar, well rinsed and drained
2 cocktail gherkins (cornichons), finely chopped
freshly milled black pepper

You will also need a 7½ inch (19 cm) diameter fluted quiche tin with a removable base, 1¼ inches (3 cm) deep, very lightly buttered, and a small, solid baking sheet.

First of all sift the flour with the pinch of salt into a large bowl, holding the sieve up high to give them a good airing. Then add the lard and butter and, using only your fingertips, lightly and gently rub the fat into the flour, again lifting the mixture up high all the time to give it a good airing. When everything is crumbly, add the Parmesan and then sprinkle in some cold water – about 1 tablespoon. Start to mix the pastry with a knife and then finish off with your hands, adding more drops of water till you have a smooth dough that will leave the bowl clean. Then pop the pastry into a polythene bag and let it rest in the refrigerator for 30 minutes.

Meanwhile, pre-heat the oven to gas mark 5, 375°F (190°C) and pop the baking sheet in to pre-heat on the centre shelf.

After that, roll the pastry out into a circle on a surface lightly dusted with flour, and as you roll, give it quarter turns to keep the round shape, rolling it as thinly as possible. Now transfer it, rolling it over the pin, to the tin. Press it lightly and firmly all over the base and sides of the tin, easing any overlapping pastry back down to the sides, as it is important not to stretch it too much. Now trim the edges and press the pastry up about ¼ inch (5 mm) above the rim of the tin all round. Then prick the base all over with a fork and, after that, brush some of the beaten egg for the filling all over the base and sides. Now place the tin on the baking sheet and bake it for 20-25 minutes or until the pastry is crisp and golden. Check halfway through the cooking time to make sure that the pastry isn't rising up in the centre. If it is, just prick it again a couple of times and press it back down again with your hands.

When the pastry is cooked, remove the tin from the oven and lower the temperature to gas mark 3, 325°F (170°C).

For the filling, put the haddock and kipper in a medium-sized saucepan, along with the milk, bay leaf and mace. Now bring it up to simmering point, cover with a lid and poach gently for about 2 minutes, then remove the fish from the milk. Discard the bay leaf, but reserve the milk.

Then lightly whisk the eggs and egg yolks together with a seasoning of black pepper and nutmeg, but no salt, as the fish will be fairly salty. Then heat the reserved milk, whisking in the crème fraîche or double cream. Then, when it has come to simmering point, pour it over the beaten eggs, whisking well. Now divide the cooked haddock and kipper into flakes about ½ inch (1 cm) in size and arrange them in the cooked pastry case, along with the smoked salmon trimmings. Next scatter the capers and gherkins all over and slowly pour half the cream and egg mixture in, allowing the liquid to settle between each addition. Then place the baking sheet in the oven, gradually add the remainder of the filling and cook for 30-35 minutes or until the surface is golden brown and feels firm in the centre.

When you have removed it from the oven, let it rest for 10 minutes, then ease it away from the edges using a small knife and place it on a suitable-sized jar, which will allow you to carefully ease the sides away. Then slide a palette knife or wide fish slice underneath and ease the tart carefully on to a plate or board ready to serve, or simply cut it into portions straight from the tin base.

Smoked Fish Tart with a Parmesan Crust; cooked, left, and uncooked, below

Pumpkin Pie

This recipe uses another version of shortcrust pastry that is used for sweet open-faced flans and tarts. It's richer than shortcrust, but very crisp, and the eggs give it a shortbread quality. Nuts can sometimes be added; here there are toasted pecans, although walnuts or hazelnuts can be used, or the pastry can be made without nuts if you prefer. In autumn I love the velvet texture of pumpkin, but this tart could be made with butternut squash.

Serves 8

For the pastry:

1½ oz (40 g) pecan nuts
6 oz (175 g) plain flour, plus a little extra for dusting
½ oz (10 g) icing sugar
pinch of salt
3 oz (75 g) softened butter
a little cold water
1 large egg yolk

For the filling:

1 lb (450 g) prepared weight pumpkin flesh, cut into 1 inch (2.5 cm) chunks
2 large eggs plus 1 yolk (reserve the white)
1 tablespoon molasses
3 oz (75 g) soft dark brown sugar
1 teaspoon ground cinnamon
½ teaspoon freshly grated nutmeg
½ teaspoon ground allspice
½ teaspoon ground cloves
½ teaspoon ground ginger
10 fl oz (275 ml) double cream

You will also need a 9 inch (23 cm) diameter fluted flan tin, 1½ inches (4 cm) deep, with a loose base, lightly greased, and a medium-sized solid baking sheet.

Pre-heat the oven to gas mark 4, 350°F (180°C).

To begin this you need to toast the pecan nuts. First of all, when the oven has pre-heated, spread the nuts out on the baking sheet and toast them lightly for 8 minutes, using a timer so that you don't forget them. After that, remove them from the oven to a chopping board (turning the oven off for now) and let them cool a little. Then either chop them really finely by hand or in a processor using the pulse action. Be careful here, though, because if you overdo it they will go oily.

For the pastry, first of all sift the flour, icing sugar and the pinch of salt into a large bowl, holding the sieve up high to give them a good airing. Then add the butter and start cutting it into the flour using a knife, then, using only your fingertips, lightly and gently rub it into the flour, again lifting the mixture up high all the time to give it a good airing.

When everything is crumbly, add the chopped nuts, then sprinkle in about 1 tablespoon of water and the egg yolk. Start to mix the pastry with a knife and then finish off with your hands, lightly bringing it together (you may need to add more water) until you have a smooth dough that will leave the bowl clean. Then pop it into a polythene bag and let it rest in the refrigerator for 30 minutes.

Meanwhile, pre-heat the oven to gas mark 4, 350°F (180°C) with the baking sheet inside. Now place a steamer over a pan of simmering water, add the pumpkin, put a lid on and steam for 15-20 minutes, until the pieces feel tender when tested with a skewer. After that, place a large, coarse sieve over a bowl and press the pumpkin through it to extract any seeds or fibres.

By this time the pastry will have rested, so now remove it from the fridge. Roll it out into a circle on a surface lightly dusted with flour, and as you roll, give it quarter turns to keep the round shape. Roll it into a circle approximately 12 inches (30 cm) in diameter, as thinly as possible. Now transfer it, rolling it over the pin, to the tin. Press it lightly and firmly all over the base and sides of the tin, easing any overlapping pastry back down the sides, as it is important not to stretch this bit too much. Now trim the edge, leaving ¼ inch (5 mm) above the rim of the tin all round. Then prick the base all over with a fork and brush it and the sides with the reserved egg white, lightly beaten. Now place the tin on the pre-heated baking sheet on the centre shelf of the oven and bake it for 20-25 minutes, until the pastry is crisp and golden. Check halfway through the cooking time to make sure that the pastry isn't rising up in the centre. If it is, just prick it again a couple of times and press it back down again with your hands.

Now for the filling. First lightly whisk the eggs and extra yolk together in a large bowl. Next measure the molasses (lightly greasing the spoon first, as this makes things easier), then just push the molasses off the spoon with a rubber spatula into a saucepan. Add the sugar, spices and the cream, then bring it up to simmering point, giving it a whisk to mix everything together. Then pour it over the eggs and whisk it again briefly. Now add the pumpkin purée, still whisking to combine everything thoroughly, then pour the filling into a jug. When the pastry case is ready, remove it from the oven on the baking sheet using an oven glove. Then pour half the filling in, return it to the oven, then, with the shelf half out, pour in the rest of the filling and slide the shelf back in. Bake the pie for 35-40 minutes, by which time it will puff up round the edges but still feel slightly wobbly in the centre. Then remove it from the oven and place the tin on a wire cooling rack.

I prefer to serve this chilled (stored loosely covered in foil in the fridge) with some equally chilled crème fraîche, but warm or at room temperature would be fine. In America, ice cream is the preferred accompaniment.

Old-Fashioned English Custard Tart

This old-fashioned Custard Tart needs a thick, wobbly filling, so I've used a round tin with sloping sides and a rim, which gives a good depth. The nutmeg is very important to the flavour, so always use it freshly grated and grate it on to a piece of foil, which helps when you have to sprinkle it on quickly when it goes into the oven.

Serves 6
For the shortcrust pastry:
5 oz (150 g) plain flour, plus a little extra for dusting
pinch of salt
1 oz (25 g) softened lard
1½ oz (40 g) softened butter
a little cold water

For the filling:
1 pint (570 ml) single cream
3 large eggs, plus 2 large egg yolks, lightly beaten
2 oz (50 g) caster sugar
½ teaspoon vanilla extract
1½ whole nutmegs, freshly grated
1 teaspoon softened butter

You will also need a 2 inch (5 cm) leaf cutter, a tin that has a rim and sloping sides (1½ inches/4 cm deep, with a 7 inch/18 cm base and a ½ inch/1 cm rim), lightly greased, and a medium-sized, solid baking sheet.

To make the pastry, first of all sift the flour with the pinch of salt into a large bowl, holding the sieve up high to give it a good airing. Then add the lard and butter and, using only your fingertips, lightly and gently rub the fat into the flour, again lifting the mixture up high all the time to give it a good airing.

When everything is crumbly, sprinkle in about 1 tablespoon of cold water. Start to mix the pastry with a knife and then finish off with your hands, adding a few more drops of water, till you have a smooth dough that leaves the bowl clean. Then pop the pastry into a polythene bag and let it rest in the refrigerator for 30 minutes. Meanwhile, pre-heat the oven to gas mark 5, 375°F (190°C) and pop the baking sheet in to pre-heat on the centre shelf.

After that, roll the rest of the pastry out into a circle, giving it quarter turns to keep its round shape; it's a good idea at this stage to put the tin lightly on top of the pastry – the size needs to be 1 inch (2.5 cm) bigger all round. Now transfer it, rolling it over the pin, to the tin, and press it lightly and firmly around the base, sides and rim. Now take a sharp knife and trim the overlapping pastry. Then press the rim of the pastry so that about ¼ inch (5 mm) overlaps the edge. Next, roll the trimmings and cut out about 24 leaves, making veins in them with the blunt side of the knife. Now brush the whole surface of the pastry case with some of the beaten eggs, arranging the leaves all around the rim, overlapping them. Brush these, too, with beaten egg. Now prick the base of the tart with a fork, then place it on the baking sheet and bake on the centre shelf for 20 minutes, until the pastry is crisp and golden. Check after 4 minutes to make sure that the pastry isn't rising up in the centre. If it is, prick it again a couple of times, pressing it back down with your hands. After 20 minutes, remove it from the oven, leaving the baking sheet there, and reduce the temperature to gas mark 3, 325°F (170°C).

Now place the cream in a saucepan and bring it up to a gentle simmer, then whisk the beaten egg mixture and sugar together in a large heatproof jug using a balloon whisk – but not too vigorously because you don't want to make bubbles. Then pour the hot liquid over the beaten eggs, add the vanilla extract and half the nutmeg and whisk briefly again.

Now place the pie tin back on the baking tray with the oven shelf half out and have ready the rest of the grated nutmeg on a piece of foil. Carefully pour the filling into the pastry case (it will be very full) and scatter the rest of the nutmeg all over, then dot with the softened butter and bake in the oven for 30-40 minutes, until the filling is golden brown, firm in the centre and slightly puffed up. Serve either warm or, as I actually prefer it, cold.

Apple and Raisin Parcels

This is yet another version of a good old apple pie, but the great thing about this recipe is that it bakes into individual portions, so it's much easier when you come to serve it. Raisins are a good winter addition, but in autumn you could replace them with 4 oz (110 g) of blackberries or, in summer, make the whole thing with 1 lb (450 g) of gooseberries, adding 3½oz (95 g) sugar.

Serves 8

For the shortcrust pastry:

12 oz (350 g) plain flour
pinch of salt
3 oz (75 g) softened lard
3 oz (75 g) softened butter
a little cold water

For the filling:

8 oz (225 g) Bramley apples (unpeeled),
cored and cut into ½ inch (1 cm) dice
4 oz (110 g) Cox's apples (unpeeled),
cored and cut into ½ inch (1 cm) dice
3 oz (75 g) raisins, soaked overnight in
4 fl oz (120 ml) dry cider
8 teaspoons semolina
16 whole cloves
2 oz (50 g) golden caster sugar, plus an
extra teaspoon for sprinkling
1 egg white, lightly beaten

You will also need a non-stick baking tin measuring 10 x 6 inches (25.5 x 15 cm) and 1 inch (2.5 cm) deep.

Start this recipe the night before by soaking the raisins in the cider. The next day, start the pastry, and to do this sift the flour with the pinch of salt into a large bowl, holding the sieve high. Add the lard and butter and, using your fingertips, lightly rub the fat into the flour, lifting the mixture up to give it a good airing. When the mixture is crumbly, add about a tablespoon of cold water. Start mixing the pastry with a knife, then finish off with your hands, adding a little more water, till you have a smooth dough that leaves the bowl clean. Now pop it in a polythene bag and chill for 30 minutes.

Meanwhile, pre-heat the oven to gas mark 6, 400°F (200°C). Remove the pastry from the fridge, then divide it into four pieces. Dust your work surface lightly with flour, then roll each into a length about 10 x 5 inches (25.5 x 13 cm) and trim each piece into two 5 inch (13 cm) squares. Working with two squares at a time, scatter a teaspoon of semolina over each pastry square, then mix both varieties of apple together and add 2 tablespoons of chopped apples, 2 cloves, 2 teaspoons of sugar and some drained raisins to each square. Now brush the edges of each square with some of the beaten egg white, then loosely fold the corners over. Then, using a fish slice to help you, lift each parcel into the tin, tucking them neatly into the corners, and repeat with the remaining squares so that they all fit snugly in the tin. If you have any fruit left over, carefully lift the corners of each parcel and add some more apples and raisins. Now either leave the parcels open or squeeze the pastry corners together a little more (for the closed version see the photo on page 100). Next brush the pastry with the remaining beaten egg white and scatter the rest of the sugar over, along with the extra teaspoon of sugar. Bake in the oven on the shelf just above centre for 50 minutes, then serve warm with cream, ice cream or Traditional English Custard (see page 62), and don't forget to warn your guests that there are a few whole cloves lurking.

Note: If you're using blackberries, gooseberries, rhubarb or blackcurrants, use a level dessertspoon of semolina in each parcel to absorb the extra juice.

Quick and easy flaky pastry

Clever chefs and professional pâtissiers make proper puff pastry and sometimes call it *millefeuille* (meaning 'thousand leaves'). It involves rolling and folding the pastry several times to trap the air, and letting it rest between rollings. It is a labour of love and dedication – and can be therapeutic if you have time to lock yourself away for a few hours – but it is not something for the fraught cook, trying to juggle this with the rest of life happening outside the kitchen. Yet all is not lost because there is a quick and easy version – crisp, light and, if you close your eyes, you won't know whether you are eating 50 or 1,000 leaves, because the taste will be the same.

Quick flaky pastry is really a cheat's version, because it doesn't involve the turning, rolling, resting and all the palaver that goes into the real thing. The advantage is that what you get is a home-made pastry made purely with butter, which gives you a texture and flavour that is quite unique and special but, at the same time, doesn't involve either a lot of time or – believe it or not – a lot of skill. The secret is grating partly frozen butter, then mixing it with flour (so no boring rubbing in). It really does involve the minimum of skill but, at the same time, produces spectacular results.

What should perfect flaky pastry be like? Answer: as light as possible, wafer-thin and so crisp it eats like a whisper so that you hardly know it's there. So if you don't believe that it's incredibly easy to achieve, here are the detailed instructions. I promise you will be so pleased with the results that you will probably make four more batches to put in the freezer for a rainy day.

Flour should always be soft, plain and sifted, lifting the sieve high as you do so and letting it fall into a large, roomy bowl. I have said it before, but there is no harm in underlining that the most important ingredient in pastry is air. Sifting the flour like this gives it a good airing.

Butter Because the butter is going to be coarsely grated, it needs to be almost frozen. So measure it out, then wrap it in foil and place it in the freezer or freezing compartment of the fridge for 30-45 minutes. If it is too soft, it won't grate properly.

Resting Like all pastries, quick flaky pastry must be rested after it has been mixed – that means putting it in a polythene bag in the refrigerator and leaving it there for 30 minutes.

Baking Because this pastry has a high fat content, it's essential to have a high oven temperature, which is important if you want to achieve that lovely light, crisp effect, so do be sure to pre-heat the oven before baking the pastry.

Texture Quick flaky pastry is not puff pastry, so don't expect it to rise up like a thousand leaves. It is light-textured and flaky, though, and will puff and rise fractionally when it is cooking.

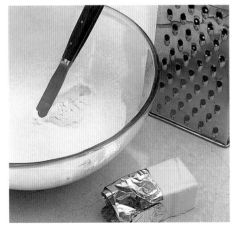

Your secret weapons in this cheat's flaky pastry are frozen butter and a grater…

To begin the recipe, first of all remove a pack of butter from the fridge, weigh out 4 oz (110 g), then wrap it in a piece of foil and return it to the freezer or freezing compartment of the fridge for 30-45 minutes.

Then, when you are ready to make the pastry, sift the flour and salt into a large, roomy bowl. Take the butter out of the freezer, fold back the foil and hold it in the foil, which will protect it from your warm hands. Then, using the coarse side of a grater placed in the bowl over the flour, grate the butter, dipping the edge of the butter on to the flour several times to make it easier to grate. What you will end up with is a large pile of grated butter sitting in the middle of the flour. Now take a palette knife and start to distribute the gratings into the flour – don't use your hands yet, just keep trying to coat all the pieces of fat with flour. Now sprinkle 2 tablespoons of cold water all over, continue to use the palette knife to bring the whole thing together, and finish off using your hands. If you need a bit more moisture, that's fine – just remember that the dough should come together in such a way that it leaves the bowl fairly clean, with no bits of loose butter or flour anywhere. Now pop it into a polythene bag and chill for 30 minutes before using. Remember, this, like other pastries, freezes extremely well, in which case you will need to defrost it thoroughly and let it come back to room temperature before rolling it out on a lightly floured surface.

For the pastry:
4 oz (110 g) butter
6 oz (175 g) plain flour
pinch of salt
a little cold water

All you do is grate the frozen butter into the flour using the coarse side of the grater

Once the butter is distributed, add water and use a palette knife to combine

Finish off with your hands, adding a little more water if the pastry needs it

Tomato and Goats' Cheese Galettes

Galettes are very thin discs of pastry which, unlike conventional tarts, have no sides. The concept is a good one because the pastry is barely there, yet it gives a light, very crisp background to all kinds of toppings, both savoury and sweet. There's no limit to what you can put on top of them – the combinations are endless, and you can serve them for a light lunch, as a first course, on a picnic or for a dessert. What I often do is freeze the pastry circles raw, interleaved with foil or greaseproof paper, so you can just whip some out for an impromptu meal any old time at all. If you don't have the right-sized cutter, just cut around a saucer of the same size.

The first of my recipes for galettes calls for lovely ripe red tomatoes for colour, and the preferred cheese in our house is Crottin de Chavignol, but any firm goats' cheese will do.

*Serves 3 as a light lunch
or 6 as a first course*
quick flaky pastry made with 6 oz (175 g) plain flour and 4 oz (110 g) butter (see page 119)
12 medium tomatoes
7 oz (200 g) firm goats' cheese
18 large basil leaves, plus 6 sprigs for garnish
a little olive oil, for drizzling
salt and freshly milled black pepper

You will also need two solid baking sheets measuring 14 x 11 inches (35 x 28 cm), lightly greased, and a 6 inch (15 cm) plain pastry cutter.

Pre-heat the oven to gas mark 7, 425°F (220°C).

Make the pastry as described on page 119 and chill for 30 minutes in the fridge. Meanwhile, you need to skin the tomatoes, so pour boiling water over them and leave for exactly 1 minute before draining and slipping off the skins (protect your hands with a cloth if they are too hot). Next, on a lightly floured surface, roll out the pastry very thinly to ⅛ inch (3 mm), cut out six 6 inch (15 cm) discs and place these on the baking sheets.

Now scatter the large basil leaves over the pastry, tearing them first if they're very large. Next, thinly slice the tomatoes and arrange them in circles overlapping each other on top of the basil. Peel the goats' cheese and crumble it over the tomatoes, then pour some olive oil on to a saucer and dip the reserved basil leaves in it, placing one on each tart. Then season well and drizzle each one with a little extra olive oil. Now bake the galettes in the oven, one tray on a high shelf, the other on the next one down, for 10-12 minutes or until the tomatoes are tinged brown and the cheese is bubbling, swapping the baking sheets over halfway through. Serve warm straight from the oven, or they're still excellent cold, cooled on a wire tray.

Feta Cheese, Spinach and Pine Nut Galettes

This is a very Greek combination where, authentically, the filling gets wrapped in pastry parcels. I now prefer this version, though, which has less pastry and is much prettier to look at.

Make the pastry as described on page 119 and chill it for 30 minutes in the fridge. Meanwhile, cook the spinach by placing it in a saucepan with a lid on, then place it over a medium heat. Just let it collapse down into its own juices, timing it for 2-3 minutes and turning it over halfway through. Drain the spinach in a colander, pressing it with a saucer to extract every last bit of juice, then season with a little nutmeg. Next roll out the pastry on a lightly floured surface to ⅛ inch (3 mm), cut out six 6 inch (15 cm) discs and place these on the baking sheets. Finely chop the spinach and divide it between the pastry circles, spreading it out towards the edges of the pastry but leaving a small uncovered rim around the edge. Next scatter the Feta over the spinach, then sprinkle over the pine nuts. Now cook the galettes for 10-12 minutes, one tray on the high shelf, the other on the next one down, until golden brown, swapping the baking sheets over halfway through. Remove from the oven, sprinkle the Parmesan over and serve warm, or cool on a cooling tray.

Serves 3 as a light lunch or 6 as a first course

quick flaky pastry made with 6 oz (175 g) plain flour and 4 oz (110 g) butter (see page 119)
4½ oz (125 g) Feta cheese, chopped into small cubes
8 oz (225 g) young leaf spinach
1 oz (25 g) pine nuts
a little freshly grated nutmeg
1 oz (25g) Parmesan (Parmigiano Reggiano), finely grated

You will also need two solid baking sheets measuring 14 x 11 inches (35 x 28 cm), lightly greased, and a 6 inch (15 cm) plain pastry cutter.

Pre-heat the oven to gas mark 7, 425°F (220°C).

Tomato and Goats' Cheese Galette, far left; Feta Cheese, Spinach and Pine Nut Galette, left

Apricot Galettes with Amaretto

Serves 6
quick flaky pastry made with 6 oz
(175 g) plain flour and 4 oz (110 g)
butter (see page 119)
27 ready-to-eat dried apricots
6 teaspoons amaretto liqueur
18 whole blanched almonds, toasted
and cut into slivers (optional)
6 heaped teaspoons demerara sugar

To serve:
a little icing sugar, sieved
7 fl oz (200 ml) crème fraîche

You will also need two 12 x 10 inch
(30 x 25.5 cm) solid baking sheets,
lightly greased, and a 4 inch (10 cm)
plain pastry cutter.

Dried apricots are great for this in the winter, but in summer it's also good with fresh apricots, in which case you'll need the same quantity of small apricots, halved and stoned.

Make the pastry as described on page 119 and chill for 30 minutes in the fridge. Then roll the pastry out on a lightly floured surface to ⅛ inch (3 mm), cut out six 4 inch (10 cm) discs and place these on the baking sheets. Meanwhile, pre-heat the oven to gas mark 7, 425°F (220°C).

Now cut the apricots in half, then place nine apricot halves on each round of pastry, topped by a few almond slivers (if using). Sprinkle a teaspoon of amaretto over each one, then sprinkle them all with the demerara sugar. Bake for 10-12 minutes in the oven, one tray on the highest shelf, the other on the next one down, until the pastry is crisp and brown and the apricots have browned and caramelised a little at the edges, swapping the baking sheets over halfway through. Serve straight from the oven, sprinkled with icing sugar and the chilled crème fraîche, or leave to cool.

Prune and Apple Galettes

Serves 6
quick flaky pastry made with 6 oz
(175 g) plain flour and 4 oz (110 g)
butter (see page 119)
15 mi-cuit prunes, halved lengthways
3 small Cox's apples (unpeeled)
a little ground cinnamon
2 tablespoons runny honey
cream or crème fraîche, to serve

You will also need two 12 x 10 inch
(30 x 25.5 cm) solid baking sheets,
lightly greased, and a 4 inch (10 cm)
plain pastry cutter.

If you can get mi-cuit plums, the lovely squashy half-dried Agen prunes from France, so much the better. If not, then pitted dried Agen prunes will be fine.

Make the pastry as described on page 119 and chill for 30 minutes in the fridge. Then roll out the pastry on a lightly floured surface to ⅛ inch (3 mm), cut out six 4 inch (10 cm) discs and arrange them on the baking sheets. Meanwhile, pre-heat the oven to gas mark 7, 425°F (220°C).

Now cut each apple into quarters, core and then cut each quarter into two. Then arrange five prune halves and four slices of apple in a circle on top of each pastry round, then sprinkle over a little ground cinnamon. Now place the baking sheets in the oven for 10-12 minutes, one tray on the highest shelf, the other on the next one down, until the galettes are golden brown, swapping them over halfway through. Remove from the oven and, while they are still warm, glaze each one by brushing a little of the runny honey over the prunes and apples. Serve warm with cream or crème fraîche.

Poached Pear Galettes

These are exceptionally pretty to look at, and I like to serve them as a sweet ending to a special meal. They're a bit more trouble, but still very easy to make and assemble.

Make the pastry as described on page 119 and chill for 30 minutes in the fridge. Meanwhile, find a lidded saucepan that will fit the pears comfortably, laying them in the pan on their sides. Now mix the wine with the sugar and pour this over the pears, then add the cinnamon stick and ½ vanilla pod. Put the lid on the pan and gently simmer the pears for 45 minutes, until tender when tested with a skewer. Turn them over halfway through the cooking time so the other half sits in the wine and they colour evenly. Towards the end of the cooking time, pre-heat the oven to gas mark 7, 425°F (220°C). Then roll the pastry out to ⅛ inch (3 mm) thick and cut it into six 4 inch (10 cm) circles, then arrange them on the baking sheets.

Now lift the pears from the liquid and halve them by first making a slit in the stalk as you press it on to a flat surface. Then stand each pear upright and cut through the split stalk, halve the pears and remove the cores. Now you need to slice each half into a fan, so take a sharp knife and, starting from the top of the stalk end, about ½ inch (1 cm) in, slice the pear downwards and at a slight angle so you end up with the slices of pear fanning out but still attached to the stalk. Now place each half pear on to a pastry base and fan it out, then place the baking sheets in the oven for 10-12 minutes, one on the top shelf, the other on the next one down, swapping them over halfway through the cooking time.

Meanwhile, you need to reduce the poaching liquid, so first remove the cinnamon stick and vanilla pod, then place the saucepan over a high heat and let it bubble for about 5 minutes. Then, in a cup, mix the arrowroot with a little cold water until you have a smooth paste, then add this to the saucepan, whisking with a balloon whisk all the time. This will thicken the sauce slightly, then remove it from the heat and leave it to cool.

When the tarts are ready, remove them from the oven. Serve hot or cold but, just before serving, pour a little of the sauce over each tart to give them a pretty glaze.

Serves 6

quick flaky pastry made with 6 oz (175 g) plain flour and 4 oz (110 g) butter (see page 119)
3 firm unripe pears, peeled but with the stalks left on
10 fl oz (275 ml) red wine
1 oz (25 g) caster sugar
½ cinnamon stick
½ vanilla pod
1 teaspoon arrowroot

You will also need two 12 x 10 inch (30 x 25.5 cm) solid baking sheets, lightly greased, and a 4 inch (10 cm) plain pastry cutter.

From top: Poached Pear Galette; Prune and Apple Galette; Apricot Galette with Amaretto

Wild Mushroom Tartlets with Poached Quails' Eggs

This is my version of one of the most brilliant first courses I've ever eaten. It was created by Michel Bourdin, head chef at London's prestigious Connaught Hotel. His version has boiled quails' eggs, but I can't bear the fiddle of peeling them, so I now poach them, which cuts out a great deal of time and work. I also have Michel's approval, as he told me that he originally did them like this. It's still not the swiftest, easiest course, but when you want something really special for a celebration, this is it.

Serves 6
quick flaky pastry made with 4 oz
(110 g) flour and 3 oz (75 g) butter
(see page 119)
18 quails' eggs
1 quantity Foaming Hollandaise
(see page 71)

For the mushroom filling:
10 oz (275 g) small, dark-gilled
mushrooms
¾ oz (20 g) dried porcini mushrooms,
soaked in boiling water and drained
5 shallots, peeled
1 oz (25 g) butter
⅓ whole nutmeg, grated
sea salt and freshly milled black pepper

You will also need six ½ inch (1 cm)
deep fluted quiche tins with a base
diameter of 3 inches (7.5 cm) and a
top diameter of 3½ inches (9 cm),
greased with a little melted butter, a
medium-sized solid baking sheet, and
a 4 inch (10 cm) plain cutter.

First, place the fresh and soaked mushrooms and shallots in a food processor till finely chopped. Now melt the butter in a medium-sized pan over a high heat, add the mushroom mixture, nutmeg and seasoning, reduce the heat and gently sauté for 20-25 minutes, until all the juices have evaporated. Then remove from the heat and allow to cool.

On a lightly floured surface, roll out the pastry to ⅛ inch (3 mm) thick and cut out six rounds with the cutter, re-rolling the pastry if necessary. Now line each tin with the pastry, pushing it down from the tops so the pastry doesn't shrink during cooking. Trim the pastry around the tops to ¼ inch (5 mm) and prick the bases with a fork, then refrigerate for 30 minutes.

Pre-heat the oven to gas mark 6, 400°F (200°C). Now place the tins on the baking sheet and bake them on the top shelf of the oven for 15 minutes. (All this can be done well in advance. The mushroom mixture should be cooled, then covered and stored in the fridge, and the pastry cases carefully removed from their tins and stored in an airtight container. The Foaming Hollandaise can also be made in advance and kept at room temperature.)

Then, in a medium-sized frying pan half-filled with boiling water from the kettle, you can begin to poach the eggs. Place the pan over a gentle heat and have a bowl of cold water ready. Now, as soon as the pan has fine bubbles all over the base, make a slit in 6 quails' eggs with a small serrated knife, carefully slipping the eggs in to poach. Put a timer on for 1½ minutes, then, after this time and using a draining spoon, remove them, starting with the first one that went in. Transfer them to the bowl of cold water, then repeat the whole process twice until all the eggs are poached.

With everything ready – the mushroom filling, the tartlet cases, hollandaise and the poached eggs – you can now assemble the tartlets.

When you are ready to serve the tartlets, pre-heat the grill to its highest setting. Next, place the tartlet cases on a baking sheet, cover with foil and pop them under the grill 6 inches (15 cm) from the heat to warm through for 5 minutes. Then, while this is happening, re-heat the mushroom mixture in a small saucepan and get it really hot. Then fill the pastry cases with the mushroom mixture and top each one with 3 quails' eggs, using a draining spoon and a wodge of kitchen paper to drain off any water. Next spoon the Foaming Hollandaise over, then pop the whole lot back under the grill again, at least 6 inches (15 cm) from the heat, and watch like a hawk – it should take only 30 seconds for the sauce to warm through and brown slightly. Then switch the grill off and serve on warm plates as quickly as possible.

This is a beautiful bite-sized version of mince pies, and I think not as fiddly. If you don't have a pastry wheel you can forgo the frilly edge and use a sharp knife to cut the pastry.

First make the pastry as described on page 119 and chill for 30 minutes. Then remove the rested pastry from the fridge on to a floured surface and shape it into an oblong. Cut the oblong into two, one piece slightly larger than the other, then, on a lightly floured surface, first roll the smaller piece into a rectangle 12 x 10 inches (30 x 25.5 cm), roll it around the rolling pin and transfer it to the baking sheet.

Next brush the surface of the pastry with the beaten egg, then, with the oblong turned lengthways, place 5 level teaspoons of mincemeat along one top edge and carry on with another row until you end up with six rows of mincemeat blobs. Now roll the larger piece of pastry into another oblong approximately 13 x 11 inches (32.5 x 28 cm), transfer this again by wrapping it around the rolling pin, and lay it carefully over the bottom piece of pastry, being careful not to trap too much air. Now gently press the pastry together to seal the little squares, then trim the edges and cut the whole lot into little squares using the pastry wheel. Next, with a pair of small scissors, make 2 little snips in each one to allow the air to escape. Now bake the whole lot in the oven for 15 minutes or until golden brown.

To serve, pre-heat the grill to its highest setting for at least 10 minutes, then sprinkle the ravioli liberally with the sifted icing sugar and place them under the grill, very close to the heat source, for 40-60 seconds. What will happen is the icing sugar will caramelise to a lovely shiny glaze. Then serve dusted with a little more icing sugar as soon as they have cooled enough to eat, or cool and serve cold. Alternatively, re-heat and serve warm later.

Makes 30
quick flaky pastry made with 8 oz (225 g) plain flour and 6 oz (175 g) butter (see page 119)
7 oz (200 g) good-quality mincemeat
1 large egg, beaten
1 oz (25 g) icing sugar, sifted, plus extra for dusting

You will also need a solid baking sheet measuring 16 x 12 inches (40 x 30 cm), lightly greased, and a pastry wheel.

Pre-heat the oven to gas mark 6, 400°F (200°C).

6

Cakes and biscuits for beginners

If you think you can't make a cake, let me tell you now that you most certainly can. Cake-making is not the minefield of possible disaster that many people imagine it to be. Basically, there are only two things you have to remember: number one is to always follow the rules, and number two is to always follow the recipe. Making a cake can never be a throw-it-all-in-and-see-what-happens affair, and people who boast about never following recipes are, I suspect, happy with a good deal of mediocrity. The perfect cake, as I've said, needs close attention to the rules, and once you know what they are, it makes the whole thing blissfully clear and simple.

When making cakes, it's vital that the butter you use is extremely soft

The all-in-one method means that all the ingredients go into the bowl together…

…then are whipped to a smooth, soft consistency using a hand-held whisk

The case for making a cake

A home-made cake has a lot going for it on days when life seems to lack that special edge. So instead of attempting to treat yourself to something bland and boring made in a factory, why not try the real thing? Home baking transports you psychologically to a world of comfort and wellbeing – the quality of life seems utterly assured as your home is filled with the warm, evocative aroma of something quietly and happily baking in the oven.

In my *Book Of Cakes*, published way back in 1977, I wrote: 'A cake is a symbol of love and friendship – if someone actually goes to the trouble of baking a cake specially for family and friends, they can't fail to feel spoiled and cared for.' I haven't changed my mind on that, but perhaps the simplest way to start venturing towards a lifetime of happy cakemaking is to take the rules on board and try to memorise them.

The top five rules of cakemaking

1 It is absolutely crucial to use the correct-sized tin
2 You must have a reliable recipe
3 You need to weigh the ingredients correctly
4 Once the cake is in the oven, don't open the door
5 Make sure your oven is functioning correctly

Tin size

This is where 99 per cent of cakemaking goes wrong. I have, over the years, struggled to encourage manufacturers to standardise tin sizes so that people like me, who write and test recipes, are able to communicate in such a way that as many people as possible can enjoy making cakes. Well, I'm sorry to report that until now I have failed, due, I think, to the unacceptable face of commercialism, which also seeks to undercut the competition.

Let me explain. The most popular everyday cake is probably a sponge cake. Well, it's all quite simple: three eggs and a 6 oz (175 g) flour mix fit an 8 inch (20 cm) tin that's 1½ inches (4 cm) deep; two eggs and a 4 oz (110 g) flour mixture fit a 7 inch (18 cm) tin with the same depth. But out there in the high street you will find 7½, 8¾, 7¾ inches. Why? Because the way manufacturers undercut on price is to make tins fractionally smaller and thus cheaper. There is quite a lot of pile-it-high, sell-it-cheap rubbish out there that claims to be baking equipment, so my advice is to only buy the right-sized tins, which thankfully one manufacturer has guaranteed to make, and though quality is costly in the beginning, it *will* last a lifetime. The cheap versions, which need to be constantly replaced, work out to be a lot more expensive.

Depth of tin

This is also crucial, so a sponge tin has to be at least 1½ inches (4 cm) deep because depth of support at the sides encourages the cakes to rise up and be as light and airy as possible.

Larger cake tins

These seem more easily available. An 8 inch (20 cm) round cake tin is a good average size, but remember that if you use a square tin, the same mixture will fit 7 inches (18 cm); the rule is that square tins should always be 1 inch (2.5 cm) smaller than round ones.

Loaf tins

These change like the wind and vary between manufacturers, but thankfully old-fashioned bread tins, as used in Chapter 4, are always available, so I use these for loaf cake recipes. They come in a 2 lb/900 g (7¼ x 4½ x 3½ inches/ 18.5 x 11.5 x 9 cm) or 1 lb/450 g (6 x 3¾ x 2¾ inches/15 x 9.5 x 7 cm) size.

Weighing ingredients

Provided you have a reliable recipe and the right-sized tin, the next step is to weigh everything carefully. The best scales are the balance kind; they will last a lifetime and never let you down. Weighing ingredients in cakemaking is absolutely vital, so never attempt to make a cake if you don't have any means of weighing the ingredients.

Lining sponge tins

Whether or not you use non-stick tins, it's important to line them with non-stick silicone paper (baking parchment), which gives the cake some protection but also makes it easier to remove from the tin. The way to line a sponge tin is shown in the photograph, above right.

Cooling trays

In most cases, once cakes are cooked it's important to cool them with air circulating around them, so a wire cooling tray is a vital piece of equipment.

Please leave it alone!

One of the perennial problems of beginning to cook is curiosity. You've done it, you've made the cake, but it's now out of your sight sitting behind a closed oven door, and even if it's glass, you can't see over the rim of the tin, so you feel anxious, cut off and all you want to do is just have one little peep. Please don't, because it will be a disaster! Without being too technical, what happens to the cake mixture is that the heat causes the air bubbles within it to push up and expand the mixture, making a light, airy cake, and this only happens if the heat is constant until finally the cake has reached a point where it can't expand any more and the structure is set. What happens if you open the oven door is that you send a rush of cold air in, which diminishes the heat and interrupts the expansion process. So instead of rising to great heights, the cake collapses and sinks into heaviness. So now you know *never* to open the door of the oven until at least three-quarters of the cooking time has elapsed.

It's important that the base of the tin is lined with silicone paper (parchment)

Once the mixture is in the tin, level it off using the back of a spoon

Once cooked, turn the cake on to a wire rack, then peel off the base paper

How do I know if it's cooked?

For years, and when I first started cooking, the rule of thumb here was to stick a skewer in the centre of the cake and, if it came out clean, the centre was cooked. But I have changed my mind on that particular rule, firstly because I never found it reliable, and secondly, if the cake had fruit in it, then obviously if the skewer had passed through a sticky raisin it wouldn't be coming out clean, even if the cake was cooked. Now I feel the best test is to press lightly on the centre surface of the cake with your finger (doesn't matter which one), then, if the cake springs back without leaving an impression, it's cooked; if not, give it another 5 minutes.

Cake ingredients

Because I have attempted to simplify things and make cakemaking easily accessible to absolute beginners, I have only included recipes for cakes that are made by the all-in-one method. This means everything is mixed together in just one mixing, so a few notes on the ingredients might be useful here.

Butter and other fats

This must be very soft indeed (see the picture on page 128) so the flat blade of a knife can make a deep impression all the way through immediately. Therefore, I always leave the butter out of the fridge to stay at room temperature overnight, which works beautifully – but as I said in Chapter 5, you may need to leave a note on the fridge door to remind you. Other fats, such as soft margarine or whipped white vegetable fats, need only be out of the fridge for 30 minutes; they produce excellent results but don't, in my opinion, have the flavour of butter.

Flours and raising agents

In most cases cakes are made with self-raising flour, which already has a raising agent, but all-in-one mixtures need a little extra help, so baking powder is also used. Always sift the flour, lifting the sieve up high to give it lots of air as it falls down into the bowl, as air is an important ingredient.

Eggs

Cakes require large eggs (as do all my recipes), and if you keep them in the fridge, remember to remove them one hour before you start baking as they blend more easily with the other ingredients if they're not too cold.

Ovens

As a cookery writer struggling to give people foolproof recipes, all I can say is if I could wave a magic wand so that we all had the same oven, life would be so simple, but every single oven seems to vary. We have fan ovens, fan-assisted ovens, ovens without fans and then all the Aga-type cookers and so on. A cake is a very good test of an oven – if it browns too much on one side and not on the other, it's not your fault – you need to have your oven checked. If cakes are overcooked or undercooked, the temperature thermostat may be faulty. Remember, it's very simple to have it tested professionally, and it only takes about 5 minutes. Alternatively, what I find really useful is having my own thermometer. You can pop this in the oven when you pre-heat it and it will tell you simply and clearly if your oven temperature is true. If it isn't, then you really must have the oven checked.

Fan ovens

Here you must follow the manufacturer's instructions. Because fan ovens vary from manufacturer to manufacturer, it's impossible for me to give correct timings for all of them. So the answer here is to calculate the cooking time according to your oven instruction manual; ie, in a fan oven the heat temperature will be lower and the cooking time will be slightly reduced, and no pre-heating will be needed.

Conventional ovens

This is my preferred choice, and here it is necessary to pre-heat the oven about 10-20 minutes before the cake goes in.

To line a round, greased cake tin, cut a strip of greaseproof paper slightly longer than the circumference of the tin and 3 inches (7.5 cm) higher. Fold it back about 1 inch (2.5 cm) along its length, then snip it at a slight angle at intervals up to the fold. Now press the paper around the sides – the snipped edge will overlap on the base of the tin for a snug fit. Finally, cut a circle out – using the tin as a template – to fit over the snipped paper over the base

To line a square tin, cut a piece of greaseproof paper to size by first measuring the length and width of the tin and then adding twice its depth. Centre the tin on the sheet of paper, then make four cuts from the paper's edge right up to the corners of the tin. Grease the tin and fit the greaseproof paper inside, folding and overlapping it at the corners. For the base paper, cut a square out, again using the tin as a template, and fit it in the base

A Classic Sponge Cake (with Passion-Fruit Filling)

This sponge cake could also be made in a 7 inch (18 cm) tin (just use two eggs and 4 oz/110 g each of flour, sugar and butter). It can then be filled with jam and cream. And while the soft fruits of summer, when they're available, are perfect for filling sponge cakes, in winter, passion fruit fulfil all the criteria needed, ie, something sharp, fragrant and acidic to contrast with the richness of the cake and cream.

Serves 8
For an 8 inch (20 cm) cake:
6 oz (175 g) self-raising flour
1 rounded teaspoon baking powder
3 large eggs at room temperature
6 oz (175 g) very soft butter
6 oz (175 g) golden caster sugar
½ teaspoon vanilla extract
1 dessertspoon caster sugar
a little sifted icing sugar, for dusting

For the filling:
6 passion fruit
9 oz (250 g) Mascarpone
7 fl oz (200 ml) fromage frais
1 dessertspoon golden caster sugar
1 teaspoon vanilla extract

You will also need two 8 inch (20 cm) 1½ inch (4 cm) deep sponge tins, lightly greased and the bases lined with silicone paper (parchment).

Pre-heat the oven to gas mark 3, 325°F (170°C).

Take a very large mixing bowl, put the flour and baking powder in a sieve and sift it into the bowl, holding the sieve high to give it a good airing as it goes down. Now all you do is simply add all the other cake ingredients to the bowl and, provided the butter is really soft, just go in with an electric hand whisk and whisk everything together until you have a smooth, well-combined mixture, which will take about 1 minute. If you don't have an electric hand whisk, you can use a wooden spoon, using a little bit more effort. What you will now end up with is a mixture that drops off a spoon when you give it a tap on the side of the bowl. If it seems a little too stiff, add a little more water and mix again.

Now divide the mixture between the 2 tins, level it out and place the tins on the centre shelf of the oven. The cakes will take 30-35 minutes to cook, but don't open the oven door until 30 minutes have elapsed. To test whether the cakes are cooked or not, touch the centre of each lightly with a finger: if it leaves no impression and the sponges spring back, they are ready.

Next, remove them from the oven, then wait about 5 minutes before turning them out on to a wire cooling rack. Carefully peel off the base papers, which is easier if you make a fold in the paper first, then pull it gently away without trying to lift it off. Now leave the sponges to get completely cold, then add the filling.

To make this, first slice the passion fruit into halves and, using a teaspoon, scoop all the flesh, juice and seeds into a bowl. Next, in another bowl, combine the Mascarpone, fromage frais, sugar and vanilla extract using a balloon whisk, which is the quickest way to blend them all together. After that, fold in about two-thirds of the passion fruit. Now place the first sponge cake on the plate or cake stand you are going to serve it on, then spread half the filling over it, drizzle the rest of the passion fruit over that, then spread the remaining filling over the passion fruit. Lastly, place the other cake on top, press it gently so that the filling oozes out at the edges, then dust the surface with a little sifted icing sugar.

Banana and Walnut Loaf

This is a lovely, moist cake that keeps well and is perfect for picnics or packed lunches. In the summer it's brilliant served cut in thick slices and spread with clotted cream.

Begin, as soon as the oven has pre-heated, by spreading the nuts out on a baking sheet and toasting them lightly in the oven for 7-8 minutes – use a timer so that you don't forget them. After that, remove them from the oven to a chopping board, let them cool briefly, then chop them fairly roughly. Now, in a bowl, peel and mash 3 of the bananas to a purée with a fork, and peel and chop the other one into ½ inch (1 cm) chunks.

Next you need to take a large mixing bowl and sift the salt, baking powder, cinnamon and both the flours into it, holding the sieve up high to give it a good airing, then adding the bran that's left in the sieve. Now simply add all the remaining ingredients (except the chopped banana and nuts) and, using an electric hand whisk, begin to beat the mixture, first on a slow speed for about half a minute, then increasing the speed to mix everything thoroughly and smoothly. Then lightly fold in the chopped banana and walnuts. You may need to add a drop of milk to give a mixture that drops easily off a spoon when you give it a sharp tap on the side of the bowl.

Next pile the mixture into the tin, level the top with the back of a spoon and sprinkle on the demerara sugar. Bake in the centre of the oven for 1¼-1½ hours, until the cake feels springy in the centre. After that, remove it from the oven and let it cool for about 5 minutes before turning it out on to a wire tray. Then let it get completely cold before serving or transferring it to a cake tin.

Serves 8
4 medium bananas (approximately 12 oz/350 g)
6 oz (175 g) walnut pieces
pinch of salt
1 rounded teaspoon baking powder
1 teaspoon ground cinnamon
4 oz (110 g) plain flour
4 oz (110 g) wholewheat flour
grated zest 1 orange
grated zest 1 lemon
4 oz (110 g) butter at room temperature
6 oz (175 g) soft dark brown sugar
2 large eggs at room temperature

For the topping:
1 tablespoon demerara sugar

You will also need a 2 lb (900 g) loaf tin, lightly buttered.

Pre-heat the oven to gas mark 4, 350°F (180°C).

Austrian Coffee and Walnut Cake with Coffee Cream

This is unashamedly rich and luscious. Firstly, coffee and walnuts have a great affinity; secondly, so do coffee and creaminess; and thirdly, because the cake is soaked in coffee syrup, it's also meltingly moist.

First of all you need to toast all the walnuts, so spread them on a baking sheet and place in the pre-heated oven for 7-8 minutes. After that, reserve 10 halves to use as decoration later and finely chop the rest. Take a very large mixing bowl, put the flour and baking powder in a sieve and sift it into the bowl, holding the sieve high to give it a good airing as it goes down.

Now all you do is simply add all the other ingredients (except the coffee and walnuts) to the bowl and, provided the butter is really soft, just go in with an electric hand whisk and whisk everything together until you have a smooth, well-combined mixture, then fold in the coffee and chopped walnuts. This will take about 1 minute but, if you don't have an electric hand whisk, you can use a wooden spoon and a little bit more effort. What you should end up with is a soft mixture that drops off the spoon easily when you give it a sharp tap; if not, add a spot of water. Divide the mixture between the prepared sandwich tins, spreading the mixture around evenly. Then place the tins on the centre shelf of the oven and bake them for 30 minutes.

While the cakes are cooking you can make up the syrup and the filling and topping. For the syrup, first place the coffee and sugar in a heatproof jug, then measure the boiling water into it and stir briskly until the coffee and sugar have dissolved, which will take about 1 minute. Next, the filling and topping, and all you do here is place all the ingredients, except the reserved walnuts, in a bowl and whisk them together till thoroughly blended. Then cover the bowl with clingfilm and chill till needed.

When the cakes are cooked, ie, feel springy in the centre, remove then from the oven but leave them in their tins and prick them all over with a skewer while they are still hot. Now spoon the syrup as evenly as possible over each one and leave them to soak up the liquid as they cool in their tins. When they are absolutely cold, turn them out very carefully and peel off the base papers – it's a good idea to turn one out on to the plate you're going to serve it on. Then spread half the filling and topping mixture over the first cake, place the other cake carefully on top and spread the other half over. Finally, arrange the reserved walnut halves in a circle all around. It's a good idea to chill the cake if you're not going to serve it immediately.

Serves 8

For the sponge cake:
1½ tablespoons instant coffee mixed with 2 tablespoons boiling water
3 oz (75 g) walnut halves
6 oz (175 g) self-raising flour
1½ teaspoons baking powder
6 oz (175 g) softened butter
6 oz (175 g) golden caster sugar
3 large eggs at room temperature

For the syrup:
1 tablespoon instant espresso coffee powder
2 oz (50 g) demerara sugar
2 fl oz (55 ml) boiling water

For the filling and topping:
1 tablespoon instant espresso coffee powder
1 rounded tablespoon golden caster sugar
10 walnut halves, reserved from the sponge cake
9 oz (250 g) Mascarpone
7 fl oz (200 ml) 8 per cent fat fromage frais

You will also need two 8 inch (20 cm) sandwich tins, 1½ inches (4 cm) deep, lightly greased and the bases lined with silicone paper (parchment).

Pre-heat the oven to gas mark 3, 325°F (170°C).

Fresh Coconut Layer Cake

The optimum word here is 'fresh'. If you've ever suffered cakes made with dry, dull desiccated coconut, let me transport you to a different world. Fresh coconut is very moist and has a fragrant, slightly sour, sweet flesh that is perfect for this cake.

Before you start this cake, you'll first have to deal with the coconut. Not half as impenetrable as it might seem, as all you do is first push a skewer into the three holes in the top of the coconut and drain out the milk. Then place the coconut in a polythene bag and sit it on a hard surface – a stone floor or an outside paving stone. Then give it a hefty whack with a hammer – it won't be that difficult to break. Now remove the pieces from the bag and, using a cloth to protect your hands, prise the top of a knife between the nut and the shell. You should find that you can force the whole piece out in one go. Now discard the shell and take off the inner skin using a potato peeler. The coconut is now ready to use. The best way to grate coconut flesh is with the grating disc of a food processor, but a hand grater will do just as well.

To make the cake, sieve the flour and baking powder into a large bowl, holding the sieve high to give them a good airing. Now just add all the other ingredients, except the grated coconut, to the bowl and go in with an electric hand whisk and combine everything until you have a smooth mixture, which will take about 1 minute. If you don't have an electric hand whisk, use a wooden spoon, using a little more effort. What you should now have is a mixture that drops off a spoon when you give it a tap on the side of the bowl. If it seems a little stiff, add a drop of water and mix again. Finally, stir in the finely grated coconut and divide the mixture between the tins. Now place them on the centre shelf of the oven for 30-35 minutes. To test whether the cakes are cooked, lightly touch the centre of each with a finger: if it leaves no impression and the sponges spring back, they are ready.

Next, remove them from the oven, then wait about 5 minutes before turning them out on to a wire cooling rack. Carefully peel off the base papers, and when the cakes are absolutely cold, carefully divide each one horizontally into two halves using a very sharp serrated knife.

Now make up the frosting by simply whisking all the ingredients together in a bowl to combine them. Next select the plate or stand you want to serve the cake on – you'll also need a palette knife – then simply place one cake layer on first, followed by a thin layer of frosting (about a fifth), followed by the next layer of cake and frosting, and so on. After that, use the rest of the frosting to coat the sides and top of the cake. Don't worry how it looks: the good thing is that it's all going to be covered with the rest of the grated coconut next. And that's it!

Serves 8

For the cake:
3 oz (75 g) finely grated fresh coconut
6 oz (175 g) self-raising flour
1 rounded teaspoon baking powder
3 large eggs at room temperature
6 oz (175 g) very soft butter
6 oz (175 g) golden caster sugar
1 teaspoon vanilla extract

For the coconut frosting:
1½ oz (40 g) finely grated fresh coconut
9 oz (250 g) Mascarpone
7 fl oz (200 ml) fromage frais
1 teaspoon vanilla extract
1 dessertspoon golden caster sugar

For the topping and sides:
2 oz (50 g) coarsely grated fresh coconut

You will also need two 8 inch (20 cm) sandwich tins with a depth of 1½ inches (4 cm), lightly greased and the bases lined with silicone paper (parchment).

Pre-heat the oven to gas mark 3, 325°F (170°C).

Low-Fat Moist Carrot Cake

I have been making carrot cake for years, and each time it seems to improve with a little tinkering here and there. Last year I attempted a low-fat version rather reluctantly, not believing it was possible. Now I have to admit it's become one of my favourites. It's also one of the quickest, easiest cakes ever.

Serves 12

6 oz (175 g) dark brown soft sugar, sifted

2 large eggs at room temperature

4 fl oz (120 ml) sunflower oil

7 oz (200 g) wholemeal self-raising flour

1½ teaspoons bicarbonate of soda

3 rounded teaspoons mixed spice

grated zest 1 orange

7 oz (200 g) carrots, peeled and coarsely grated

6 oz (175 g) sultanas

For the topping:

9 oz (250 g) Quark (skimmed-milk soft cheese)

¾ oz (20 g) caster sugar

2 teaspoons vanilla extract

1 rounded teaspoon ground cinnamon, plus a little extra for dusting

For the syrup glaze:

juice ½ small orange

1 dessertspoon lemon juice

1½ oz (40 g) dark brown soft sugar

You will also need a non-stick baking tin measuring 10 x 6 inches (25.5 x 15 cm) and 1 inch (2.5 cm) deep, the base lined with silicone paper (parchment).

Pre-heat the oven to gas mark 3, 325°F (170°C).

Begin by whisking the sugar, eggs and oil together in a bowl using an electric hand whisk for 2-3 minutes. Then sift together the flour, bicarbonate of soda and the mixed spice into the bowl, tipping in all the bits of bran that are left in the sieve. Now stir all this together, then fold in the orange zest, carrots and sultanas. After that pour the mixture into the prepared tin and bake on the centre shelf of the oven for 35-40 minutes, until it is well risen and feels firm and springy to the touch when lightly pressed in the centre.

While the cake is cooking, make the topping by mixing all the ingredients in a bowl until light and fluffy, then cover with clingfilm and chill for 1-2 hours or until needed.

Now you need to make the syrup glaze, and to do this whisk together the fruit juices and sugar in a bowl. Then, when the cake comes out of the oven, stab it all over with a skewer and quickly spoon the syrup over as evenly as possible. Now leave the cake on one side to cool in the tin, during which time the syrup will be absorbed. Then, when the cake is completely cold, remove it from the tin, spread the topping over, cut it into 12 squares and dust with a little more cinnamon.

Spiced Apple Muffin Cake with Pecan Streusel Topping

I have included this because I still get letters from people saying they can't make muffins. My message to them is don't try too hard – undermixing is the golden rule and, once mastered, the American muffin mix makes the lightest cakes in the world. In the summer, you could always substitute the apples for 12 oz (350 g) of fresh apricots, stoned and chopped, or, in the autumn, 12 oz (350 g) of plums, stoned and chopped. In both cases, though, weigh after stoning. This recipe will also make 24 mini or 12 large muffins, cooking them for 20 and 30 minutes respectively.

First of all place the butter in a small saucepan and put it on a gentle heat to melt. Then, as with all muffin mixtures, you need to sift the dry ingredients twice, so place the flour, baking powder, salt, cinnamon, cloves and grated nutmeg in a sieve and sieve them into a bowl. Then, in another large mixing bowl, whisk the eggs, sugar and milk together, pour the melted butter into the egg mixture and give it all another good whisk. Now sift the flour mixture again straight in on top of the egg mixture and fold it in using as *few* folds as possible. Ignore the horrible lumpy mixture you're now faced with and don't be tempted to overmix. I think this is where people go wrong: they can't believe that what looks like a disaster can possibly turn into something *so* light and luscious. Now fold in the chopped apple and then spoon the whole lot into the tin, levelling off the surface.

Next, make the topping, and you can use the same bowl. Just add the flour, sugar and cinnamon and rub the butter in with your fingertips until crumbly. Finally, sprinkle in the nuts and cold water, then press the mixture loosely together. Again, it will be quite lumpy – no problem! Now spoon the topping over the surface of the cake, then bake on the centre shelf of the oven for about 1¼ hours, until it feels springy in the centre. Allow the cake to cool in the tin for 30 minutes before removing the sides, then gently slide a palette knife under the base and transfer the cake to a wire rack to finish cooling. Serve this as fresh as possible, either on its own or warm as a dessert with whipped cream, crème fraîche or vanilla ice cream.

Serves 10-12

12 oz (350 g) Bramley apples (weight after peeling and coring), chopped into ½ inch (1 cm) cubes
4 oz (110 g) butter
10 oz (275 g) plain flour
1 tablespoon plus 1 teaspoon baking powder
½ teaspoon salt
1 heaped teaspoon ground cinnamon
1 teaspoon ground cloves
½ whole nutmeg, grated
2 large eggs at room temperature
3 oz (75 g) golden caster sugar
6 fl oz (175 ml) milk

For the pecan streusel topping:
2 oz (50 g) pecan nuts, roughly chopped
3 oz (75 g) self-raising flour
3 oz (75 g) demerara sugar
1 rounded teaspoon ground cinnamon
1 oz (25 g) soft butter
1 tablespoon cold water

You will also need a 9 inch (23 cm) springform cake tin, lightly greased and the base lined with silicone paper (parchment).

Pre-heat the oven to gas mark 5, 375°F (190°C).

Irish Whiskey Christmas Cakes

*Makes four 4 inch (10 cm) square cakes
or an 8 inch (20 cm) square cake*
For the pre-soaking:
10 fl oz (275 ml) Irish whiskey
1½ teaspoons Angostura bitters
1 lb (450 g) raisins
8 oz (225 g) currants
4 oz (110 g) stoned no-soak prunes
2 oz (50 g) glacé cherries
2 oz (50 g) unblanched almonds
4 oz (110 g) mixed candied peel
½ rounded teaspoon ground cinnamon
½ teaspoon freshly grated nutmeg
½ teaspoon ground cloves
1½ teaspoons vanilla extract
1 tablespoon molasses sugar
grated zest 1 orange
grated zest 1 lemon
½ teaspoon salt

For the cake:
9 oz (250 g) self-raising flour, sifted
9 oz (250 g) demerara sugar
9 oz (250 g) unsalted butter, softened
5 large eggs at room temperature
1 heaped tablespoon apricot jam
1 tablespoon Irish whiskey

For the icing:
1lb 2 oz (500 g) marzipan (in a block)
1 lb 4 oz (570 g) unrefined golden icing
sugar, plus a little extra for rolling
1 large egg white
1 dessertspoon molasses syrup or
black treacle
2½ tablespoons Irish whiskey

You will also need an 8 inch (20 cm)
square cake tin, greased, the base and
sides lined with a double thickness of
silicone paper (parchment) to sit 4
inches (10 cm) deep.

If you've never made a Christmas cake before, this one is dead easy, and you won't be disappointed. I now prefer the much thinner layer of marzipan and icing, and the flavour of the Irish whiskey in the icing, as well as the cake, is brilliant. The instructions here are for four small cakes; measurements for the large one are in the caption opposite. If you want to keep the cake for any length of time, let the marzipan dry out (covered with a clean tea cloth) for a week before icing.

One week before you intend to bake the cake, measure out the whiskey, bitters and 3 tablespoons of water into a large saucepan, then roughly chop the prunes, cherries and almonds and finely dice the mixed candied peel. Add these, along with the rest of the pre-soaking ingredients, to the pan, ticking them as you go to make sure nothing gets left out. Now stir and bring the mixture up to simmering point, then, keeping the heat low, simmer very gently, without a lid, for 15 minutes. After that, allow everything to cool completely, then pour the mixture into a large jar with a lid or an airtight plastic container and leave it in the fridge for seven days, giving it a little shake from time to time.

When you're ready to bake the cake, pre-heat the oven to gas mark 1, 275°F (140°C). If you are using a gas oven that was made after 1992, you will need to cook this cake at gas mark 2.

All you need to do is measure out the flour, sugar and butter into a very large bowl, then add the eggs and either whisk or beat with a wooden spoon until everything is evenly blended. Now gradually fold in the fruit mixture until it is evenly distributed. Then spoon the mixture into the prepared tin, levelling the surface with the back of the spoon. Bake in the centre of the oven for 3 hours without opening the door, then cover the cake with a double thickness of greaseproof paper and continue to bake it for a further 30 minutes or until the centre feels springy when lightly touched.

Cool the cake for 45 minutes in the tin, then remove it to a wire rack to finish cooling. When it's completely cold, wrap it in a double layer of greaseproof paper, then foil, and store it in an airtight container.

When you are ready to finish the cake, first take a sharp knife and cut the cake into quarters so you end up with four smaller 4 inch (10 cm) square cakes. Then melt the jam with the whiskey in a small saucepan and stir it a few times until all the lumps have dissolved. Now, using a brush, coat the surface of each cake quite generously with it. Take the marzipan and cut off a quarter of the block, then, on a surface lightly dusted with icing sugar, roll the piece into an 8 inch (20 cm) square. Now, with a sharp knife, cut the square into quarters so you end up with four 4 inch (10 cm) square pieces. Gently take each square and place one on top of each cake, lightly pressing the marzipan down. Next, cut the remaining piece of marzipan in half and roll each half into a strip measuring 6 x 16 inches (15 x 40 cm), then cut each strip in half lengthways so you are left with four strips: one for the sides of each cake. Press each strip lightly around the edges of each cake and pinch to seal at the join with the top piece of marzipan.

For the icing, sieve the icing sugar, then place the egg white and molasses (or black treacle) in a large bowl and, using an electric hand whisk, whisk together thoroughly. Now, with the whisk running, add a tablespoon of icing sugar at a time and keep adding it until the mixture thickens. As it begins to crumble, add a tablespoon of the Irish whiskey to combine the mixture, then carry on adding more icing sugar until it becomes thick. Add another tablespoon of whiskey, then the rest of the icing sugar and whiskey, and keep whisking until everything is blended together.

Now divide the icing into four and, using a palette knife, smooth it over the top and down the sides of each cake, dipping the knife into a small saucepan of simmering water to make it easier to spread. To give the cakes a nice finish, dip the knife in the simmering water once more and make swirls with the knife over the cakes, then leave them to dry overnight. Wrap each cake in greaseproof paper, then in foil, and keep in an airtight container. To decorate the cakes, you'll need four lengths of ribbon, each 4 ft (1.2 m) long and 1½ inches (4 cm) wide. When you're ready to finish the cakes, carefully place a length of ribbon around each one, tying the ends in a bow.

For the 8 inch (20 cm) cake, take the marzipan and cut off a quarter of the block, then roll this piece out to an 8 inch (20 cm) square. Cut the remaining piece in half and roll each half into a strip measuring 3 x 16 inches (7.5 x 40 cm), then use these strips to cover the sides of the cake. To decorate the cake, you will need a length of ribbon 6½ ft (2 m) long and about 1½ inches (4 cm) wide

Irish Tea Bread

It's always hard for me to believe that this simple little fruit loaf can taste so good. When we were testing recipes, this one disappeared the fastest – none of us could resist just one more little bit. It's good all by itself or spread with butter, and it's quite brilliant toasted. The recipe makes two loaves, so you can pop the other one in the freezer and keep it for a rainy day.

Begin this the evening before by placing all the fruits, including the candied peel, in a bowl, then dissolve the sugar in the hot tea, pour this over the fruits, cover the bowl and leave it overnight so the fruits become plump and juicy.

The next day, pre-heat the oven to gas mark 3, 325°F (170°C), then place the nuts on a baking sheet and pop them into the oven for 6-8 minutes (use a timer, as they burn easily). Then, when they're cool, roughly chop them. Next, add the beaten egg mixture to the bowl containing the fruits. Then sift in the flour, add the toasted nuts and give everything a really good mixing. Now divide the mixture between the prepared loaf tins and bake them in the centre of the oven for 1¼-1½ hours, until they feel springy in the centre. Then straight away, loosen them with a palette knife and turn them out on to a wire rack to cool. Then have patience – it won't be long before you can taste some.

Makes 2 small loaves
8 oz (225 g) raisins
8 oz (225 g) currants
8 oz (225 g) sultanas
4 oz (110g) whole candied peel,
cut into ¼ inch (5 mm) pieces
8 oz (225 g) demerara sugar
10 fl oz (275 ml) Lapsang Souchong,
Earl Grey or any other hot tea
4 oz (110 g) pecan nuts
1 large egg at room temperature,
lightly beaten with 2 tablespoons milk
1 lb (450 g) self-raising flour

You will also need two 1 lb (450 g) loaf tins, the bases lined with silicone paper (parchment).

Although you can now buy really good-quality biscuits and American cookies, making them at home still has the edge, and as biscuits are so easy, it's a very good place to start if you are a beginner in home baking. I've used 'adult' chocolate in these, but for children, chocolate chips would do fine.

First of all, using a sharp knife, chop the chocolate into small chunks about ¼ inch (5 mm) square. Now put the butter, sugar and syrup in a saucepan, place it on the gentlest heat possible and let it all dissolve, which will take 2-3 minutes. Meanwhile, chop the nuts into small chunks about the same size as the chocolate pieces. When the butter mixture has dissolved, take it off the heat. In a large mixing bowl, sift in the flour and salt and add the porridge oats and half the chocolate and nuts, then give this a quick mix before pouring in the butter mixture. Now, using a wooden spoon, stir and mix everything together, then switch from a spoon to your hands to bring everything together to form a dough. If it seems a bit dry, add a few drops of cold water.

Now take half the dough and divide it into nine lumps the size of a large walnut, then roll them into rounds using the flat of your hand. Place them on a worktop and press gently to flatten them out into rounds approximately 2½ inches (6 cm) in diameter, then scatter half the remaining chocolate and almonds on top of the biscuits, pressing them down lightly. Once you have filled one tray (give them enough room to spread out during baking), bake them on the middle shelf of the oven for 15 minutes whilst you prepare the second tray. When they're all cooked, leave them to cool on the baking sheets for 10 minutes, then transfer them to a wire rack to finish cooling. You could store the biscuits in a sealed container, but I doubt you'll have any left!

Crunchie variations

For *Apricot Pecan Crunchies*, use 2 oz (50 g) of dried apricots and 1½ oz (40 g) of pecans, chopped, instead of the chocolate and almonds.
For *Cherry and Flaked-Almond Crunchies*, use 2 oz (50 g) of dried sour cherries and 1½ oz (40 g) of flaked almonds.
For *Raisin Hazelnut Crunchies*, use 2 oz (50 g) of raisins and 1½ oz (40 g) of hazelnuts.

Makes 18
2 oz (50 g) dark continental chocolate
(75 per cent cocoa)
4 oz (110 g) butter
3 oz (75 g) demerara sugar
1 dessertspoon golden syrup
1½ oz (40 g) whole almonds,
unblanched
4 oz (110 g) self-raising flour
pinch of salt
4 oz (110 g) porridge oats

You will also need two baking sheets measuring 14 x 11 inches (35 x 28 cm), lightly greased with groundnut or another flavourless oil.

Pre-heat the oven to gas mark 3, 325°F (170°C).

From top: Chocolate Almond Crunchie, Apricot Pecan Crunchie, Cherry and Flaked-Almond Crunchie

7

Flour-based sauces and batter

Don't, whatever you do, be daunted by the subject of saucemaking. How the enormous amount of fear that's attached to the subject was first generated it's hard to say, but now is the time to sweep it away, along with all those packets of strange-sounding chemicals and ingredients that masquerade under the name of sauce. So stop thinking too thin, too thick or, worst of all, what about the lumps; instead, make your mind up to get to grips with it, learn how to do it once and for all and then enjoy a lifetime of making and enjoying perfect sauces any time you want to.

Although the entire art of saucemaking is a vast subject, covering many different methods and approaches (see Hollandaise Sauce on page 70 and Traditional English Custard on page 62), here we are concerned with flour-based sauces, which, when you've understood the rules and learned how to master them, will give you a good grounding in the rest of saucemaking.

More power to your elbow

I'm not sure if this old cliché came into being through the subject of saucemaking or not, but it does say something wise, and that is this: when flour, fat and liquid are combined and heated, they always need extremely vigorous whisking. As I said in the chapter on pastry, it's the brain that gives out signals to the hands (or arms in this case) and commands either gentleness or forcefulness, and with sauces it's the latter, so the more vigorously you whisk the better. With all flour-based sauces, once you know this and put it into practice, everything will be within your control – because in the end it's the whisk that controls. Learning in the first place begins with a decision: I will always do what Delia says and whisk like mad!

Lumps are a thing of the past

Flour-based sauces, it has to be admitted, have suffered a bad press. I well remember a few years ago Anne Robinson on the BBC's *Points Of View* programme repeatedly showing a TV chef making a horrible lumpy white sauce in close-up. Yes, it was funny, because the chef at the time was saying how smooth and silky it was. Knowing the hazards of television cooking and the heat not always being right when the director says go, I could sympathise. It's a shame in this case that he (the director) didn't think to look at the monitor. But making a sauce at home is nowhere near as hazardous as it is on television, so lumps really are within your control.

In a classic white sauce and all other flour-based sauces, there's only one rule apart from determined whisking, and that is the fat content: it's the flour blended with the fat that ensures lump-free results, so never attempt to blend hot liquid and flour without the presence of fat, as this is what causes lumps.

It is all quite straightforward, a case of once you understand the rules, lumps should never occur. But so what? If you do happen to slip up on the rules or get distracted, then don't forget why sieves were invented.

Now let's first have a look at some of the rules. You need to remember the three ways to make a white sauce.

1 The roux method

Roux is the name given to the mixture of butter and flour that forms the basis of the classic white sauce called béchamel. The butter is melted in the pan, the flour is then stirred in to make a smooth, thick paste, and finally, the liquid is added a little at a time with continual whisking. This is the only way to make a sauce if the liquid is hot, because hot liquid can only be combined with flour if it's first blended with fat, so if you want to make a sauce with hot liquid, ie, fish-poaching liquid, hot vegetable stock or infused milk, remember to use the roux method described here.

2 The all-in-one method

What happens here is that if you are using cold liquid you can simply place all the ingredients, ie, butter, flour and liquid, in a saucepan and whisk continuously and vigorously over the heat until the heat thickens the sauce. By the time the heat penetrates, the butter will have been blended with the flour enough to prevent lumps and the finished sauce will be silky smooth and exactly the same as in the roux method above.

3 The fat-free, no-lump flour method

Yes, it's true. For the first time in history we have an utterly new and quite phenomenal way of making a white sauce, which has changed all the rules somewhat. It's with a flour called *sauce flour*, which has been invented by an extremely clever flour miller who was watching me on television emphasising the absolutely essential presence of fat to avoid lumps. We need not get scientific here, but what he did was work out what it was that made the sauce go lumpy, and then develop a specific type of sauce flour that did not need the presence of fat, and this, thankfully, is now available in supermarkets. After that he sent me some samples to test, and the happy conclusion is that, sure enough, using the all-in-one method above with cold milk, you can now make a white sauce without any butter at all. Of course, there is some fat in the milk, but there's still a vast difference in the total fat content, which is wonderful news for those on a low-fat diet.

Obviously the richness and flavour of butter is what makes a classic creamy white sauce the star it is, but it's good to have the choice of not adding butter on occasions, and I think this is a huge step forward. You can now make a creamy, silky-smooth white sauce with skimmed or semi-skimmed milk and flour with no butter. Amazing.

What's the best saucepan?

A vexed question that has occupied me for years. The absolute truth is that a white sauce is probably the very best test of a saucepan. Why? Because what you want is a saucepan in which the sauce won't catch. If it does you will find that, as you whisk, little bits of scorched sauce will begin to appear. For years I have searched and searched, and at long last I've found what I can only describe as a little gem, left. Since I first started cooking I've always known that heavy-gauge aluminium is the very best conductor of heat in cooking, and now, thankfully, it has at last been declared safe (see page 42).

It provides the perfect pan for making sauces and it's not mega expensive. Not particularly glamorous to look at, but light-years ahead of anything else on performance.

How long should you cook a flour-based sauce?

When you use flour in a sauce, although it will thicken to a smooth creaminess very quickly, it then has to be cooked. This is because the flour can at first taste a little raw. Therefore it's important to remember that all sauces using flour must have 5 minutes' cooking time over the gentlest possible heat, except if you're going to continue to cook the sauce in the oven, as in a lasagne, for example, which means you can cut this initial cooking to 2 or 3 minutes.

Can you make it ahead?

Yes, you certainly can, but a few things to remember first. When the sauce is made, place some clingfilm directly over the surface to prevent a skin from forming, then either keep it warm by placing it over a pan of barely simmering water or, if you want to make it a long way ahead, re-heat it using the same method and don't remove the clingfilm until you are ready to serve. If you find it has thickened a little, this is easy to rectify by adding a little more liquid – milk, stock or cream – to bring it back to the right consistency.

Opposite, clockwise from top right: fatless white sauce, all-in-one white sauce, roux

Classic White Béchamel Sauce

This is the classic way of making a white sauce, using what the French call a roux (see page 147).

Makes about 15 fl oz (425 ml)
15 fl oz (425 ml) milk
a few parsley stalks
1 bay leaf
1 blade of mace or a pinch of
powdered mace (optional)
10 whole black peppercorns
1 slice onion, ¼ inch (5 mm) thick
1½ oz (40 g) butter
¾ oz (20 g) plain flour
salt and freshly milled black pepper

First place the milk in a small saucepan and add the parsley stalks, bay leaf, mace (if using), peppercorns and onion. Then place it over a low heat and let it come very slowly up to simmering point, which will take approximately 5 minutes. Then remove the saucepan from the heat and strain the milk into a jug, discarding the flavourings.

All this can be done ahead of time, but when you want to make the sauce, use the same washed pan and place it over a gentle heat. Begin by melting the butter gently – don't over-heat it or let it brown, as this will affect the colour and flavour of the sauce. As soon as the butter melts, add the flour and, over a medium heat and using a small pointed wooden spoon, stir quite vigorously to make a smooth, glossy paste. Now begin adding the infused milk a little at a time – about 1 fl oz (25 ml) first of all – and stir again vigorously. Then, when this milk is incorporated, add the next amount and continue incorporating each bit of liquid before you add the next. When about half the milk is in, switch to a balloon whisk and start adding large amounts of milk, but always whisking briskly. Your reward will be a smooth, glossy, creamy sauce.

Now turn the heat down to its lowest setting and let the sauce cook for 5 minutes, whisking from time to time. While that's happening, taste and season with salt and freshly milled black pepper. If you wish to keep the sauce warm, all you do is pour it into a warmed jug and cover the surface with clingfilm to stop a skin from forming, then place the jug in a pan of barely simmering water.

All-In-One White Sauce

The golden rule here, as explained earlier, is to use cold milk. So if you want to infuse the milk, pour it into a bowl and let it get completely cold before you begin.

Makes about 15 fl oz (425 ml)
15 fl oz (425 ml) milk – this can be infused (see page 150) but must be cold
¾ oz (20 g) plain flour
1½ oz (40 g) butter
salt and freshly milled black pepper

When you're ready to make the sauce, put the milk in a saucepan, then simply add the flour and butter and bring everything gradually up to simmering point, whisking continuously with a balloon whisk, until the sauce has thickened and becomes smooth and glossy.

Then turn the heat down to its lowest possible setting and let the sauce cook very gently for 5 minutes, stirring from time to time. Meanwhile, taste and add seasoning.

Any Kind of Cheese Sauce

Yes, it's true – any kind of cheese can be used. If you want a mild lactic flavour use a Lancashire, or for something more assertive, how about a sharp Gorgonzola? Or, instead of Cheddar and Parmesan, try Gruyère and Parmesan. Cheese sauce is also very obliging when it comes to odd bits of cheese lurking in the refrigerator, in which case you can use a mixture.

Makes about 1 pint (570 ml)
1 pint (570 ml) milk
1½ oz (40 g) plain flour
1½ oz (40 g) butter
pinch of cayenne pepper
2 oz (50 g) mature Cheddar, grated
1 oz (25 g) Parmesan (Parmigiano Reggiano), finely grated
a little freshly grated nutmeg
salt and freshly milled black pepper

All you do is place the milk, flour, butter and cayenne pepper into a medium saucepan and place it over a gentle heat. Then, using a balloon whisk, begin to whisk while bringing it to a gentle simmer. Whisk continually until you have a smooth, glossy sauce, and simmer very gently for 5 minutes. Then add the cheeses and whisk again, allowing them to melt. Then season with salt, freshly milled black pepper and some freshly grated nutmeg.

Fatless White Sauce

Okay, so you don't get the buttery flavour, but you do get a lovely creamy-smooth, milky white sauce by using sauce flour (see page 147), which is most helpful for those needing to cut the fat content of their diet.

Makes about 10 fl oz (275 ml)
10 fl oz (275 ml) milk – this can be infused (see page 150) but must be cold
¾ oz (20 g) sauce flour
salt and freshly milled black pepper

All you do to make this sauce is place the milk in a small saucepan, then simply add the flour and, over a medium heat, bring everything gradually up to simmering point, whisking vigorously and continuously with a balloon whisk until the sauce has thickened to a smooth, rich creaminess. Then add seasoning and allow it to cook very gently for 5 minutes on the lowest possible heat.

Cauliflower and Broccoli Gratin with Blue Cheese

The cheese we used for the sauce in this recipe, as pictured on the following page, was Gorgonzola, but Roquefort, below, is also extremely good.

Begin by heating the oil in the frying pan over a medium heat, then add the onions and let them cook for 3-4 minutes, until lightly tinged brown. Next stir in the rice – there's no need to wash it – and turn the grains over in the pan so they become lightly coated and glistening with oil. Then add the boiling stock, along with the salt, stir once only, then cover with the lid, turn the heat to its very lowest setting and cook for 40-45 minutes. Don't remove the lid and don't stir the rice during cooking, because this is what will break the grains and release their starch, making the rice sticky.

While the rice is cooking, make the sauce, and all you do here is place the milk, butter, flour and cayenne pepper in a saucepan and, using a balloon whisk, whisk on a medium heat, continuing until the sauce becomes thick, smooth and glossy. Then turn the heat to its lowest setting and give it 5 minutes to cook. After that, whisk in the cheese until it has melted, then season with the nutmeg, salt and freshly milled black pepper.

Next, pre-heat the grill to its highest setting, then place a saucepan on the heat, add some boiling water from the kettle, fit a steamer in it and add the cauliflower. Put a lid on and time it for 4 minutes. After that, add the broccoli to join the cauliflower, lid on again, and time it for another 4 minutes.

Now arrange the cooked rice in the baking dish, then top with the cauliflower and broccoli florets. Next pour the sauce over, then, finally, mix the Parmesan with the breadcrumbs and parsley. Sprinkle this all over the top, then place the whole thing under the grill and cook for 2-3 minutes, until the sauce is bubbling and golden brown.

Serves 4

10 oz (275 g) cauliflower florets
10 oz (275 g) broccoli florets
1 tablespoon olive oil
2 medium onions, peeled and sliced into 8 through the root
10 fl oz (275 ml) brown basmati rice
1 pint (570 ml) boiling vegetable stock
1 rounded teaspoon salt

For the blue cheese sauce:
4 oz (110 g) Roquefort, cubed
1 pint (570 ml) milk
1½ oz (40 g) butter
1½ oz (40 g) plain flour
pinch of cayenne pepper
a little freshly grated nutmeg
salt and freshly milled black pepper

For the topping:
1 oz (25 g) Parmesan (Parmigiano Reggiano), finely grated
½ oz (10 g) fresh breadcrumbs
1 tablespoon finely chopped fresh parsley

You will also need an ovenproof baking dish with a base measurement of 8 x 6 inches (20 x 15 cm), 2 inches (5 cm) deep, and a 10 inch (25.5 cm) frying pan with a lid.

Roasted Vegetable and Brown Rice Gratin

This, like the previous recipe, is obviously a supper dish for non-meat-eaters, but I have served it to the most dedicated carnivores who, after initial apprehension, have loudly sung its praises.

Serves 4
For the rice:
10 fl oz (275 ml) brown basmati rice
1 tablespoon olive oil
2 medium onions, peeled and finely chopped
1 pint (570 ml) boiling vegetable stock
1 rounded teaspoon salt

For the vegetables:
10 oz (275 g) peeled butternut squash
5 oz (150 g) each celeriac, swede, carrots and parsnip (peeled weight)
2 medium red onions, peeled
1 heaped tablespoon chopped mixed fresh herbs: parsley, thyme and tarragon, for example
1 fat clove garlic, peeled and crushed
2 tablespoons olive oil
salt and freshly milled black pepper

For the cheese sauce:
2 oz (50 g) mature Cheddar, grated
1 oz (25 g) Parmesan (Parmigiano Reggiano), finely grated
1 pint (570 ml) milk
1½ oz (40 g) plain flour
1½ oz (40 g) butter
a little cayenne pepper
a little freshly grated nutmeg
salt and freshly milled black pepper

You will also need a 16 x 12 inch (40 x 30 cm) baking sheet, a 8 x 6 inch (20 x 15 cm) based ovenproof dish and a 10 inch (25.5 cm) lidded frying pan.

Pre-heat the oven to gas mark 8, 450°F (230°C).

For the vegetables, begin by cutting the squash, celeriac, swede, carrots and parsnip into 1 inch (2.5 cm) cubes. Place them and the red onions, each cut into six through the root, in a large bowl, along with the herbs, garlic, a good seasoning of salt and pepper and the olive oil, then toss them around so they get a good coating of oil and herbs. Now arrange them evenly all over the baking sheet, then place this on the highest shelf of the oven to roast for about 30 minutes, or until they are nicely brown at the edges. As soon as they are ready, take them out and reduce the oven temperature to gas mark 6, 400°F (200°C).

For the rice, begin by warming the frying pan over a medium heat, then add the oil and the onions and let them cook for 3-4 minutes, until lightly tinged brown. Next stir in the rice – there's no need to wash it – and turn the grains over in the pan so they become lightly coated and glistening with oil. Then add the boiling stock, along with the salt, stir once only, then cover with the lid, turn the heat to the very lowest setting and cook for 40-45 minutes. Don't remove the lid and don't stir the rice during cooking, because this is what will break the grains and release their starch, which makes the rice sticky.

Meanwhile, make the cheese sauce by placing the milk, flour, butter and a pinch of the cayenne pepper into a medium-sized saucepan, then whisk it all together over a gentle heat until you have a smooth, glossy sauce. Let it cook on the lowest heat for 5 minutes, and after that add half the cheeses. Whisk again and allow them to melt into it, then season the sauce with salt, freshly milled black pepper and freshly grated nutmeg.

When the vegetables and rice are cooked, arrange the rice in the ovenproof dish, then the vegetables on top of that, followed by the sauce, pouring it over and around the vegetables as evenly as possible. Finally, scatter over the remaining cheeses with a sprinkling of cayenne pepper, then return the dish to the oven and give it about 20 minutes or until the sauce is browned and bubbling.

Opposite, top: Roasted Vegetable and Brown Rice Gratin; bottom, Cauliflower and Broccoli Gratin with Blue Cheese

Roast Lamb with Garlic and Rosemary

Serves 6-8
1 leg of lamb weighing about 4 lb (1.8 kg)
3 large cloves garlic, peeled and thinly sliced lengthways into about 24 slivers
2 large stems fresh rosemary, cut into about 24 small sprigs
1 small onion, peeled
salt and freshly milled black pepper

You will also need a solid roasting tin with a base measuring 11 x 9 inches (28 x 23 cm) and 2 inches (5 cm) deep.

Pre-heat the oven to gas mark 5, 375°F (190°C).

I have included this recipe for roast lamb here in the sauce section because it is served with two sauces: Traditional Gravy on page 163 and the Rosemary and Onion Sauce below. I find that the Oven-Sautéed Potatoes Lyonnaises on page 188 make an excellent accompaniment.

Begin by making about 24 small, deep cuts in the skin of the lamb using a small, sharp knife. Then push a sliver of garlic, followed by a small sprig of rosemary, into each cut, and season the meat generously with salt and freshly milled black pepper. Next, cut the onion in half and place it in the bottom of the roasting tin, then transfer the lamb to the tin to sit on top of the onion halves. Cover the tin loosely with foil, then cook in the oven on a high shelf for 1½ hours. After this, take the foil off and let it cook for another 30 minutes.

Remove the lamb from the oven, cover loosely with foil again and allow it to rest for about 20 minutes. Meanwhile, make the gravy (see page 163).

Rosemary and Onion Sauce

Makes about 1 pint (570 ml)
1 rounded tablespoon rosemary leaves
1 large onion, peeled and finely chopped
1 oz (25 g) butter
1 oz (25 g) plain flour
6 fl oz (175 ml) milk
6 fl oz (175 ml) vegetable stock
2 tablespoons crème fraîche
salt and freshly milled black pepper

This is good with the roast lamb above, lamb chops, or served with bangers and mash.

In a small saucepan, melt the butter and cook the onions over a very gentle heat for about 5 minutes – it's important not to let them colour, so keep an eye on them. While that's happening, bruise the rosemary leaves with a pestle and mortar to release their oil, then chop them very, very finely and add them to the onion. Then continue to cook as gently as possible for a further 15 minutes, again, without letting the onions colour too much. Next, using a wooden spoon, stir the flour into the onions and their buttery juices till smooth, then gradually add the milk, a little at a time, still stirring, followed by the stock, bit by bit, whilst vigorously whisking with a balloon whisk.

Now taste and season the sauce with salt and pepper and let it barely simmer on the lowest possible heat for 5 minutes. Next, remove it from the heat, then liquidise or process half of it, then return it to the saucepan to join the other half. Then re-heat gently, add the crème fraîche and pour it into a warmed serving jug.

Roast Lamb with Garlic and Rosemary served with Oven-Sautéed Potatoes Lyonnaises

English Parsley Sauce

Yes, it's old-fashioned nursery food, but I sometimes think that things like this need a revival. I love it with baked cod cutlets and creamy mashed potatoes, and it's also excellent with gammon. Here, though, I've included my favourite recipe for Salmon Fishcakes specially for the parsley sauce.

Place the milk and the next five ingredients in a small pan, bring everything slowly up to simmering point, then pour the mixture into a bowl and leave aside to get completely cold. When you're ready to make the sauce, strain the milk back into the pan, discard the flavourings, then add the flour and butter and bring everything gradually up to simmering point, whisking continuously with a balloon whisk until the sauce has thickened and is smooth and glossy. Then turn the heat down to its lowest possible setting and let the sauce cook gently for 5 minutes, stirring from time to time. To serve the sauce, add the parsley, cream and lemon juice, taste and season, then serve in a warm jug.

Makes about 15 fl oz (425 ml)
15 fl oz (425 ml) milk
a few parsley stalks
1 bay leaf
1 slice onion, ¼ inch (5 mm) thick
1 blade of mace or a pinch of powdered mace (optional)
10 whole black peppercorns
¾ oz (20 g) plain flour
1½ oz (40 g) butter
4 heaped tablespoons finely chopped fresh parsley
1 tablespoon single cream
1 teaspoon lemon juice
salt and freshly milled black pepper

Salmon Fishcakes

The thing to remember here is that good-quality tinned salmon makes better fishcakes than fresh, so don't be tempted to cook some salmon just for this.

First of all boil the potatoes in salted water for about 25 minutes or until they're absolutely tender when tested with a skewer. (Be careful, though – if they are not tender you will get lumps.) Then drain the potatoes and mash them to a purée with the mayonnaise using an electric hand whisk, then add some seasoning.

Now, in a large mixing bowl, simply combine all the ingredients for the fishcakes together. Mix really thoroughly, then taste and season again if it needs it. After that, allow it to cool thoroughly, then cover the bowl and place it in the fridge, giving it at least 2 hours to chill and become firm.

When you are ready to cook the fishcakes, lightly flour a work surface, then turn the fish mixture on to it and, using your hands, pat and shape it into a long roll, 2-2½ inches (5-6 cm) in diameter. Now cut the roll into 12 round fishcakes, pat each one into a neat, flat shape and then dip them, one by one, first into the beaten egg and then into the matzo meal (or breadcrumbs), making sure they get a nice, even coating all round.

Now, in a large frying pan, heat the oil and butter over a high heat and, when it is really hot, add half the fishcakes to the pan, then turn the heat down to medium and give then 4 minutes' shallow frying on each side. Then drain on crumpled greaseproof paper and keep warm. Repeat with the rest of the fishcakes, adding a little more oil and butter if needed. Serve immediately on hot plates with the parsley sauce, sprigs of parsley and some lemon wedges.

Salmon Fishcakes with English Parsley Sauce

Makes 12 (serves 6)
For the fishcakes:
15 oz (425 g) red salmon
10 oz (275 g) Desirée or King Edward potatoes, peeled and cut into large chunks
2 tablespoons mayonnaise
2 heaped tablespoons chopped fresh parsley
2 heaped tablespoons salted capers or capers in vinegar, drained and chopped
6 pickled gherkins (cornichons), drained and chopped
2 large eggs, hard-boiled and chopped small
1 dessertspoon anchovy paste or 4 anchovies, mashed up
2 tablespoons lemon juice
¼ teaspoon powdered mace
¼ teaspoon cayenne pepper
salt and freshly milled black pepper

For the coating and frying:
a little flour for dusting
1 large egg, beaten
3 oz (75 g) matzo meal or fresh white breadcrumbs
about 2 tablespoons groundnut or other flavourless oil
about ½ oz (10 g) butter

To serve:
1 quantity English Parsley Sauce (see opposite)
a few sprigs fresh parsley
lemon wedges

Moussaka with Roasted Aubergines and Ricotta

Once you've mastered the art of a perfect white sauce you can use it for any number of recipes. This one is a Greek classic, but the little hint of Italy I've added in the shape of Ricotta cheese makes the very best moussaka topping I've tasted. Also, roasting the aubergines is much less tiresome than standing over a frying pan watching them soak up masses of oil.

Serves 6

1 lb (450 g) minced lamb
2 medium-sized aubergines
2 tablespoons olive oil
2 medium onions, peeled and chopped small
2 cloves garlic, peeled and chopped
1 heaped tablespoon chopped fresh mint
1 heaped tablespoon chopped fresh parsley
1 teaspoon ground cinnamon
2 rounded tablespoon tomato purée
3 fl oz (75 ml) red wine
salt and freshly milled black pepper

For the topping:

9 oz (250 g) Ricotta
10 fl oz (275 ml) whole milk
1 oz (25 g) plain flour
1 oz (25 g) butter
¼ whole nutmeg, grated
1 bay leaf
1 large egg
1 tablespoon grated Parmesan (Parmigiano Reggiano)
salt and freshly milled black pepper

You will also need an ovenproof baking dish measuring 10 x 8 inches (25.5 x 20 cm), 2 inches (5 cm) deep, and a 14 x 11 inch (35 x 28 cm) baking sheet.

First of all you need to prepare the aubergines to get rid of their high water content and concentrate their flavour. To do this, remove the stalks and, leaving the skins on, cut them into approximately 1½ inch (4 cm) chunks. Then place them in a colander and sprinkle them with about 1 level dessertspoon of salt. Now put a plate on top of them and weigh it down with something heavy, then put another plate underneath to catch the juices. Leave them like this for 1 hour. Then, shortly before the end of this time, pre-heat the oven to its highest setting. When the hour is up, squeeze out any of the excess juice from the aubergines with your hands and dry them as thoroughly as you can in a clean cloth. Next, spread them out on the baking sheet, drizzle 1 tablespoon of the olive oil over them and toss them around to get a good coating. Now pop the baking sheet in the oven and roast the aubergines for 30 minutes or until they are tinged brown at the edges.

Meanwhile, heat the remaining olive oil in your largest frying pan and fry the onions and garlic gently for about 5 minutes. After that, turn the heat up high, add the minced lamb and brown it for a few minutes, turning it and keeping it on the move. Now cook the whole lot, stirring all the time, for 2-3 minutes. Then reduce the heat and, in a small bowl, mix the mint, parsley, cinnamon, tomato purée and red wine. When they're thoroughly combined, pour them over the meat, season well and cook the whole lot very gently for about 20 minutes, stirring from time to time so it doesn't catch on the base of the pan.

Now remove the aubergines from the oven and reduce the temperature to gas mark 4, 350°F (180°C). It's a good idea to leave the oven door open to cool it down a bit.

Next, make the topping by placing the milk, flour, butter, nutmeg and bay leaf in a saucepan. Using a balloon whisk, whisk over a medium heat until everything comes up to simmering point and the sauce becomes smooth and glossy. Now turn the heat down to its lowest setting and let the sauce cook gently for 5 minutes. Then taste and season, discarding the bay leaf, remove the saucepan from the heat and let it cool a little before whisking in the Ricotta and egg. Give it a good whisk to blend everything thoroughly.

Finally, combine the roasted aubergines with the meat mixture and transfer it all to the baking dish. Then pour the topping over, sprinkle the surface with the Parmesan and bake on the centre shelf of the oven for 50 minutes, by which time the top will be golden brown. Let it stand for 10 minutes to settle, then serve with brown rice and a Greek-style salad of cucumber, tomatoes, olives and crumbled Feta cheese dressed with olive oil and fresh lemon juice.

Gravy training

What is gravy?

Apparently, originally in the 14th century it was a bit of a copy error. The French (who by no means have the last word in cooking) had the word *grane*, and someone at some stage mistakenly copied over the 'n' as a 'v', and for some unknown reason the English kept the 'v' and added a 'y'. Thus, in a 14th-century cookbook we find that oysters, for instance, were stewed 'in their own gravy', meaning with their own juices, plus wine broth, almonds and rice flour, and similar gravies appeared from then on. So the French still, to this day, have only sauce or *jus* (juices), whilst the British have gravy, which is a sauce made from juices and other ingredients. So in all our most prestigious cookbooks, literature, food journals and diaries throughout the centuries, gravy is prominently featured.

British sauce

It is therefore hardly surprising that even our modern generation undoubtedly still has a latent passion for it. True, if you're a food snob, the word does not have such a fashionable ring to it as the French *jus* that dominates restaurant menus, along with perfumed broths, essences and other such pretensions. But it has to be said that gravy is part of our heritage; it comes from a long line of careful cooks who knew how to prepare a perfectly flavoured sauce by utilising precious juices, adding thickening for creamy smoothness and other flavour-enhancing ingredients to provide a beautiful sauce.

Gravy again

Now we can come to the crux of all this, and that is how, since everyone wants to enjoy proper gravy, they are at the same time deeply afraid of attempting to make it. I have written about it and demonstrated it countless times, but still people ask, 'How do you make gravy?'

Witness the horrors that line our supermarket shelves: cubes, packets and granules with long lists of chemicals, producing alien artificial flavour and instant gelatinous gloop – it's no wonder doctors are prescribing more antidepressants with people introducing such gloominess into their lives. But now is the time to move on and, once and for all, with the aid of this book plus the TV demonstration that accompanies it, everyone everywhere who wants to can make proper gravy for ever and ever. It really isn't hard, and there's nothing to be afraid of, so here goes.

Traditional Gravy

First of all remove the meat or poultry from the roasting tin and have a bowl ready, then tilt the tin and you will see quite clearly the fat separating from the darker juices. So now you need to spoon off the fat into the bowl using a tablespoon, but remember, you need to leave 1-1½ tablespoons of fat in the tin. Then, using a wooden spoon, scrape the sides and base of the tin to release any crusty bits, which are very important for flavour. Next, place the tin over direct heat turned fairly low and, when the fat and juices begin to sizzle, add the flour, then quickly dive in with the wooden spoon using brisk circular movements. Speed is of the essence – gentle, faint-hearted stirring is not what's needed here: you should be mixing in the manner of a speeded-up film!

Soon you will have a smooth paste, so now begin to add the hot stock, a little at a time, whisking briskly and blending after each addition. Now turn the heat up to medium and you will find that, as the stock is added and it reaches simmering point, the gravy will have thickened.

Now your own preference comes into play. If the gravy is too thin, let it bubble and reduce a little; if it's too thick, add a little more liquid. Finally, taste and season with salt and freshly milled black pepper, then pour the gravy into a warmed jug ready for the table.

For *pork*, which has pale juices, add onion to the roasting tin. This will caramelise during cooking and give colour to the juices. The onion may also be used with other joints and poultry to give colour.

For *lamb*, add a teaspoon of mustard powder with the flour, a tablespoon of redcurrant jelly to melt into the gravy, and some red wine to add body.

For *duck*, add the grated zest and juice of a small orange, along with a glass of port.

For *beef*, add a wineglass of Sercial Madeira – this enriches the beef flavour magically.

For *instant gravy without a joint*, see the recipe for Roasted-Onion Gravy on page 165.

Makes about 1 pint (570 ml)
the juices left in the roasting tin from cooking meat or poultry
1 rounded tablespoon plain flour
approximately 1 pint (570 ml) hot stock (potato or other vegetable water, for example), but the exact amount will depend on how thick you like your gravy
salt and freshly milled black pepper

You will also need a solid-based, flameproof roasting tin.

Begin by spooning off most of the fat from the roasting tin, leaving a little behind

Now add the flour and briskly mix it in using circular movements

Once you have a smooth paste, add the stock, a little at a time, blending as you go

Increase the heat; you will now see that the gravy will begin to thicken

Toad in the Hole with Roasted-Onion Gravy

I can't give this high enough accolades – it's a simply wonderful creation from the humble origins of British cooking. If only you could order it in a restaurant, though. Can I persuade anyone? It is, after all, a sort of fusion food – a fusion of light, crispy, crunchy batter and plump, meaty pork sausages, all moistened with a generous amount of roasted-onion jus. Here's hoping!

Begin by making the batter, and to do this sieve the flour into a large bowl, holding the sieve up high to give the flour a good airing. Now, with the back of a spoon, make a well in the centre, break the egg into it and add some salt and pepper. Now, measure the milk and water in a measuring jug, then, using an electric hand whisk on a slow speed, begin to whisk the egg into the flour – as you whisk, the flour around the edges will slowly be incorporated. Then add the liquid gradually, stopping to scrape the flour into the mixture. Whisk until the batter is smooth. Now the batter is ready for use, and although it's been rumoured that batter left to stand is better, I have never found this, so just make it whenever it's convenient.

Now place the sliced onions in a bowl, add 1 teaspoon of the oil and the sugar and toss the onions around to get the lightest coating, then spread them on the baking tray. Next arrange the sausages in the roasting tin, then place the onions on to a high shelf in the oven, with the sausages on a lower shelf, and set a timer for 10 minutes. When the timer goes off, remove the sausages from the oven but leave the onions in for a further 4-5 minutes – they need to be nicely blackened round the edges. When they are ready, remove them and leave to one side.

Now place the roasting tin containing the sausages over direct heat turned to medium and, if the sausages haven't released much fat, add the tablespoon of oil. When the tin is really hot and the oil is beginning to shimmer – it must be searing hot – quickly pour the batter in all around the sausages. Immediately return the roasting tin to the oven, this time on the highest shelf, and cook the whole thing for 30 minutes.

Now for the gravy. First add the Worcestershire sauce and mustard powder to the stock, then add the onions from the baking tray to a medium-sized pan. Now add the second teaspoon of oil, then, using a wooden spoon, stir in the plain flour. Stir all this together over a medium heat and then switch to a whisk, then gradually add the stock to the pan, whisking all the time, until it's all in. Then bring it up to simmering point and gently simmer for 5 minutes. Taste to check the seasoning, then pour into a warmed serving jug. When the toad is ready, it should be puffed brown and crisp and the centre should look cooked and not too squidgy. Serve it immediately with the gravy, and it's absolutely wonderful with mashed potato.

Serves 2-3
6 good-quality pork sausages – about 14 oz (400 g)
1 tablespoon groundnut or other flavourless oil (if necessary)

For the batter:
3 oz (75 g) plain flour
1 large egg
3 fl oz (75 ml) semi-skimmed milk
2 fl oz (55 ml) water
salt and freshly milled black pepper

For the onion gravy:
8 oz (225 g) onions, peeled and sliced
2 teaspoons groundnut or other flavourless oil
1 teaspoon golden caster sugar
1 dessertspoon Worcestershire sauce
1 teaspoon mustard powder
1 rounded dessertspoon plain flour
15 fl oz (425 ml) vegetable stock made from 1½ teaspoons Marigold Swiss vegetable bouillon powder dissolved in 15 fl oz (425 ml) boiling water
salt and freshly milled black pepper

You will also need a solid flameproof roasting tin with a base of 9 x 6 inches (23 x 15 cm), 2 inches (5 cm) deep, and a baking tray 14 x 10 inches (35 x 25.5 cm).

Pre-heat the oven to gas mark 7, 425°F (220°C).

Canadian Buttermilk Pancakes with Maple Syrup

Canada is where this profoundly unique syrup made from the sap of maple trees is made, and these are the pancakes that a certain Madame Lafond made for me when I was in Quebec; delightfully easy but tasting so light and fluffy. I love the way they puff up, crinkle and get really crisp at the edges. Serve these, as she did, straight from the pan on to warm plates, then absolutely drench them with maple syrup and add a generous dollop of crème fraîche.

Makes about 6
5 oz (150 g) plain flour
½ teaspoon baking powder
pinch of salt
4 fl oz (120 ml) buttermilk
3 fl oz (75 ml) cold water
3 large eggs, beaten
1-2 oz (25-50 g) lard

To serve:
lots of pure maple syrup and crème fraîche

First sieve the flour, baking powder and salt together in a roomy bowl and make a well in the centre. After that, whisk the buttermilk and water together in a jug and gradually whisk this into the bowl, slowly incorporating the flour with each new addition of liquid. Finally, add the eggs a little at a time until you have a smooth batter.

Now place a large, solid frying pan over a medium heat, add 2 teaspoons of the lard and heat it until the fat shimmers. Then, using a tablespoon of batter per pancake, place 2 or 3 spoonfuls into the pan.

They will take about 1 minute to turn golden brown, then turn them over using a spatula and fork, being careful not to splash yourself with the hot fat. Give them another 45 seconds on the other side, by which time they should have puffed up like little soufflés, then briefly rest them on some kitchen paper to absorb any excess fat.

Repeat this with the rest of the batter, adding a little more lard if necessary. They will keep warm in a low oven, but to enjoy them at their best, have everyone seated to eat them as soon as they come out of the pan.

8
Real potatoes

'Cuisine is when things taste like themselves' wrote Curnonsky, a distinguished 19th-century French food writer, and therein lies the whole truth about the art of cooking – how to make something really taste like itself. This is the real challenge that's set before anyone who wants to cook, and never was it more true than in the art of cooking potatoes. So the question is precisely this: how to make a potato really taste like a potato? The answer begins by perhaps rediscovering a healthy respect for what a potato actually is: no longer the humble 'also ran' of the meat-and-two-veg syndrome or something used as a filler to eke out the meat, but now hopefully re-emerging as a solo star on the food stage, loved and valued in its own right.

Potatoes make a comeback

Well, in a way this is true, because in my younger days potatoes were the enemy of the perfect waistline in a less nutritionally enlightened era; it was starch that made you fat, and starchy foods like bread and potatoes had to be avoided. Thankfully, bread and potatoes have now been rescued from this scenario; fat has now emerged as the number one culprit and the major cause of being overweight. This means that large portions of potatoes (without fat) are nutritious, healthy, high in energy-giving carbohydrate and low in calories – only about 70 per 100 g (approximately 4 oz), and, added to that, they are the single most important source of vitamin C in our diet. So potatoes are very 'in' at the moment and it's therefore more important than ever to learn how to make the best of them.

The importance of flavour

Before you even think about how to cook potatoes, as with many other foods, the key to flavour begins in the market place or, more specifically, in the earth. I well remember growing my first crop of new potatoes and discovering that straight from the ground into the cooking pot they were both soggy and tasteless and ended up being a huge disappointment. Why? I had simply grown the wrong variety, one with a high yield but absolutely no flavour.

This problem is a commercial one, too, and high-yield, disease-resistant, good-storage varieties do not always produce good flavour. So for the cook, choosing the right kind of potato is first on the list.

Varieties

Thankfully there are now many more varieties of potato to choose from; we could even be in danger of designer potatoes, like salad leaves, as I have seen both black-fleshed and purple varieties (neither of which have great flavour). But whilst we hear an awful lot about the texture of potatoes – which is measured by two things, waxiness and fluffiness, and the suitability of either of these in certain dishes – we hear very little about flavour. I would therefore like to see potatoes catch up with tomatoes on this, with varieties grown specifically for flavour. But since we are learning how to cook potatoes, here is not the place to study the long lists of various varieties that appear throughout the year, but I would like to point you in the direction of a few varieties which, in my experience, are among the best available at the moment.

New potatoes

Jersey Royal (April to June)

These, of course, have outstanding flavour, more so when they're a little more mature and larger than the tiny marbles that appear in early April. Choose them unwashed with the earth still clinging to them, and they need to be as fresh as possible, so that when you push a piece of skin with your thumb it slides away from the flesh instantly. These are the finest new potatoes of all for steaming and serving hot or cold in a potato salad.

Pentland Javelin (May to July)

These new potatoes also have a firm texture and excellent flavour and, depending on the weather, begin to come into season when the Jerseys finish. I have also grown these and they have excellent flavour.

Salad potatoes

These now appear regularly all year and, as their name suggests, are best eaten cold. Some specialised salad potatoes, though, are more difficult to find: Ratte is an old French variety that has a delicate, nutty, chestnut-like flavour, and Pink Fir Apple a more intense potato flavour with a pink skin and a firm, waxy flesh.

Main-crop potatoes

Desirée

This has always been my all-round reliable favourite because it has the best flavour of all commercially grown potatoes. It has a yellow, creamy, waxy flesh and bright-pink skin. I use it for boiling, jacket potatoes, roast potatoes, chunky chips and oven sautéeing, and I even like Desirée made into mash because of its depth of potato flavour.

King Edward

This is an old favourite and is the best variety if you want floury fluffiness. It's not suitable for boiling, as it tends to break, but it's wonderful for light, fluffy mash and for jacket potatoes where you want a really fluffy inside. This is also my choice for potato gnocchi because it makes them extra light.

Waxy or floury?

The above potatoes all have good flavour, but texture is sometimes a personal choice. I like to ring the changes and so sometimes I want, say, a firm, waxy, full-flavoured jacket potato, so I choose Desirée, and sometimes a more floury one, so it would be King Edward. The same applies to mashed potatoes, and what I would recommend is that you experiment to find out what you personally prefer.

How to cook potatoes

To peel or not to peel?

This is a much-debated question and I have given it a great deal of thought and consideration. My conclusions are these: yes, it's best to leave the skins on, and I never scrape new potatoes, but with main-crop potatoes – and it's a big but – if you're not going to peel them you must then have evenly sized potatoes so they all cook in the same amount of time.

The idea of leaving the skins on is to protect the flesh from the water or steam, which rob the potatoes of flavour. Once you start cutting them into even-sized pieces, that protection is lost. Also, if skins are left on for cooking, I would say that you should then serve the potatoes with their skins, as peeling hot potatoes while holding them in a cloth is okay if it's for one or two people, but for six servings it's quite awkward and hazardous. In Ireland, boiled potatoes are served with skins on and people who don't want to eat them leave them on the side of their plate, and I think this is a good option for steamed or boiled potatoes. I have compared steaming without skins and boiling with and found very little difference in flavour. If you are going to peel the potatoes, then please, please use a potato peeler. All the best of the flavour is near the skin, so you need to pare it off as thinly as possible.

Water – the enemy

I have a beautiful old cookbook called *Henderson's House Keeper Instructions*, and in it potatoes are boiled thus: '…in so small a quantity of water as will be sufficient to keep the saucepan from burning. Keep them close covered and as soon as the skins crack they are enough.'

Need I say more? Remember that having got hold of the perfect-flavoured potatoes, it's water that's going to take away their precious flavour. I have witnessed potatoes being murdered – covered with gallons of water, put on a low heat and left for an hour or even more, like the Victoria Wood joke about British cooking and the lady who put the sprouts on for the Christmas lunch in November! (We've all, I'm sure, experienced it.)

The number one rule here is, first of all, if you are peeling potatoes, don't let them sit around in water for hours before they're needed. If you peel them then try to do so just before you need them.

For cooking, the best way I have found to retain the flavour of the potatoes is not to boil them at all but to steam them. Firstly pour boiling water from the kettle into a pan fitted with a fan steamer (see the photograph, right), then place the potatoes in the steamer, sprinkle with salt (about 1 rounded teaspoon per 1 lb/450 g), and if they're new potatoes tuck in a few sprigs of mint. Then put a tight lid on and let them steam over a lowish heat, which is just needed to keep the water gently boiling until the potatoes are tender. This will take 20-25 minutes, and the best way to test whether the potatoes are tender is to use a thin skewer inserted in the thickest part.

After that, drain off any water beneath the steamer, then place a cloth over the potatoes for 5 minutes, which will absorb some of the excess steam that tends to cling to the potatoes and make them soggy. If you prefer to boil rather than steam, then use as little water as possible, add it boiling from the kettle and put a close lid on. The lid keeps the heat in and they will cook more quickly so spend less time in the water.

Steamed or boiled potatoes – pure and simple

In the recipes that follow I have attempted to give you a good grounding in all the most popular ways of serving potatoes. But don't forget that, cooked with a little care, plain steamed or boiled potatoes can, just on their own, be quite special. And they don't need lashings of butter; a little is a nice addition, but don't drown them with butter as some restaurants still insist on doing. All that does is swamp the delicate natural flavour of the potatoes. Gilding the lily is a sign of insecurity in cooking, and I feel it's so important to renew our confidence in the simplicity of things.

Jacket Potatoes

Could there possibly be anyone in the wide world who doesn't drool at the thought of jacket potatoes with really crisp, crunchy skins and fluffy, floury insides with something lovely melted into them? I'm not speaking of the insipid microwave versions of convenience fame, but the hallowed, reverenced beauty of the real thing. Life is too short, and therefore we need to savour every moment by spoiling ourselves with what is best and not some pale imitation that fails to satisfy. If you ever feel like treating yourself and want something supremely soothing and comforting that costs almost nothing (forget chocolate bars and the like), just bake yourself the biggest potato you can lay your hands on (see the method below), then cut it in half and, as you do, listen carefully to the inviting crackle and crunch of the skin as the knife goes in. Next, with a fork, fluff the floury insides, then add a generous amount of butter and watch it melt and disappear into the clouds of fluffiness. Add rock salt and crushed black pepper, then eat and savour it alone in all its humble, simple glory.

The secret of perfect jacket potatoes like the one described above is not to hurry them – give them up to 2 hours to get the really crunchy skin, learn to use the time when you're out, so they can be ready when you come home, or go and do something else and forget about them till they're ready. Below I have included the master recipe, and this is followed by some ideas for fillings and toppings.

Serves 2
2 large Desirée potatoes, 8-10 oz (225-275 g) each
a little olive oil
rock salt, crushed
a little butter
salt and freshly milled black pepper

Pre-heat the oven to gas mark 5, 375°F (190°C).

First you need to wash the potatoes and dry them very thoroughly with a cloth, then leave them aside to dry as much as possible. If you're using ready-washed potatoes you need not do this, as the high heat will purify them. Next, prick the skins a few times with a fork, then put a few drops of olive oil over each one and rub it all over the skin. After that, rub in some crushed salt – this will draw out the moisture from the skin and, together with the oil, provide more crunchiness.

Now place the potatoes straight on to the centre shelf of the oven and let them bake for 1¾-2 hours, or until the skins are really very crisp. When you are ready to serve, slit each potato in half lengthways and top with the butter and seasoning. Serve immediately because, after you remove jacket potatoes from the oven, they lose their crispness very quickly, so don't let them hang around.

Soured cream and chive topping

5 fl oz (150 ml) soured cream
approximately ½ oz (10 g) fresh chives
salt and freshly milled black pepper

This simple but great dressing for jacket potatoes was invented in the US, and it's still my number one favourite. All you do is snip the chives with some scissors into a bowl containing the soured cream. Add some seasoning and leave it for about 1 hour before serving, so that the soured cream has time to absorb the flavour of the chives.

Stuffed Jacket Potatoes with Leeks, Cheddar and Boursin

In this recipe the potato is scooped out, mixed with soft cheese and topped with leeks and melted cheese.

To prepare the leek, slice it almost in half lengthways, then fan it out under a running tap to wash away any trapped dirt. Now slice each half into four lengthways, then into ¼ inch (5 mm) slices. After that, put the Boursin into a medium-sized bowl and cut the potatoes in half lengthways. Protecting your hands with a cloth, scoop out the centres of the potatoes into the bowl containing the Boursin, add the milk or cream and season well with salt and freshly milled black pepper. Now quickly mash or whisk everything together, then pile the whole lot back into the potato skins. Now scatter the leeks on top, followed by the grated Cheddar – pressing it down lightly with your hand – then place on the baking sheet and bake in the oven for 20 minutes or until the leeks are golden brown at the edges and the cheese is bubbling.

Serves 2

2 large baked potatoes, 8-10 oz (225-275 g) each (see basic recipe left)
1 leek about 4 inches (10 cm) long, trimmed and cleaned
1½ oz (40 g) mature Cheddar, coarsely grated
1 x 80 g pack *Ail & Fines Herbes* Boursin
1 tablespoon from the top of the milk or single cream
salt and freshly milled black pepper

You will also need a baking sheet measuring 12 x 10 inches (30 x 25.5 cm).

Pre-heat the oven to gas mark 4, 350°F (180°C).

Welsh Rarebit Jacket Potatoes

Serves 2
2 large baked potatoes, 8-10 oz
(225-275 g) each (see page 174)
3 oz (75 g) mature Cheddar, grated
1 tablespoon Red Onion, Tomato and
Chilli Relish (see page 188)
1 heaped teaspoon finely grated onion
1 large egg, lightly beaten
1 tablespoon finely snipped fresh chives

Pre-heat the grill to its highest setting for
10 minutes before the potatoes are ready.

The same topping that goes with toasted bread goes perfectly with jacket potatoes and makes a lovely lunch dish served with a salad. You can make your own relish for this (see page 188), or you could buy it ready-made.

All you do here is combine all the filling ingredients together in a bowl. Then, when the potatoes are ready, cut them in half lengthways and make some criss-cross slits in them, being careful not to cut through the skins and using a cloth to protect your hands. Then divide the topping mixture between the potatoes, place them on the grill pan and grill 2 inches (5 cm) from the heat for 3-4 minutes, until the cheese has puffed up and turned golden brown on top.

Perfect Mashed Potato

This is now my standard all-time mashed potato recipe, adapted and revised from the Winter Collection.

Serves 4
2 lb (900 g) Desirée or King Edward
potatoes
1 dessertspoon salt
2 oz (50 g) butter
4 tablespoons whole milk
2 tablespoons crème fraîche
salt and freshly milled black pepper

Use a potato peeler to pare off the potato skins as thinly as possible, then cut the potatoes into even-sized chunks – not too small; if they are large, quarter them, and if they are small, halve them. Put the potato chunks in a steamer fitted over a large pan of boiling water, sprinkle the salt all over them, put a lid on and steam the potatoes until they are absolutely tender – they should take 20-25 minutes. The way to tell whether they are ready is to pierce them with a skewer in the thickest part: they should not be hard in the centre, and you need to be careful here, because if they are slightly underdone you do get lumps.

When the potatoes are cooked, remove them from the steamer, drain off the water, return them to the saucepan and cover with a clean tea cloth for about 4 minutes to absorb some of the steam, then add the butter, milk and crème fraîche. When you first go in with the whisk, use a slow speed to break the potatoes up, then increase it to high and whip them up to a smooth, creamy, fluffy mass. Taste and, if they need it, season. Note: To make low-fat mashed potatoes, replace the butter, milk and crème fraîche with 5 oz (150 g) of Quark (skimmed-milk soft cheese) and 2-3 tablespoons of semi-skimmed milk.

Perfect mashed potatoes begin with steaming the potato chunks until tender. With the addition of butter, milk and crème fraîche, the result, once whisked, is a smooth, creamy, fluffy mass

Pork Sausages Braised in Cider with Apples and Juniper

Braised sausages seem to have turned up many times in my books over the years, and because I love them so much, here is yet another version – a lovely, comforting, warm, winter supper dish that needs copious amounts of fluffy mashed potato to spoon the sauce over. Crushing the juniper berries releases their lovely flavour.

Serves 3-4

6 large pork sausages, weighing about
1 lb (450 g), preferably outdoor-reared
15 fl oz (425 ml) strong dry cider
1 tablespoon cider vinegar
1 Bramley apple, cored and sliced
into rings (unpeeled)
1 Cox's apple, cored and sliced
into rings (unpeeled)
1 dessertspoon juniper berries, crushed
slightly either in a pestle and mortar or
with the back of a tablespoon
2 dessertspoons olive oil
8 oz (225 g) onions, peeled and sliced
into rings
1 large clove garlic, peeled and
chopped
8 oz (225 g) lean smoked bacon,
roughly chopped
1 tablespoon plain flour
a few sprigs fresh thyme
2 bay leaves
salt and freshly milled black pepper

You will also need a 4 pint (2.25 litre)
flameproof casserole dish measuring
8 inches (20 cm) in diameter, 3 inches
(7.5 cm) deep, with a tight-fitting lid.

Begin by taking a large, heavy-based frying pan, place it on a medium heat and add 1 dessertspoon of the oil to it. As soon as it's hot, fry the sausages until they are nicely browned on all sides, then, using a draining spoon, transfer them to a plate. Now add the onions, garlic and bacon to the frying pan and cook these until they have also browned at the edges – about 10 minutes.

Meanwhile, place the casserole on to another heat source, again turned to medium, add the other dessertspoon of oil, then, when it's hot, add the apple rings and brown these on both sides, which will take 2-3 minutes. After that, add the sausages, followed by the bacon, onion and garlic, then sprinkle the flour in to soak up the juices, stirring it gently with a wooden spoon. Next add the cider and cider vinegar, a little at a time, stirring after each addition. Then add the thyme, bay leaves and crushed juniper berries, season with salt and pepper, but not too much salt because of the bacon. After that, put the lid on and simmer very gently on the lowest possible heat for 1 hour. Serve with mashed potato.

*Pork Sausages Braised in Cider with
Apples and Juniper served with
Perfect Mashed Potato (see page 176)*

Aligot (Mashed Potatoes with Garlic and Cheese)

I first ate this mashed potato with cheese in southwest France, in the Tarn region, and it was, quite simply, the best mashed potato I've ever eaten. Research on my return revealed that it involved a special, lovely cheese called Cantal, not generally available – but after many experiments I have, I think, come up with something comparable, made with farmhouse Lancashire, which has a lovely, fresh, lactic flavour.

Serves 2
1 lb (450 g) Desirée or King Edward
potatoes
2 fat cloves garlic, peeled and halved
lengthways
1 oz (25 g) butter
8 oz (225 g) Lancashire cheese, grated
salt and freshly milled black pepper

Begin this by placing the garlic in a small saucepan with the butter, then leave it on the gentlest heat possible to melt and infuse for 30 minutes. Meanwhile, thinly pare and discard the skins of the potatoes and cut them into even-sized chunks, or cut any large potatoes into quarters and small ones into halves. Place the potatoes in a steamer, then pour some boiling water straight from the kettle into a saucepan. Fit the steamer over, sprinkle the potatoes with 1 dessertspoon of salt, put a lid on and let them steam for 20-25 minutes, until tender in the centre when tested with a skewer. After this, remove them, transfer to a large bowl (preferably a warm one) and cover with a cloth to absorb some of the steam.

Now, with an electric hand whisk, switch to slow and begin to break up the potatoes, then add the butter and garlic, some black pepper and a handful of the grated cheese. Now switch the speed to high and continue adding the cheese, a handful at a time, while you whisk. There's a lot of cheese, but what will happen is that, as you whisk it in, the potatoes will turn translucent and glossy and, as you lift and whisk, it will form stiff, glossy peaks. When all the cheese is in, serve very quickly. The marinated steak recipe opposite is the perfect accompaniment, but it's also great with sausages.

Note: As the cheese goes in, the mixture becomes stiff and clings to the whisk, but keep going and it will part company with the whisk eventually. Also, if you want to keep it warm, place the bowl over a pan of simmering water, but don't leave it too long.

Having added the butter, garlic and seasoning, throw in a handful of cheese

Increase the speed of the whisk and continue adding the cheese, a handful at a time

As you whisk, the potatoes will turn into a translucent mass, forming glossy peaks

This is oh, so simple, but oh, so good. Great if you're organised and can leave the steaks in the marinade the day before you need them, but failing that, a few hours will do. The recipe was created specially to serve with Aligot, but it needs two to eat and two to cook: one to do the steaks and one to whip the potatoes!

Put the steaks in the shallow dish or polythene box, then mix the red wine, Worcestershire sauce and garlic together and pour this over the steaks. Cover with clingfilm or put the lid on, then place in the fridge for a few hours or, preferably, overnight. When you're ready to cook the steaks, drain and dry them carefully with kitchen paper, reserving the marinade.

Now take a medium frying pan, place it on a high heat and heat the oil until it's very hot. Then sear the steaks for 4 minutes on each side and, 2 minutes before the time is up, add the reserved marinade to the pan and let it bubble and reduce by about half. When the steaks are cooked, remove them from the pan to warm serving plates, then, using your sharpest knife, cut them into slices diagonally (see below) and spoon the sauce over. Garnish with the watercress and serve immediately with the Aligot.

Serves 2
2 x 7-8 oz (200-225 g) rump steaks
3 fl oz (75 ml) red wine
3 fl oz (75 ml) Worcestershire sauce
1 large clove garlic, peeled and crushed
1 teaspoon groundnut or other flavourless oil

To garnish:
a few sprigs fresh watercress

You will also need a shallow dish or lidded polythene box large enough to hold the steaks closely and comfortably.

Marinated Rump Steak served with Aligot

Mashed Potato with Three Mustards

This is the perfect accompaniment to gammon steaks, rich beef casseroles or spicy meat casseroles, and, as always, is great with bangers.

Serves 4

2 lb (900 g) Desirée or King Edward potatoes, peeled and steamed as for the Perfect Mashed Potato recipe (see page 176)

1½ tablespoons grain mustard

2 tablespoons French's American mustard

1 tablespoon hot mustard powder

2 rounded tablespoons crème fraîche

2 oz (50 g) butter

3-4 tablespoons from the top of the milk or single cream

salt and freshly milled black pepper

Whilst the potatoes are cooking, mix the crème fraîche with the three mustards in a small bowl. Drain the potatoes and return them to the hot pan, cover with a clean tea cloth for 4 minutes to absorb some of the steam, then add the mustard mixture, butter and some freshly milled black pepper. Then, using an electric hand whisk on a slow speed, break the potatoes up, then increase the speed and whisk them to a light, fluffy mash, adding the milk or single cream. Taste to check the seasoning before serving.

Green Parsley Mash

This is a quite stunning colour and the flavour of the parsley has an amazing affinity with potatoes. This is the perfect mash to serve with fish recipes, but it's also very good with boiled ham or grilled gammon steaks.

Serves 4

2 lb (900 g) Desirée or King Edward potatoes, peeled and steamed as for the Perfect Mashed Potato recipe (see page 176)

2 oz (50 g) fresh curly parsley

5 fl oz (150 ml) milk

salt and freshly milled black pepper

While the potatoes are cooking, place the parsley, with its stalks, into a small saucepan, add the milk and bring very slowly up to the gentlest simmer possible for 5 minutes or until the parsley is wilted and tender. Then place the whole lot into a liquidiser or processor and blend on a high speed until the parsley is blended into the milk and has turned it a bright green colour – 2-3 minutes – then strain it through a sieve to remove any bits of stalks and return to the pan to keep warm. When the potatoes are tender, drain them and cover with a clean tea cloth and leave for 4 minutes. Then, using an electric hand whisk on a slow speed, start to mash the potatoes, then increase the speed of the whisk and gradually add the parsley milk and a good seasoning of salt and freshly milled black pepper. Whisk until the mash is light and fluffy.

*This is another recipe for mashed potato that's great served with fish.
I love it with some freshly grilled mackerel or herring, and it's also
extremely good with smoked fish.*

When the potatoes are tender, drain them and cover with a clean tea cloth
and leave for 4 minutes, then add the butter, milk and crème fraîche. Now,
using an electric hand whisk, begin to whisk slowly to break them up, then
add the watercress, increase the speed of the whisk and continue whisking
until the potatoes are smooth and fluffy. Next, stir in the lemon juice and
capers and add the seasoning, though you may not need much salt if you
are using salted capers.

Serves 4

2 lb (900 g) Desirée or King Edward
potatoes, peeled and steamed as for
the Perfect Mashed Potato recipe
(see page 176)
5 oz (150 g) watercress, stalks removed
1 heaped tablespoon salted capers or
capers in vinegar, thoroughly washed
and drained
2 oz (50 g) butter
2 tablespoons milk
2 tablespoons crème fraîche
2 tablespoons lemon juice
salt and freshly milled black pepper

*Clockwise from top: Aligot, Mashed
Potato with Three Mustards, Watercress
and Caper Mash, Green Parsley Mash*

183

Crunchy Roast Potatoes with Saffron

This is my old favourite recipe for roast potatoes but with a new twist, and that's a flavouring of saffron – not too much, just a hint – and with the added dimension of a deep saffron colour, which makes this look even more irresistible.

Serves 4

2 lb (900 g) Desirée or King Edward potatoes, peeled and cut into approximately 1½ inch (4 cm) pieces
1 teaspoon saffron stamens
1 tablespoon olive oil
salt

You will also need a solid baking tray measuring 16 x 11 inches (40 x 28 cm).

Pre-heat the oven to gas mark 7, 425°F (220°C) and place the baking tray with 2 tablespoons of oil in it to pre-heat as well.

First of all crush the saffron to a powder with a pestle and mortar. Then place the potatoes in a saucepan with sufficient boiling water to almost cover them, add a dessertspoon of salt and half the saffron powder, cover with a lid and simmer gently for 6 minutes. Use a timer, as it's important not to overcook them at this stage.

When the time is up, lift a potato out using the skewer to see if the outer edge is fluffy. You can test this by running the point of a skewer along the surface – if it stays smooth, give them 2 or 3 more minutes. Then drain off the water, place the lid back on the pan and, holding the lid firmly and protecting your hand with a cloth, shake the saucepan vigorously. This is to create a fluffy surface so the finished potatoes will be really crunchy.

Now mix the oil with the rest of the saffron powder, then remove the tray from the oven and place it over a direct medium heat. Next, using a long-handled spoon, carefully but quickly lift the potatoes into the hot fat, tilt the tray and baste them well, then, using a small brush, quickly paint the potatoes with the saffron oil, making sure they are well coated. Now return the tray to the highest shelf of the oven for 40-50 minutes, until the potatoes are golden and crunchy. Sprinkle with a little salt before serving with meat or fish or with the marinated chicken recipe on the next page. Note: Classic plain roast potatoes are cooked in exactly the same way, minus the saffron, and don't forget, it's always important to serve them straight away, before they lose their crunchiness.

Marinated Chicken with Honey and Ginger served with Mango and Sultana Salsa

This is another quick and easy recipe that's helpful for busy people because it needs to be prepared ahead and can then be cooked alongside the Crunchy Roast Potatoes with Saffron on page 184 at the same temperature. So, in theory, you could come home from work and have supper for four ready in about an hour.

Begin this by making two cuts in each chicken breast, about ¼ inch (5 mm) deep, then place the chicken breasts neatly in the ovenproof dish. Now combine all the marinade ingredients in a bowl, whisking them together, then pour this over the chicken breasts, turning them around in the marinade to get them well coated. You now need to cover the dish with clingfilm and leave it in the fridge overnight.

Next, place the sultanas for the salsa with the lime zest and juice in a small bowl so they can plump up overnight. Cover them with clingfilm and store in the fridge.

When you are ready to cook the chicken, pre-heat the oven to gas mark 7, 425°F (220°C). Then remove the clingfilm from the chicken and baste each breast with the marinade. Bake on a high shelf of the oven (or the next one down from the potatoes) for 20-30 minutes.

While the chicken is cooking, remove the skin from the mango using a potato peeler or sharp knife. Then slice all the flesh away from the stone and chop it into small pieces – about ¼ inch (5 mm) dice. Then add it to the sultanas, along with the remaining salsa ingredients, and garnish just before serving with the coriander leaves. Serve the cooked chicken with some of the salsa spooned over and the rest served separately, along with a bowl of the saffron-roasted potatoes.

Serves 4
4 x 6 oz (175 g) bone-in chicken breasts, skin on
salt and freshly milled black pepper

For the marinade:
2 tablespoons runny honey
1 inch (2.5 cm) piece root ginger, peeled and finely grated
1 teaspoon ground ginger
2 cloves garlic, peeled and crushed
zest and juice ½ lime
salt and freshly milled black pepper

For the salsa:
1 medium or ½ large mango
2 oz (50 g) sultanas
zest and juice 1 lime
½ red pepper, deseeded and chopped
½ medium red onion, peeled and finely chopped
1 medium green chilli, deseeded and finely chopped

To garnish:
½ oz (10 g) fresh coriander leaves

You will also need an ovenproof dish measuring 8 x 6 inches (20 x 15 cm) and 1¾ inches (4.5 cm) deep.

Marinated Chicken with Honey and Ginger served with Mango and Sultana Salsa and Crunchy Roast Potatoes with Saffron

Potatoes Boulangères with Rosemary

These potatoes are so named because in France they were given to the local baker to place in a bread oven to cook slowly. The nice thing is that you can pop them in your oven and just forget about them until you are ready to serve, and, unlike other potato dishes, they don't mind being kept warm.

Begin by preparing the rosemary, which should be stripped from the stalks then bruised in a pestle and mortar. After that, take two-thirds of the leaves and chop them finely. Now cut the onions in half and then the halves into the thinnest slices possible; the potatoes should be sliced, but not too thinly. All you do is arrange a layer of potatoes, then onions, in the dish, followed by a scattering of rosemary, then season. Continue layering in this way, alternating the potatoes and onions and finishing with a layer of potatoes that slightly overlap. Now mix the stock and milk together and pour it over the potatoes. Season the top layer, then scatter over the whole rosemary leaves. Now put little flecks of the butter all over the potatoes and place the dish on the highest shelf of the oven for 50-60 minutes, until the top is crisp and golden and the underneath is creamy and tender.

Serves 6

2 lb 8 oz (1.15 kg) Desirée or Romano potatoes, peeled
½ oz (10 g) fresh rosemary
2 medium onions, peeled
10 fl oz (275 ml) vegetable stock
5 fl oz (150 ml) milk
1½ oz (40 g) butter
sea salt and freshly milled black pepper

You will also need an ovenproof dish measuring 11 x 8 x 2 inches (28 x 20 x 5 cm), lightly buttered.

Pre-heat the oven to gas mark 4, 350°F (180°C).

Oven-Sautéed Potatoes Lyonnaises

Let's face it, though sautéed potatoes are much loved, they are a bother – someone has to stand there and cook, and for four to six people you'll need, at best, four frying pans. The kitchen gets all greasy, too. Until now, that is, because you can, I've discovered, just pop them in the oven and forget about them till they're ready. They're particularly good alongside the Roast Lamb with Garlic and Rosemary on page 156.

Serves 4-6
2 lb (900 g) Desirée potatoes, peeled and, if large, halved
1 dessertspoon salt
3 tablespoons olive oil
1 medium onion, peeled, halved, then cut into ¼ inch (5 mm) slices
rock salt

You will also need a flameproof baking tray measuring 16 x 11 inches (40 x 28 cm).

Pre-heat the oven to gas mark 7, 425°F (220°C).

Place the potatoes in a steamer over boiling water and sprinkle them with the dessertspoon of salt, then put a lid on and let them steam for 10 minutes using a timer. When the time is up, remove the steamer, cover the potatoes with a clean tea cloth and allow them to cool slightly. Meanwhile, place the baking tray plus 2 tablespoons of the oil on to a high shelf of the oven to pre-heat for 10 minutes. Then, when the potatoes are cool enough to handle, slice them into rounds about ⅓ inch (7 mm) thick.

Next, remove the baking tray from the oven and place it over a medium direct heat. Now spoon the potatoes on to the tray and turn and baste them well so they get a good coating of oil, then pop them back in the oven, high shelf again, for 10 minutes. While that's happening, toss the onion slices with the remaining tablespoon of oil in a bowl. When the 10 minutes are up, remove the baking tray from the oven and scatter the onion amongst the potato slices, then return them to the same shelf of the oven for a further 10 minutes. Have a look after this time to make sure they are not becoming too brown, but give them a further 5 minutes if they are not quite brown enough. Then, when they're ready, sprinkle with rock salt and serve immediately.

Red Onion, Tomato and Chilli Relish

This is a recipe I devised especially for the chunky potato chips opposite, which I feel are all the better for some kind of dipping sauce.

Serves 4
1 small red onion, peeled and finely chopped
8 oz (225 g) ripe red tomatoes
½ small red chilli, deseeded and finely chopped
1 clove garlic, peeled and crushed
1 tablespoon dark brown soft sugar
4 fl oz (120 ml) balsamic vinegar
salt and freshly milled black pepper

First you need to skin the tomatoes, so pour boiling water over them and leave for exactly 1 minute before draining them and slipping off the skins (protect your hands with a cloth if they are too hot). Put the onion, chilli, garlic and tomatoes in a food processor and blend until finely chopped, then place the mixture in a saucepan and add the sugar and vinegar. Place the pan over a gentle heat and simmer very gently, without a lid, for 2 hours, by which time the mixture will have reduced to a thick sauce. Towards the end of the cooking time, stir frequently so the sauce doesn't stick to the bottom of the pan. Then taste to check the seasoning and serve hot or cold. Covered in the fridge, the relish will keep for several days.

Oven-Roasted Chunky Chips

These are, believe it or not, low fat – just one dessertspoon of oil between four to six people, so not quite as wicked as it would first seem.

First wash the potatoes very thoroughly, then dry in a clean tea cloth – they need to be as dry as possible; if they're ready-washed, just wipe them with kitchen paper. Leaving the peel on, slice them in half lengthways and then cut them again lengthways into chunky wedges approximately 1 inch (2.5 cm) thick. Dry them again in a cloth, then place them in a large bowl with the oil and a sprinkling of salt. Now toss them around a few times to get them well covered with the oil, then spread them out on the baking tray and place in the oven on a high shelf to roast for about 30 minutes. They should be golden brown and crisp after this time; if not, give them a few more minutes. Finely sprinkle with a little more salt, then serve absolutely immediately.

Serves 4-6
2 lb (900 g) Desirée potatoes
1 dessertspoon olive oil
salt

You will also need a solid baking tray measuring approximately 16 x 11 inches (40 x 28 cm).

Pre-heat the oven to gas mark 8, 450°F (230°C).

For Oven-Roasted Chunky Chips with Garlic and Rosemary (add to the basic recipe above):
2 cloves garlic, peeled and crushed
2 tablespoons bruised and chopped rosemary leaves

Oven-Roasted Chunky Chips served with Red Onion, Tomato and Chilli Relish

Gnocchi with Sage, Butter and Parmesan

Once again it's the Italians who are so clever at inventing such simple things out of what seem to be fairly ordinary ingredients but then become something quite outstanding. Thus it is with gnocchi – little dumplings made from potatoes, flour and egg. Not very exciting, you might think, but like real pasta made in the old-fashioned way, gnocchi have a texture and flavour of their own which can absorb and complement other flavours. This recipe is very simple, served with just butter, sage and Parmesan (but is also great with four cheeses, as overleaf). Always make the gnocchi the day you are going to serve them, because they will discolour if left overnight.

Serves 2-3

10 oz (275 g) King Edward potatoes
(about 2 medium-sized potatoes)
3½ oz (95 g) plain flour, sifted, plus
a little extra for rolling
1 large egg, lightly beaten
salt and freshly milled black pepper

For the sauce:
2 oz (50 g) butter
1 large clove garlic, peeled and crushed
8 fresh sage leaves

To serve:
3-4 tablespoons freshly grated
Parmesan (Parmigiano Reggiano)

You will also need a shallow ovenproof
serving dish measuring about 10 x 7
inches (25.5 x 18 cm).

First place the potatoes, with their skins on, in a suitably sized saucepan, almost cover with boiling water, add some salt, then put a lid on and simmer for 20-25 minutes, until tender. Then drain well and, holding them in your hand with a tea cloth, quickly pare off the skins using a potato peeler. Then place the potatoes in a large bowl and, using an electric hand whisk on a slow speed, start to break the potatoes up, then increase the speed and gradually whisk until smooth and fluffy. Now let them cool.

Next, add the sifted flour to the potatoes, along with half the beaten egg, season lightly and, using a fork, bring the mixture together. Then, using your hands, knead the mixture lightly to a soft dough – you may need to add a teaspoonful or so more of the egg if it is a little dry. Now transfer the mixture to a lightly floured surface, flour your hands and divide it into quarters. Now roll each quarter into a sausage shape approximately ½ inch (1 cm) in diameter, then cut it, on the diagonal, into 1 inch (2.5 cm) pieces, placing them on a tray or plate as they are cut. Cover with clingfilm and chill for at least 30 minutes, but longer won't matter.

After that, using a fork with the prongs facing upwards, press the fork down on to one side of each gnocchi so that it leaves a row of ridges on each one; at the same time, ease them into crescent shapes. The ridges are there to absorb the sauce effectively. Now cover and chill the gnocchi again until you are ready to cook them.

To cook the gnocchi, firstly bring a large, shallow pan of approximately 6 pints (3.5 litres) of water to a simmer and put the serving dish in a low oven to warm through. Then drop the gnocchi into the water and cook for about 3 minutes; they will start to float to the surface after about 2 minutes, but they need 3 altogether. When they are ready, remove the gnocchi with a draining spoon and transfer them to the warm serving dish. To serve, melt the butter with the garlic over a gentle heat until the garlic turns nut brown in colour – about 1 minute. Next add the sage leaves and allow the butter to froth while the sage leaves turn crisp – about 30 seconds – then spoon the butter mixture over the warm gnocchi. Sprinkle half the Parmesan over and serve the rest separately.

Spinach Gnocchi with Four Cheeses

I dream about eating this recipe on a warm, sunny summer's day outside, but in winter it's still an excellent lunch for two people or as a first course for four. For a variation, instead of using all cheese, halve the amount and add 6 oz (175 g) of crisp, crumbly bacon or pancetta.

Serves 2-3

1 medium King Edward potato –
about 6 oz (175 g)
8 oz (225 g) young leaf spinach
6 oz (175 g) Ricotta
a little freshly grated nutmeg
1 oz (25 g) plain flour, plus a little
extra for rolling
1 large egg
2 oz (50 g) Mascarpone
1 heaped tablespoon freshly
snipped chives
2 oz (50 g) creamy Gorgonzola,
roughly cubed
2 oz (50 g) Fontina, cut into
small cubes
2 oz (50 g) Pecorino Romano,
finely grated
salt and freshly milled black pepper

You will also need a shallow ovenproof serving dish measuring about 10 x 7 inches (25.5 x 18 cm).

First boil the potato, leaving the skin on, which will take about 25 minutes. Meanwhile, pick over the spinach, remove the stalks, then rinse the leaves. Place them in a large saucepan over a medium heat and cook briefly with a lid on for 1-2 minutes, until wilted and collapsed down. Then drain in a colander and, when cool enough to handle, squeeze all the moisture out and chop finely.

When the potato is cooked, drain and, holding it in a tea cloth, peel off the skin and sieve the potato into a bowl. Next add the spinach, Ricotta, nutmeg and flour to join the potato, then beat the egg and add half, together with some seasoning. Now, gently and lightly using a fork, bring the mixture together. Finish off with your hands and knead the mixture lightly into a soft dough, adding a teaspoonful or more of the beaten egg if it is a little dry. Then transfer the mixture to a floured surface and divide it into four. Roll each quarter into a sausage shape approximately ½ inch (1 cm) in diameter, then cut it on the diagonal into 1 inch (2.5 cm) pieces, placing them on a tray or plate as they are cut. Cover with clingfilm and chill for at least 30 minutes, but longer won't matter.

After that, using a fork with the prongs facing upwards, press the fork down on to each gnocchi, easing it into a crescent shape, so that it leaves a row of ridges on each one. Now cover and chill the gnocchi again until you are ready to cook them.

To cook the gnocchi, have all the cheeses ready. Pre-heat the grill to its highest setting, then bring a large, shallow pan of approximately 6 pints (3.5 litres) of water up to simmering point and put the serving dish near the grill to warm through. Now drop the gnocchi into the water and cook them for 3 minutes; they will start to float to the surface after about 2 minutes, but they need an extra minute. When they are ready, remove them with a draining spoon and transfer them straight to the serving dish. When they are all in, quickly stir in first the Mascarpone and chives, then sprinkle in the Gorgonzola and Fontina, then add some seasoning and cover the whole lot with the grated Pecorino. Now pop it under the grill for 3-4 minutes, until it is golden brown and bubbling. Serve absolutely immediately on hot plates.

Note: The plain gnocchi on page 190 can also be served with four cheeses, as above.

Potato Salad with Roquefort

This potato salad, with creamy, piquant Roquefort and the added crunch of celery and shallots, is good to eat all by itself, but I also like to serve it with cold cuts at a buffet lunch. It's therefore a very good recipe to have around at Christmas.

Place the potatoes in a steamer over boiling water and sprinkle them with a dessertspoon of salt, then put a lid on and let them steam for 20-25 minutes.

Meanwhile, make the dressing. To do this, place the garlic, along with the teaspoon of salt, into a mortar and crush it to a creamy mass, then add the mustard and work that in. Next add the lemon juice, vinegar and, after that, the oil, then whisk everything together thoroughly. Now, in a medium-sized bowl, first combine the crème fraîche and mayonnaise, then gradually whisk in the dressing. When it's thoroughly blended, add the cheese and season with freshly milled black pepper.

When the potatoes are cooked, remove the steamer and place a cloth over them for about 4 minutes to absorb the steam. Then cut any larger potatoes in half, transfer them to a large bowl and, while they are still warm, pour the dressing over them, along with the shallots and celery. Give everything a good gentle mixing, then, just before serving, crumble over the rest of the Roquefort and the spring onions.

Serves 6-8
2 lb (900 g) small new potatoes or salad potatoes
1 oz (25 g) Roquefort, crumbled
4 shallots, peeled and finely chopped
2 celery sticks, trimmed and chopped into ¼ inch (5 mm) pieces
4 spring onions, trimmed and finely chopped
salt

For the dressing:
1½ oz (40 g) Roquefort, crumbled
1 clove garlic, peeled
1 teaspoon salt
1 heaped teaspoon grain mustard
1 tablespoon lemon juice
2 tablespoons balsamic vinegar
2 tablespoons olive oil
5 fl oz (150 ml) half-fat crème fraîche
2 tablespoons mayonnaise
freshly milled black pepper

9
All kinds of rice

If you want to cook perfect rice – the kind that always stays light and fluffy, with absolutely every grain remaining separate – then I can teach you. But first you will have to make a promise, and that is to memorise three simple little words: *leave it alone!* If you can do this you will always be able to cook long-grain rice perfectly, and never have to worry about it.

The enemy

The number one enemy of fluffy, separate rice is the wooden spoon or, more specifically, the anxious cook who wields it. It is nervous prodding, poking and constant stirring that ruins rice. So there you are – that's the basic principle for the most common type of rice you'll have to cook, long-grain rice, but, of course, there are other kinds of rice that need different kinds of cooking. So for the beginner it's crucial to know your rice before you attempt to buy or cook it.

Know your rice

The simplest approach to rice cooking is to think in terms of four types of eating categories: first there's the fluffy, separate kind we've talked about; secondly there's the creamy, soupy kind used in risottos; then the clingy, sticky kind used in the Far East; and lastly what I'd call speciality rices, which have a distinctive characteristic of their own and are therefore not really in any of the categories already mentioned.

Brown or white?

Grains of rice, like wheat grains, are sometimes milled, which means the germ and the outer bran layer are removed in the process, revealing the inner grain, which comes in different shades of creamy white to pure white, depending on the variety. If the bran and germ are left intact, the colour of the grain is a rather appealing greeny-brown – hence the name brown rice. Here the flavour is more pronounced, slightly nutty and the texture is less soft, with more bite than white rice.

The advantage is that this rice contains (as you'd expect) more fibre, vitamins and minerals, but it takes longer to cook: 40 minutes as opposed to 15. But it's good to ring the changes, and there are times when I personally prefer brown to white rice for serving with certain dishes – with chilli, for instance, or in a rice salad. On the other hand, if I'm serving curry, I always prefer white rice, but it's good to experiment to find out what your own preferences are.

The long and short of it

What usually determines the 'eating' categories is the shape of the grain (although there is the odd exception, as you will see later).

Long-grain rice is precisely that, and the longer and thinner the grain is, the better the quality. So the grains should be mega-slim, with needle-sharp points at each end: this is the type of rice needed for separate, fluffy grains, and the best quality is called *basmati*. This is more expensive than others, but since cooking is about flavour, it is the one to buy, as it has a far superior taste. Although you will see dozens of varieties of long-grain rice, I believe it's well worth paying that little bit extra for basmati. Whether you are using the brown or the white, it's quite certainly the best.

Medium- and short-grain rice

Here the grains are not long and thin, but rounder and plumper. This group comes in the creamy and sticky eating category described earlier. There are, however, various qualities and national preferences.

Italian risotto rice, sometimes called *arborio* rice, is superb, or for the finest-quality risotto rice of all, look for the names *carnaroli* or *vialone nano*. In creamy, almost soupy risottos the rice is stirred, which releases some of the starch, and it is this that creates the lovely, smooth, creamy mass. The same kind of plump grain is used in Spain, and one of the finest varieties comes from the Valencia region and is called *calasparra*, which is used to make paella, though here the grains are not stirred, so they remain firm and distinct but with a moist, creamy edge.

In Japan there are several varieties of short-grain rice, ranging from the mildly sticky to the very sticky rice used to make sushi (it makes absolute sense that in the countries where chopsticks are used, rice with a stickier, more clinging consistency is far more manageable). This is sometimes called 'glutinous' rice, but it does not, as its name might suggest, contain any gluten and I prefer to describe it as *sticky rice*, which is more accurate.

In Thailand and Southeast Asia the rice grown and preferred is sometimes called *jasmine* or *fragrant rice*, but again I think the title is a little misleading, because it isn't actually any more fragrant than other types of rice. However, the quality is very good, and though it's actually a long-grain rice and when cooked, the grains have a firm texture and a good bite, they have a faint stickiness and tend to adhere to each other. I would say in this case the rice is both fluffy and sticky, and this is how it should be.

Specialist rices

These are rice varieties with their own individual characteristics. The first is *Camargue red rice*. Though other red rices are grown in America, this one, from France, is of superior quality. It is an unmilled short-grain rice with a brownish-red colour, and I would describe its character as earthy and gutsy, with a firm, slightly chewy texture and a nutty flavour. It is excellent in salads and combined with other strong flavours. Because it is a short-grain rice it is very slightly sticky when cooked and not meant to be separate and fluffy.

Black rice, well, it's reddish black, is an Asian rice used for sweet dishes and puddings and turns purple when cooked. It's probably about to become as fashionable here as it is in Australia, where practically every smart restaurant has a special pudding made with cooked black rice dressed with a mixture of palm sugar, coconut milk and lime. If you manage to get some, follow the instructions on the packet, which vary.

Wild rice is not actually a rice grain at all but the seed of a special type of grass grown in the swamps of North America. However, it's called rice, so I've put it on my list because it is cooked and served in exactly the same

Top row, left to right: black rice, Thai fragrant rice, Japanese rice
Centre, left to right: Camargue red rice, brown basmati rice, risotto rice
Bottom row, left to right: wild rice, white basmati rice, pudding rice

way, but needs about 50 minutes. The seeds are very long and most attractive, with a shiny ebony colour, and have a subtle, smoky, nutty flavour. It's good in salads and with gutsy foods with strong flavours. When cooked, the seeds tend to burst and split slightly, but this is quite normal and not some failure in the cooking – though, as with rice grains, it's important not to overcook them.

The 'also rans'

There are, of course, a million and one types of rice, and the list I've given you has what I believe to be the best in quality. The 'also rans', in a way, perpetuate the myth that cooking rice is difficult, and people usually buy them out of fear. Hopefully, *How To Cook* will dispel the myth and we can all enjoy the best quality of flavour when we're cooking rice. Pre-cooked or par-boiled rice is actually cooked before milling: this means the grains are tougher so require more water and a much longer cooking time. This is to help it stay more separate, but in my opinion there is a loss of flavour and I would never choose it. Quick-cook or easy-cook rice has been partially cooked after milling and then dried, so all it has to do is reabsorb water. It is quicker to cook, only 8-10 minutes instead of 12-15, but the loss of character and flavour puts this in the 'sliced white' category, ie, dull and pappy.

Pudding rice

Since I was a small child – a long time ago – we have always had in Britain a variety of short-grain rice called pudding rice; this is the type used the world over in sweet dishes and is best of all, in my opinion, for good Old-Fashioned Rice Pudding (see page 212). It is very sticky when cooked and, simmered in milk, becomes deliciously soft and creamy.

Always measure your rice by volume, using double the amount of water to rice

First cook the onions, then add the rice, turning the grains to coat them in the oil

The next stage is to add the boiling water and salt to the rice in the pan

198

To wash or not to wash?

I have never washed rice since I discovered that it is possible to wash away some of the nutrients in the process, and in any case modern rice is thoroughly cleaned in the milling. What's more, the water it's cooked in will be boiling, and that, of course, will purify it. I think some of the traditional methods of cooking rice, which require long rinsing and washing, belong to past times, when the rice was not as clean as it is today.

The ten rules for cooking perfect rice

1 Always measure rice by volume and not by weight. Use a measuring jug and measure 2½ fl oz (65 ml) per person (5 fl oz or 150 ml for 2, 10 fl oz or 275ml for 4 and so on).

2 Coating the grains of rice in a little oil before adding the water can help to keep them separate, and adding a little onion (see the recipe that follows) can provide extra flavour. But this is not a necessity – rice can be cooked quite simply in water.

3 The quantity of liquid you will need is roughly double the volume of rice, so 5 fl oz (150ml) needs 10 fl oz (275ml) of water or stock. Always add hot water or stock.

4 Don't forget to add salt, about 1 level teaspoon to every 5 fl oz (150ml) of rice.

5 The very best utensil for cooking fluffy, separate rice is a frying pan with a lid. Over the years I have found that the shallower the rice is spread out during cooking the better. Buying a 10 inch (25.5 cm) pan with a lid would be a good lifetime investment for rice cooking. Failing that, try to find a large saucepan lid that will fit your normal frying pan.

Stir once only – more will break the delicate grains, resulting in sticky rice

Put a lid on, turn the heat to its lowest setting and leave for 15 minutes

Once ready, remove the pan from the heat and cover with a cloth for 5-10 minutes

6 Once the hot liquid has been added, stir once only, cover with the lid and turn the heat down to its lowest setting, Give white rice 15 minutes and brown rice 40.

7 Leave it alone! Once the lid is on, set the timer and go away. If you lift the lid and let the steam out you can slow down the cooking process, and rice should always be cooked as briefly as possible. Even worse, if you stir it you will break the delicate grains and release the starch, and then it will end up sticky.

8 Use a timer – overcooking is what spoils rice. The best way to test if it is cooked is simply to bite a grain. Another way is to tilt the pan and, if liquid collects at the edge, it will need a couple more minutes' cooking.

9 When the rice is cooked, remove the lid, turn the heat off and place a clean tea cloth over the pan for 5-10 minutes. This will absorb the steam and help keep the grains dry and separate.

10 Just before serving, use the tip of a skewer or a fork to lightly fluff up the grains.

Perfect Rice

Serves 4
white basmati rice measured up to the 10 fl oz (275 ml) level in a measuring jug
1½ teaspoons groundnut or other flavourless oil
1 small onion, peeled and finely chopped
1 pint (570 ml) boiling water
1 rounded teaspoon salt

You will also need a frying pan with a 10 inch (25.5 cm) base and a tight-fitting lid.

Begin by warming the frying pan over a medium heat, then add the oil and the onions and let them cook for 3-4 minutes, until lightly tinged brown. Next stir in the rice – there's no need to wash it – and turn the grains over in the pan so they become lightly coated and glistening with oil. Then add the boiling water, along with the salt, stir once only, then cover with the lid. Turn the heat to its very lowest setting and let the rice cook gently for exactly 15 minutes. Don't remove the lid and don't stir the rice during cooking, because this is what will break the grains and release their starch, which makes the rice sticky.

After 15 minutes, tilt the pan to check that no liquid is left; if there is, pop it back on the heat for another minute. When there is no water left in the pan, take the pan off the heat, remove the lid and cover with a clean tea cloth for 5-10 minutes before serving, then transfer the rice to a warm serving dish and fluff it lightly with a fork before it goes to the table.

Oven-Baked Risotto Carbonara

I just love pasta with carbonara sauce so much that one day I thought I'd try it with a risotto – same ingredients: pancetta, a strong-flavoured Italian bacon, eggs and sharp Pecorino cheese. The result is outstandingly good and got one of the highest votes from the crew when we were filming.

First of all, in a large, hot frying pan over a medium heat, fry the pancetta or bacon in its own fat for 4-5 minutes, until it's crisp and golden, then remove it to a plate. Next add the butter to the pan, then the onion, turn the heat down to gentle and let the onion soften in the butter for about 5 minutes. Meanwhile, heat the stock in a small saucepan. Then return the pancetta or bacon to the frying pan and, after that, stir in the rice and move it around until all the grains get a good coating of the buttery juices. Now add the hot stock to the rice, along with some salt and freshly milled black pepper. Let it all come up to a gentle simmer, then transfer the whole lot to the warmed dish, stir it once and then bake, without covering, on the centre shelf of the oven and set a timer for 20 minutes.

When the time is up, gently stir in the Pecorino, folding and turning the rice grains over, then set the timer for a further 15 minutes. Meanwhile, whisk the egg, egg yolks and crème fraîche together, then remove the risotto from the oven and gently stir in this mixture, making sure it is well mixed. Leave the risotto for about 2 minutes, by which time the eggs and crème fraîche will have thickened – but no longer, as it will get too thick. Serve on warm plates with some more Pecorino Romano sprinkled over.
Note: This recipe contains raw eggs.

Serves 2
8 fl oz (225 ml) carnaroli rice
4½ oz (125 g) cubetti pancetta
or chopped bacon
1 oz (25 g) butter
1 medium onion, peeled and
finely chopped
1¼ pints (725 ml) chicken or
vegetable stock
3 oz (75 g) finely grated Pecorino
Romano, plus some extra for
sprinkling
1 large egg
2 large egg yolks
1 heaped tablespoon crème fraîche
salt and freshly milled black pepper

You will also need a round ovenproof dish with a diameter of 9 inches (23 cm), 2 inches (5 cm) deep, placed in the oven when it's pre-heated.

Pre-heat the oven to gas mark 2, 300°F (150°C).

Chinese Stir-Fried Rice

The most important point to remember if you want to fry rice successfully is that it must be cooked but cold. I have used authentic Chinese ingredients here, which are easily obtainable if you live near speciality Chinese suppliers; if not, you can use fresh prawns instead of shrimps and fresh shiitake mushrooms instead of dried.

Serves 4

8 fl oz (225 ml) white basmati rice, cooked as for Perfect Rice (see page 200, but using 16 fl oz/450 ml boiling water), cooled
1 oz (25 g) Chinese dried shrimps
¼ oz (5 g) Chinese dried mushrooms
16 fl oz (450 ml) boiling water
1½ tablespoons groundnut or other flavourless oil
1 small onion, peeled and finely chopped
4 rashers streaky bacon, chopped into ¼ inch (5 mm) pieces
2 oz (50 g) peas, fresh if possible, defrosted if frozen
2 large eggs, lightly beaten
2 spring onions, split lengthways and finely chopped
1 tablespoon Japanese soy sauce

You will also need a wok or frying pan with a 10 inch (25.5 cm) base.

Begin by putting the shrimps and mushrooms in a small bowl, pour over the boiling water and leave them to soak for 30 minutes. Then squeeze the liquid from them, discard the mushroom stalks and slice them finely. Then heat half the oil in the wok or pan and, when it's really hot, quickly fry the onions and bacon for 3 minutes, moving them around in the pan until the bacon is crispy. Then add the shrimps, peas and mushrooms and stir-fry these for about 1 minute. Now add the remaining oil to the pan and, when it's smoking hot, add the rice and stir-fry, this time for about 30 seconds. Now spread the ingredients out in the pan and pour in the beaten eggs. It won't look very good now, but keep on stir-frying, turning the mixture over, and the eggs will soon cook into little shreds that mingle with the other ingredients. Finally, add the spring onions and soy sauce, give it one more good stir and serve.

Chinese Stir-Fried Rice served with Oriental Steamed Fish with Ginger, Soy and Sesame

This can be a quick supper dish for the family or it's exotic enough for entertaining: all you need is a fan steamer – bamboo or the old-fashioned kind.

Oriental Steamed Fish with Ginger, Soy and Sesame

You need to begin this by having a little chopping session. First the ginger, which should be thinly sliced then cut into very fine shreds. The garlic needs to be chopped small, as do the spring onions, making sure you include the green parts as well.

Now place a medium frying pan over a medium heat and, when it's hot, add the sesame seeds and toast them in the dry pan, shaking it from time to time until they're a golden brown colour – this takes only 1-2 minutes. Now transfer the seeds to a bowl.

Next add the oils to the pan and, over a medium heat, gently fry the chopped garlic and ginger – they need to be pale gold but not too brown, so take care not to have the heat too high. After that, add these to the toasted seeds, along with any oil left in the pan, then mix in the lemon juice, soy sauce and chopped spring onions.

Now season the fish, spread three-quarters of the mixture over the surface of each skinned side, roll them up quite firmly into little rolls, then spoon the rest of the mixture on top of each roll. All this can be prepared in advance, as long as the fish is kept covered in the fridge.

Then, when you're ready to cook the fish, line the base of the steamer with the lettuce leaves (or foil if you don't have any). Now place the fish on top, cover with a lid and steam over boiling water for 8-10 minutes. Serve with the Chinese Stir-Fried Rice, left.

Serves 4

1 lb 8 oz (700 g) lemon sole fillets, skinned and cut lengthways down the natural dividing line (ask the fishmonger to do this)
2½ inch (6 cm) piece root ginger, peeled
1 tablespoon Japanese soy sauce
1 rounded tablespoon sesame seeds
1 dessertspoon sesame oil
3 cloves garlic, peeled
2 spring onions
1 dessertspoon groundnut or other flavourless oil
juice 1 lemon
a few outside lettuce leaves, for lining the steamer
salt and freshly milled black pepper

You will also need a fan or bamboo steamer.

Very Red Rice

This was a recipe created for Comic Relief, hence the title, and I always have a good giggle thinking back to the filming of those hilarious cookery demonstrations that were later screened on television. It's also an excellent recipe – good with any barbecue dishes or with the pork chops opposite.

Serves 4
10 fl oz (275 ml) Camargue red rice
1 tablespoon oil
½ oz (10 g) butter
1 small red pepper, deseeded and finely chopped
1 small red onion, peeled and finely chopped
15 fl oz (425 ml) boiling water
1 teaspoon salt

To serve:
2 spring onions, trimmed and finely sliced
a few sprigs watercress

You will also need a 10 inch (25.5 cm) frying pan with a lid.

First heat the oil and butter in the pan over a medium heat. Then turn it up to high and stir-fry the chopped pepper and onion until they are softened and slightly blackened at the edges – 6-7 minutes. After that, turn the heat right down, add the red rice to the pan and stir it around to get a good coating of oil. Now pour in the boiling water and salt and stir again. When it reaches simmering point, put the lid on and let it cook very gently for 40 minutes. After that, don't remove the lid, just turn the heat off and leave it for another 15 minutes to finish off. Garnish the rice with the sliced spring onions and the watercress. Serve with the Oven-Baked Pork Chops in Maple Barbecue Sauce, opposite.

Very Red Rice served with Oven-Baked Pork Chops in Maple Barbecue Sauce

Oven-Baked Pork Chops in Maple Barbecue Sauce

Sorry about the long list of ingredients in this sauce, but it really does take only 5 minutes to make, then cooks into a heavenly, sticky, spicy goo.

First of all mix the olive oil with the lemon juice, then place the pork chops in the roasting tin with the chopped onion tucked amongst them. Season with a little salt and freshly milled black pepper, then brush the chops with the oil and lemon juice. You can, if you like, do this well in advance, just cover with a cloth and leave in a cool place.

Then, when you're ready to cook the pork chops, pre-heat the oven to gas mark 6, 400°F (200°C), then pop them in on a high shelf and cook for 25 minutes exactly. Meanwhile, combine all the sauce ingredients in a jug and, using a small whisk, blend everything thoroughly. Then, when the 25 minutes are up, remove the roasting tin from the oven, pour off any surplus fat from the corner of the tin and pour the sauce all over, giving everything a good coating.

Now back it goes into the oven for about another 25 minutes, and you will need to baste it twice during this time. After that, remove the roasting tin from the oven and place it over direct heat turned to medium. Then pour in the red wine, stir it into the sauce and let it bubble for about 1 minute. Then serve the pork chops on a bed of Very Red Rice with the sauce spooned over and garnish with the sprigs of watercress.

Serves 4
4 pork chops
1 tablespoon olive oil
1 dessertspoon lemon juice
1 medium onion, peeled and
finely chopped
salt and freshly milled black pepper

For the sauce:
2 tablespoons pure maple syrup
3 fl oz (75 ml) red wine
4 tablespoons Japanese soy sauce
2 tablespoons red wine vinegar
1 heaped tablespoon tomato purée
1 heaped teaspoon ground ginger
1 heaped teaspoon mustard powder
2 cloves garlic, peeled and crushed
1½ teaspoons Tabasco sauce

To finish:
2 fl oz (55 ml) red wine
a few sprigs watercress

You will also need a flameproof shallow roasting tin measuring 12 x 8 x 1¾ inches (30 x 20 x 4.5 cm).

Camargue Red Rice Salad with Feta Cheese

This is a lovely salad for outdoor eating on a warm, sunny summer's day.

Serves 4

10 fl oz (275 ml) Camargue red rice
7 oz (200 g) Feta cheese
1 teaspoon salt
1 pint (570 ml) boiling water
2 shallots, peeled and finely chopped
2 oz (50 g) fresh rocket leaves,
finely shredded
3 spring onions, trimmed and finely
chopped, including the green ends
salt and freshly milled black pepper

For the dressing:

1 small clove garlic, crushed
½ level teaspoon salt
1 level teaspoon grain mustard
1 tablespoon balsamic vinegar
2 tablespoons extra virgin olive oil
salt and freshly milled black pepper

You will also need a 10 inch (25.5 cm)
frying pan with a lid.

First put the rice in the frying pan with the teaspoon of salt, then pour in the boiling water, bring it back up to simmering point, then put a lid on and let it cook very gently for 40 minutes. After that, don't remove the lid, just turn the heat off and leave it for another 15 minutes to finish off.

Meanwhile, make the dressing by crushing the garlic and salt in a pestle and mortar, then, when it becomes a purée, add the mustard and work that in, followed by the vinegar and some freshly milled black pepper. Now add the oil and, using a small whisk, whisk everything thoroughly to combine it. Then transfer the warm rice to a serving dish, pour the dressing over and mix thoroughly. Taste to check the seasoning and leave aside until cold. Then add the shallots, the rocket and the spring onions. Finally, just before serving, crumble the Feta cheese all over.

Tiger Prawn Jambalaya

This is one of the easiest and nicest rice dishes, and its origins are in the traditional Cajun cooking of America. It's very easy to adapt it to whatever you have handy – fish, chicken or even pork.

Begin by bringing a pan with 1 pint (570 ml) of water to simmering point. If using raw prawns, drop them into the water for 3 minutes. After that, remove them with a draining spoon, reserving the cooking liquid. (Cooked prawns will not need this pre-cooking.) Now set aside two whole prawns and shell the rest. To do this, just remove the heads by giving them a sharp tug, then simply peel off the rest – which comes away very easily – but leave the tails intact as this makes them look nicer. Now remove the black vein from the back of each prawn, which will come away easily using the point of a sharp knife. Next place the shells in the pan of water and simmer for 30 minutes, without a lid, to make a nice prawn-flavoured stock, then drain and discard the shells. Pour the hot stock into a jug and cover with a plate to keep warm.

Now heat the frying pan over a high heat and brown the pieces of chorizo sausage, without adding any fat, then remove them from the pan to a plate and set aside. Then add a tablespoon of the oil and, when it's hot, fry the onions for 2-3 minutes to brown them a little at the edges, then return the chorizo to the pan and add the garlic, celery, chilli and sliced pepper. Continue to fry for 4-5 minutes, till the celery and pepper are also softened and lightly tinged brown at the edges, adding a little more oil if you need to. Now stir in the rice to get a good coating of oil, then measure out 12 fl oz (340 ml) of the reserved stock and add the Tabasco to it. Next add the chopped tomatoes and bay leaf to the pan, then pour in the stock. Season with salt and freshly milled black pepper, give it all one stir and push the rice down into the liquid. Now turn the heat to low, put a lid on and let it barely simmer for 20 minutes. Then, check the rice is cooked and return the shelled and the two reserved shell-on prawns to the pan, adding a little more stock if necessary. Cover with a lid for 5 more minutes, then serve garnished with the chopped parsley and spring onions.

Serves 2-3

8 raw tiger prawns, shell on, fresh or frozen and thoroughly defrosted, or you could use cooked Mediterranean prawns in their shells
4 oz (110 g) chorizo sausage, peeled and cut into ¾ inch (2 cm) pieces
1-2 tablespoons olive oil
1 medium onion, peeled and cut into ½ inch (1 cm) slices
2 cloves garlic, peeled and crushed
2 sticks celery, trimmed and sliced into ½ inch (1 cm) pieces on the diagonal
1 green chilli, deseeded and finely chopped
1 yellow pepper, deseeded and cut into ½ inch (1 cm) slices
6 fl oz (175 ml) white basmati rice
1 teaspoon Tabasco sauce
3 medium tomatoes, dropped into boiling water for 1 minute, then peeled and chopped
1 bay leaf
1 tablespoon roughly chopped flat-leaf parsley, to garnish
2 spring onions, trimmed and finely sliced, to garnish
salt and freshly milled black pepper

You will also need a 10 inch (25.5 cm) frying pan with a lid.

Spiced Pilau Rice with Nuts

I've always loved the fragrant flavour of spiced pilau rice, and could easily eat it just on its own, adding nuts to give it some crunch. However, it's also an excellent accompaniment to any spiced or curried dish, particularly the chicken recipe that follows.

Serves 4

10 fl oz (275 ml) white basmati rice
1 oz (25 g) unsalted cashew nuts
1 oz (25 g) unsalted shelled
pistachio nuts
1 oz (25 g) pine nuts
2 cardamom pods
¾ teaspoon cumin seeds
½ teaspoon coriander seeds
1½ tablespoons groundnut or other
flavourless oil
1 small onion, peeled and
finely chopped
1 pint (570 ml) boiling water
1 inch (2.5 cm) piece cinnamon stick
1 bay leaf
1 rounded teaspoon salt

You will also need a lidded frying pan with a 10 inch (25.5 cm) base.

First of all, in the pestle and mortar, crush the cardamom pods and the cumin and coriander seeds. Then, warm the frying pan over a medium heat, add the crushed spices (the pods as well as the seeds of the cardamom), turn the heat up high and toss them around in the heat to dry-roast them and draw out the flavour – this will take about 1 minute. After that, turn the heat back to medium and add the oil, onion and nuts and fry until everything is lightly tinged brown. Next, stir in the rice and turn the grains over in the pan until they are nicely coated and glistening with oil, then pour in the boiling water. Add the cinnamon, bay leaf and a good seasoning of salt, stir once only, then put the lid on, turn the heat down to its lowest setting and let the rice cook for exactly 15 minutes. After this time, take the pan off the heat, remove the lid and cover with a clean tea cloth for 5 minutes. Then empty the rice into a warm serving dish and fluff up lightly with a fork before it goes to the table.

Marinated Chicken Kebabs with Whole Spices served with Spiced Pilau Rice with Nuts

This is a heavenly combination of textures and fragrant, spicy flavours, and has the added advantage of not being too high in fat. The coriander chutney, pictured below, is a perfect accompaniment, but this dish also goes well with mango chutney if fresh coriander isn't available.

Begin by dry-roasting the cumin and coriander seeds and the cardamom pods over a medium heat for 1 minute, until the seeds begin to jump. Remove from the heat and, once cool, remove the seeds from the cardamom pods and crush them with the cumin and coriander seeds using a pestle and mortar. Next add the ginger, turmeric, garlic and salt and mix everything well.

Now cut each chicken breast into five pieces, place them in a bowl and toss them first in the groundnut or flavourless oil, then in the spice mixture, mixing everything around so they get an even coating. Next add the yoghurt, give everything a good stir and press the chicken down well into the marinade. Cover with clingfilm and refrigerate for a few hours or, preferably, overnight.

To make the chutney, simply whiz everything together in a blender, then pour into a bowl and leave aside for 2-3 hours so the flavours develop.

When you are almost ready to serve, soak the skewers in water for 20 minutes to stop them from burning, then light the barbecue or pre-heat the grill to its highest setting. Next, thread half a bay leaf on to each skewer, then a piece of chicken, a piece of onion and half a chilli. Carry on alternating the chicken, onion and chilli until you have used five pieces of chicken per kebab, then finish with half a bay leaf on each. Make sure you pack everything as tightly as possible, then season, lay the kebabs on the grill rack or barbecue and sprinkle with a little olive oil. If you're grilling, put a heatproof dish lined with foil under the rack and grill the kebabs for 10 minutes on each side, about 4 inches (10 cm) from the heat source, or simply cook over the barbecue.

Now slip the chicken and vegetables from the skewers, using a fork to ease them off, and serve with the Spiced Pilau Rice with Nuts, garnished with lime quarters, and the chutney handed round separately.

Serves 4
4 x 6 oz (175 g) boneless chicken breasts, skin on
4 bay leaves, cut in half
½ red onion, peeled, halved through the root and separated into layers
8 fresh green chillies, halved and deseeded
a little olive oil
salt and freshly milled black pepper

For the marinade:
1 teaspoon whole cumin seeds
1½ teaspoons whole coriander seeds
12 cardamom pods
1 rounded tablespoon peeled and grated root ginger
1 rounded tablespoon turmeric
3 cloves garlic, peeled and crushed
½ teaspoon Maldon sea salt or rock salt
1 tablespoon groundnut or other flavourless oil
10 fl oz (275 ml) natural yoghurt

For the fresh coriander chutney:
1 oz (25 g) fresh coriander leaves
2 tablespoons lime juice
1 fresh green chilli, halved and deseeded
1 clove garlic, peeled
1 tablespoon natural yoghurt
½ teaspoon golden caster sugar
salt and freshly milled black pepper

To garnish:
2 limes, quartered

You will also need four wooden skewers about 10 inches (25.5 cm) long.

Thai Creamed Coconut Chicken

Serves 4

1 cooked chicken weighing about
2 lb 4 oz (1 kg), stripped, or 5 cooked
chicken breasts
14 fl oz (400 ml) coconut milk
1 teaspoon coriander seeds
½ teaspoon cumin seeds
2 cardamom pods, lightly crushed
2 tablespoons groundnut or other
flavourless oil
2 medium onions, peeled
and finely sliced
2 cloves garlic, peeled and crushed
½ oz (10 g) fresh coriander
1 teaspoon turmeric
4 red chillies, deseeded and finely
chopped
1 dessertspoon finely chopped fresh
lemon grass
2 tablespoons lime juice
salt and freshly milled black pepper

The very good news about this brilliant recipe for busy people is that it's made with ready-cooked chicken. You can, of course, cook the chicken yourself, but either way it's a quick but excellent supper party dish for four people, and extra special served with the Thai Green Rice.

To prepare the chicken, remove the skin and cut the flesh into strips about 2½ inches (6 cm) long. Next the spices will need roasting, so heat a large frying pan or wok – without any fat in it – and, when it's really hot, add the coriander, cumin and cardamom pods. Allow the spices to roast briefly – about 45 seconds – shaking the pan from time to time, then tip them into a mortar, removing the seeds from the cardamom pods and discarding the husks, and crush them all fairly finely.

Now add the oil to the frying pan or wok. When it's really hot, fry the onions and garlic over a medium heat for 8-9 minutes, until they're nicely softened. Meanwhile, strip the leaves from the coriander stalks, reserve these, then chop the stalks finely.

When the onions are ready, add the turmeric, chilli, crushed spices and coriander stalks, along with the lemon grass, to the pan. Stir these thoroughly together, then pour in the coconut milk and lime juice. Add some seasoning, then simmer everything gently for about 10 minutes, uncovered, by which time the sauce should have reduced and thickened.

Now add the chicken to the sauce and simmer gently for 10 minutes or so to heat it through completely. Serve the chicken on a bed of Thai Green Rice, garnished with the coriander leaves.

Thai Green Rice

Serves 4

12 fl oz (340 ml) basmati rice
2 oz (50 g) creamed coconut
8 fl oz (225 ml) boiling water
4 cloves garlic, peeled
3 large or 2 medium-sized fresh green
chillies, deseeded

This, thankfully, is a Thai recipe that doesn't require all the speciality ingredients that are sometimes so elusive. The list of ingredients, again, seems rather long, but it is made in moments and has a lovely fragrant flavour.

Begin by dissolving the creamed coconut in the boiling water, then place it in a food processor with the garlic, chillies, ginger and coriander stalks, whizzing until everything is finely chopped.

Leave this aside while you heat the oil over a gentle heat in the frying pan, then add the cinnamon sticks, cloves, peppercorns and cashew nuts to the pan and sauté everything gently for about 1 minute. Next, add the onions and continue to cook over a medium heat until they become softened and pale gold in colour, which will take 8-10 minutes. Next add the rice, then stir once and cook for another 2-3 minutes. After that, add the coconut mixture, give everything a stir, and cook for a further 2-3 minutes. Now add the peas, salt and hot water, bring it all up to a gentle simmer, then cover with the lid. Turn the heat to low and let everything cook very gently for 8 minutes; use a timer here, and don't lift the lid.

Then remove the pan from the heat, take the lid off and cover the pan with a cloth for 10 minutes before serving. Finally, remove the pieces of cinnamon, sprinkle in the lime juice and the finely chopped coriander leaves, then fork the rice gently to separate the grains. Garnish with the reserved whole coriander leaves and serve with the Thai Creamed Coconut Chicken.

1½-inch (4 cm) cube root ginger, peeled
¾ oz (20 g) fresh coriander, leaves removed and finely chopped, the stalks reserved, with a few whole leaves reserved for the garnish
1½ tablespoons groundnut or other flavourless oil
3 x 2 inch (5 cm) pieces cinnamon stick
6 whole cloves
15 black peppercorns
1½ oz (40 g) unsalted cashew nuts, halved
2 medium onions, peeled and finely sliced
4 oz (110 g) fresh peas, or frozen and defrosted
1½ teaspoons salt, or to taste
15 fl oz (425 ml) hot water
2 tablespoons lime juice

You will also need a 9 inch (23 cm) frying pan with a close-fitting lid.

Thai Creamed Coconut Chicken served with Thai Green Rice

Old-Fashioned Rice Pudding

This is the real thing – a mass of creamy rice and a thick brown speckled nutmeg skin. Don't forget to take a sharp knife and scrape off all the bits of caramelised skin that stick to the edges – my grandmother always did that and gave everyone an equal amount.

This is simplicity itself, because all you do is mix the evaporated milk and whole milk together in a jug, then place the rice and sugar in the ovenproof dish, pour in the liquid and give it all a good stir. Grate the whole nutmeg all over the surface (it may seem a lot but it needs it), then, finally, dot the butter on top in little flecks.

Next just carefully pop the dish in the oven on the centre shelf and leave it there for 30 minutes, then slide the shelf out and give everything a good stir. Repeat the stirring after a further 30 minutes, then pop the dish back in the oven to cook for another hour, this time without stirring. At the end of this time the rice grains will have become swollen, with pools of creamy liquid all around them, and, of course, all that lovely skin! This is wonderful served warm with the Plums in Marsala, opposite.

Serves 4-6
6 fl oz (175 ml) pudding rice
14½ oz (410 g) evaporated milk
1 pint (570 ml) whole milk
1½ oz (40 g) golden granulated or
caster sugar
1 whole nutmeg
1 oz (25 g) butter

You will also need a round ovenproof dish with a diameter of 9 inches (23 cm), 2 inches (5 cm) deep, lightly buttered.

Pre-heat the oven to gas mark 2, 300°F (150°C).

Plums in Marsala

The mellow but distinctive flavour of Marsala wine, when simmered together with fruit, is something I am particularly fond of. It works well with plums, which, I think, are very good served chilled, along with the warm rice pudding opposite.

First place the plums, vanilla pod and cinnamon sticks in the baking dish, then mix the Marsala with the sugar and pour it over the plums. Now place the dish on the centre shelf of the oven and cook for 40 minutes, uncovered, turning the plums over in the Marsala halfway through the cooking time. Then remove the baking dish from the oven and strain the plums, discarding the vanilla pod and cinnamon sticks, and pour the sauce into a medium-sized saucepan. Bring it up to simmering point, then let it bubble and reduce for 5 minutes. Now mix the arrowroot with a little water in a cup to make a paste, then whisk this into the liquid. Bring the sauce back to simmering point, whisking all the time, until it has thickened slightly and is glossy – about 5 minutes. Then pour it back over the plums and serve them hot or cold.

Serves 6
3 lb (1.35 kg) fresh firm plums
1 pint (570 ml) Marsala
1 vanilla pod
2 cinnamon sticks
3 oz (75 g) golden caster sugar
2 teaspoons arrowroot

You will also need a 10 x 8 inch (25.5 x 20 cm) baking dish, 2 inches (5 cm) deep.

Pre-heat the oven to gas mark 4, 350°F (180°C).

10
Pasta revisited

I think it's about time we gave pasta a radical rethink. In the 1960s only two kinds of pasta were known to most people: spaghetti, which came in tins and was served on toast, and macaroni, which was served either in a cheese sauce or as a pudding. Yet, 30 years later, pasta has exploded into our lives with such force that it's now become almost a standard British staple – we now consume 2kg per head per year. The trouble is that a lot of this is not, in the strictest sense, real pasta; not in the way it was originally and brilliantly conceived to be. And now many modern pasta makers have, I feel, completely lost the plot.

What is real pasta?

Originally, pasta in Italy was a conception of sheer genius. It began with growing the highest-quality hard wheat, and the name given to this specific type of wheat was durum, from the Latin, meaning hard. After the pasta maker had purchased exactly the right grain, the next important stage was finding the right miller to mill the grain to a certain precise specification – and not to a fine, powdery flour but to something called semolina, which is derived from the italian for 'semi milled' and is quite unlike flour, as semolina is made up of tiny, coarse, corn-coloured granules with sharp edges.

The skill of the pasta maker was to then carefully mix the semolina with cold water. Then, after the mixing came the shaping, and the pasta was forced through special bronze dies, which gave it a specific texture. After that the pasta was dried in open-windowed lofts where either the mountain air or sea breezes – or both, depending on the region – could circulate. This carefully monitored drying process could take up to two days. It was this natural drying process, along with the specifications above, that produced a quality of pasta that had captured within it all the nuttiness and flavour of the wheat grain but also a special texture. The semolina and the effect of the bronze dies produced a roughness at the edges which, in its grand design, would provide, when cooked, the right kind of surface on which the sauce being served with it would adhere and cling and not slide off. So simple, so subtle and so wonderful.

Modern pasta (and clones)

What happened next was that, soon, everybody outside Italy wanted to eat pasta, too, and once this kind of mass production was under way, corners were cut, profit margins came into play, soft flour was added, hot instead of cold water, there were nylon dies, speeded-up hot-air quick-drying, and the whole process underwent a shift from quality to competitive price wars and then it was the 'sliced white' here-we-go-downward-spiral all over again.

But something else has crept into the frame at the same time, and that is the misguided and false conception that fresh pasta is better than dried. Yes, Italians do make and eat a very small amount of *pasta fresca*, but it is a different concept; one that more usually involves a filling, as in ravioli or tortellini. But in this country – and in America – *pasta fresca* has gone crazy. It's now a far cry from the original described above and it's a strange paradox to clone a product that has a natural shelf life of two years, then make it and sell it as fresh, then add something that will give it a longer shelf life and at the same time call the resulting slithery, slimy gloop made with soft flour and eggs pasta.

The other modern misconception is to serve more sauce than pasta. Good pasta should be enjoyed for itself, with a small amount of concentrated sauce used to merely dress it.

The case for good-quality dried pasta

If you want to enjoy cooking and eating pasta at its best, then my advice is to buy good-quality dried pasta. Yes, it does cost more, but we're not talking about great luxury here; we're talking about a main meal for two people that might cost £2 instead of £1.

There are a few artisanal pasta makers in Italy who still make the real thing, and a supplier is listed on page 232. The only fresh pastas I ever buy are ravioli, stuffed pasta shapes or lasagne sheets, which are, I think, of a far better quality than most of the dried packs. Once you taste quality dried pasta, it will be very hard for you to return to the industrially produced alternatives. It's not just the flavour: the firm, rough texture not only puts it way out in front but actually helps you to achieve that *al dente* 'firm to the teeth' texture that is the mark of well-cooked pasta. Poor quality often ends up sticky and soggy. So when you buy your pasta, make sure it says *pasta di semola di grano duro* – durum wheat semolina pasta.

There are certain dried pastas that contain eggs – *pasta all' uovo* – which add richness, but I now prefer the original semolina and water version and like to keep the richness confined to the sauce.

How to cook perfect pasta

The easiest way to communicate this is to give you a list of what is absolutely essential.

1 Always use a very large cooking pot.
2 Always make absolutely sure you have at least 4 pints (2.25 litres) of water to every 8 oz (225 g) of pasta, with 1 level tablespoon of salt added.
3 Make sure the water is up to a good fierce boil before the pasta goes in.
4 Add the pasta as quickly as possible and stir it around just once to separate it. If you're cooking long pasta, like spaghetti, push it against the base of the pan and, as you feel it give, keep pushing until it all collapses down into the water.
5 You don't need to put a lid on the pan: if it's really boiling briskly it will come back to the boil in seconds, and if you put a lid on it will boil over.
6 Put a timer on and give it 10-12 minutes for top-quality pasta, but because this timing varies according to the shape and quality of the pasta, the only real way to tell is to taste it. So do this after 8 minutes, then 9, and 10, and so on. This only applies when you cook a particular brand for the first time. After that you will always know how long it takes. Sometimes you can give it 1 minute's less boiling and then allow an extra minute's cooking whilst you combine it with the sauce.
7 Have a colander ready in the sink, then, as you are draining the water, swirl it around the colander, which will heat it ready for the hot pasta.

Below, from top: dried spaghetti, penne, macaroni and rigatoni pastas

8 Don't drain it too thoroughly: it's good to have a few drops of moisture still clinging as this prevents the pasta from becoming dry. Place the colander back over the saucepan to catch any drips.

9 Always serve it on deep warmed plates to keep the pasta as hot as possible as it goes to the table.

10 For spaghetti, the very best way to serve it is to use pasta tongs (see the photograph opposite), and always lift it high to quickly separate each portion from the rest.

11 If the pasta is going to be cooked again, in a baked dish like macaroni cheese, for example, give it half the usual cooking time to allow for the time in the oven.

12 *Presto pronto!* In Italian this means soon and quickly. Always work quickly, as pasta won't hang around – if it cools it goes sticky and gluey, so drain it quickly, serve it quickly and eat it quickly.

How to eat spaghetti and other long pastas

This is how I describe this in the *Cookery Course*. 'The big mistake here is trying to wind too much on to the fork at once. Select just two or three strands with your fork and coax them over the rim of the plate. Then, holding the fork at a right angle to the plate, simply wind the fork round and round, so that those few strands extricate themselves from the rest and are twisted round the fork in a little bite-sized bundle. Easier said than done, you're thinking? But remember – practice makes perfect.'

Spaghetti with Olive Oil, Garlic and Chilli

This one is pure pasta eaten and savoured for its own sake with the minimum amount of adornment – just a hint of garlic, chilli and olive oil.

Serves 2
8 oz (225 g) spaghetti or linguine
4 tablespoons Italian extra virgin olive oil
2 fat cloves garlic, peeled and finely chopped
1 fat red chilli, deseeded and finely chopped
freshly milled black pepper

Begin by putting the pasta on to cook. Then, just heat the olive oil in a small frying pan and, when it is hot, add the garlic, chilli and some freshly milled black pepper. Cook these very gently for about 2 minutes, which will be enough time for the flavourings to infuse the oil.

When the pasta is cooked, return it to the saucepan after draining, then pour in the hot oil. Mix well, then serve straight away on warmed pasta plates.

Linguine with Gorgonzola, Pancetta and Wilted Rocket

This is a lovely combination of assertive flavours that harmonise together perfectly.

Serves 2
8 oz (225 g) linguine
4 oz (110 g) Gorgonzola Piccante
4½ oz (125 g) cubetti (cubed) pancetta or chopped bacon
2 oz (50 g) fresh rocket
7 fl oz (200 ml) crème fraîche
1 clove garlic, peeled and crushed
4 oz (110 g) Mozzarella, cut into little cubes
a little freshly grated Parmesan (Parmigiano Reggiano), to serve
salt and freshly milled black pepper

Begin by putting the pasta on to cook and give it 1 minute less cooking time than normal, then place the Gorgonzola Piccante and the crème fraîche in a food processor and whiz it to blend together. Next place a large, solid frying pan over direct heat and, as soon as you think it is really hot, add the cubes of pancetta or chopped bacon and sauté them in their own fat for 3-4 minutes, keeping them on the move to brown all the edges evenly. Then add the garlic to the pan and toss that around for about 1 minute. Next, remove the pan from the heat and add the rocket leaves which, when you have given them a stir, will wilt in the heat of the pan.

When the pasta is ready, drain it immediately and return it to the saucepan. Now add the Gorgonzola mixture, Mozzarella and the contents of the frying pan, then return the pan to a low heat and toss everything together very thoroughly for about 1 minute. Give it a good seasoning of freshly milled black pepper and, if it needs it, a touch of salt, then serve very quickly in hot pasta bowls with some Parmesan sprinkled over.

Classic Fresh Tomato Sauce

It was once said that the greatest wines of Montrachet should be drunk kneeling with the head bowed as a sign of reverence. Well, this is how I feel about this very simple, classic sauce which, made with red, ripe, flavoursome tomatoes and served with pasta, absorbs the very essence of the tomatoes' concentrated flavour. It's still the best pasta sauce of all, and it can be made ahead and re-heated (it even freezes well).

First skin the tomatoes. To do this, pour boiling water over them and leave them for exactly 1 minute or, if the tomatoes are small, 15-30 seconds, before draining and slipping off their skins (protect your hands with a cloth if they are too hot). Now reserve 3 of the tomatoes for later and roughly chop the rest.

Next heat the oil in a medium saucepan, then add the onions and garlic and let them gently cook for 5-6 minutes, until they are softened and pale gold in colour. Now add the chopped tomatoes with about a third of the basil, torn into pieces. Add some salt and freshly milled black pepper, then all you do is let the tomatoes simmer on a very low heat, without a lid, for approximately 1½ hours or until almost all the liquid has evaporated and the tomatoes are reduced to a thick, jam-like consistency, stirring now and then. Roughly chop the reserved fresh tomatoes and stir them in, along with the rest of the torn basil leaves, and serve on pasta with a hint of Parmesan – not too much, though, because it will detract from the wonderful tomato flavour.

Note: When serving this sauce, it is a good idea to give the pasta 1 minute less cooking time than you usually would, then return it to the saucepan after draining and give 1 more minute while you mix in the sauce.

Serves 2 -3 (enough for 12 oz/350 g pasta)
2 lb 8 oz (1.15 kg) fresh, red, ripe tomatoes
1 tablespoon olive oil
1 medium onion weighing about 4 oz (110 g), peeled and finely chopped
1 fat clove garlic, peeled and crushed
approximately 12 large leaves fresh basil
a little Parmesan (Parmigiano Reggiano), to serve
salt and freshly milled black pepper

To skin the tomatoes, pour boiling water over them and leave for 1 minute

Now drain the water from the pan and slip off the tomatoes' skins

Add the ingredients to the pan and simmer on a low heat for 1½ hours

After this time, the tomatoes will have reduced to a thick, jam-like consistency

Pasta Vialli

This recipe is my adaptation of one I ate in the famous San Lorenzo Italian restaurant in Knightsbridge, which is apparently a favourite with the Chelsea Football Club players. This particular dish is named after their famous Italian star player and manager Gianluca Vialli.

Serves 2-3

12 oz (350 g) penne rigate
1 quantity Classic Fresh Tomato Sauce
(see page 221)
5 oz (150 g) Mozzarella, chopped into
¾ inch (2 cm) cubes
a little finely grated Parmesan
(Parmigiano Reggiano), to serve
a few whole basil leaves, to garnish

Start this by gently re-heating the tomato sauce and putting the pasta on to cook. When you are almost ready to eat, stir the cubes of Mozzarella into the warm sauce and let it simmer gently for 2-3 minutes, by which time the cheese will have softened and begun to melt but still retain its identity. Serve the sauce spooned over the drained pasta, sprinkle with the Parmesan and add a few fresh basil leaves as a garnish.

Penne with Wild Mushrooms and Crème Fraîche

In the Winter Collection, the Oven-Baked Wild Mushroom Risotto was a huge hit, but all the lovely concentrated mushroom flavour works superbly well with pasta, too. Because the pasta will be returned to the pan for 1 minute, don't forget to give it 1 minute less on the initial cooking time.

First pop the porcini in a small bowl, then heat the milk, pour it over the mushrooms and leave them to soak for 30 minutes. Then heat the butter in a medium frying pan over a gentle heat, stir in the shallots and let them cook gently for 5 minutes. Next, strain the porcini into a sieve lined with kitchen paper, reserving the soaking liquid, and squeeze the porcini dry. Then chop them finely and add them to the pan, along with the fresh mushrooms and the balsamic vinegar. Next, season with salt, pepper and nutmeg. Give it all a good stir, then cook gently, uncovered, for 30-40 minutes, until all the liquid has evaporated.

About 15 minutes before the mushrooms are ready, put the pasta on to cook. Then, 2 minutes before the pasta is cooked, mix the crème fraîche with the mushrooms and the mushroom soaking liquid, and warm through in a small saucepan.

Drain the pasta in a colander, return it to the hot pan and quickly mix in the mushroom mixture, then place the pasta back on a gentle heat so it continues to cook for 1 more minute while it absorbs the sauce. Take it to the table in a hot serving bowl and hand the Parmesan round separately.

Serves 4-6
1 lb 2 oz (500 g) penne rigate
1 lb (450 g) mixed fresh mushrooms (flat, chestnut, shiitake or mixed wild mushrooms, for example), finely chopped
½ oz (10 g) dried porcini mushrooms
9 fl oz (250 ml) crème fraîche
3 tablespoons milk
2 oz (50 g) butter
4 large shallots, peeled and finely chopped
2 tablespoons balsamic vinegar
¼ whole nutmeg, grated
lots of freshly grated Parmesan (Parmigiano Reggiano), to serve
salt and freshly milled black pepper

Meatballs with Spaghetti and Fresh Tomato Sauce

The Americans invented meatballs to go with spaghetti, and there are lots of ground rules, but the main criteria for any meatball is that it should have a kind of melt-in-the-mouth lightness and not be heavy and bouncy. These, I think, are just right.

Serves 4 (makes 24 meatballs)
For the meatballs:
8 oz (225 g) minced pork
1 dessertspoon chopped sage leaves
3½ oz (95 g) mortadella or
unsmoked bacon
2 tablespoons freshly grated Parmesan
(Parmigiano Reggiano)
2 tablespoons chopped fresh
parsley leaves
3 oz (75 g) white bread without crusts,
soaked in 2 tablespoons milk
1 large egg
a little nutmeg
salt and freshly milled black pepper

To cook and serve:
1-2 tablespoons groundnut or other
flavourless oil, for frying
1 lb (450 g) spaghetti
1 quantity Classic Fresh Tomato Sauce
(see page 221)
a little Parmesan (Parmigiano Reggiano)
a few fresh basil leaves

To make the meatballs, all you do is place all the ingredients into the bowl of a food processor and blend everything on a low speed until thoroughly blended. If you don't have a processor, chop everything as finely as possible with a sharp knife and blend it with a fork. Now take walnut-sized pieces of the mixture and shape them into rounds – you should end up with 24 meatballs. Then put them in a large dish or on a tray, cover with clingfilm and chill for about 30 minutes to firm up.

Meanwhile, pre-heat the oven to a low setting. Then, when you are ready to cook the meatballs, heat 1 tablespoon of the oil in a large frying pan and, over a fairly high heat, add 12 meatballs at a time and cook them until they are crispy and brown all over, adding a little more oil as necessary. This will take 4-5 minutes per batch, so as they are cooked, remove them to a plate and keep them warm, covered with foil, in the oven.

Meanwhile, cook the pasta and gently warm the tomato sauce. Then drain the pasta, return it to the pan and toss in the tomato sauce, quickly mix well and then pile it on to plates. Top with the meatballs, sprinkle with some freshly grated Parmesan and finish with a few basil leaves.

Gratin of Rigatoni with Roasted Vegetables

This recipe is another good choice for a supper dish with no meat. Oven-roasted vegetables have a magical, toasted, concentrated flavour, and they keep all their dazzling colours intact. For strict vegetarians, exclude the anchovies.

Start off by preparing the courgettes and aubergine an hour ahead of time: chop them into 1½ inch (4 cm) chunks, leaving the skins on, and layer them in a colander with a sprinkling of salt between each layer. Then put a plate on top and weight it down with something heavy, which will draw out any excess moisture from the vegetables. After an hour, squeeze then dry them in a clean tea cloth, then pre-heat the oven to its highest setting.

Now quarter the tomatoes and chop the onion and peppers into 1½ inch (4 cm) chunks. Next, arrange all the vegetables on the baking tray and sprinkle with the olive oil and chopped garlic. Give everything a good mix to coat all the pieces with the oil, then spread them out as much as possible. Season with salt and freshly milled black pepper, then roast on a high shelf in the oven for 30-40 minutes, until browned and charred at the edges. Meanwhile, put a large pan of water on to boil for the pasta.

About 5 minutes before the vegetables are ready, cook the rigatoni in the boiling water for exactly 6 minutes – no longer. Drain the pasta in a colander, transfer it to a large mixing bowl and combine it with the roasted vegetables, olives, anchovies, capers and the sauce. At this point turn the heat down to gas mark 6, 400°F (200°C), leaving the door open to let it cool down a bit quicker. Now layer the mixture into the gratin dish, a third at a time, sprinkling the Mozzarella over each layer and finishing with Mozzarella. Finally, sprinkle the mixture with the heaped tablespoon of Parmesan. Bake in the oven for another 6 minutes, and serve very hot with just a leafy salad and a sharp dressing to accompany it.

If you want to make this ahead of time, it will need 35-40 minutes in the oven at gas mark 6, 400°F (200°C) to heat it through from cold.

Serves 4
6 oz (175 g) rigatoni
1 heaped tablespoon grated Parmesan
(Parmigiano Reggiano), for the topping
1 pint (570 ml) cheese sauce (as on
page 152, omitting the Cheddar and
using 2 oz (50 g) of Parmesan

For the roasted vegetables:
2 medium courgettes
1 small aubergine
1 lb (450 g) tomatoes, skinned
1 medium onion, peeled
1 small red pepper, deseeded
1 small yellow pepper, deseeded
3 tablespoons extra virgin olive oil
2 cloves garlic, peeled and chopped
2 oz (50 g) pitted black olives, chopped
4 anchovy fillets, drained and chopped
1 heaped tablespoon salted capers or
capers in vinegar, rinsed and drained
2 oz (50 g) Mozzarella, grated
salt and freshly milled black pepper

You will also need an ovenproof baking
dish measuring 10 x 8 x 2 inches
(25.5 x 20 x 5 cm), and a baking tray
measuring 16 x 11 inches (40 x 28 cm).

Spinach and Ricotta Lasagne with Pine Nuts

This recipe is an absolute hit with everyone who eats it – even my husband, who professes not to like spinach! The combination of the four cheeses is its secret, and it is always on my top-10 list if I'm entertaining people who don't eat meat.

Serves 4-6

For the sauce:

1½ pints (850 ml) milk
2 oz (50 g) butter
2 oz (50 g) plain flour
1 bay leaf
2½ oz (60 g) Parmesan (Parmigiano Reggiano), freshly grated
salt and freshly milled black pepper

For the lasagne:

12 fresh lasagne sheets (weighing about 9 oz/250 g)
1 lb 5 oz (600 g) young leaf spinach
8 oz (225 g) Ricotta
2 oz (50 g) pine nuts
knob of butter
¼ whole nutmeg, grated
7 oz (200 g) Gorgonzola Piccante, crumbled
7 oz (200 g) Mozzarella, coarsely grated
salt and freshly milled black pepper

You will also need an ovenproof dish measuring about 9 x 9 inches (23 x 23 cm), 2½ inches (6 cm) deep, well buttered.

Pre-heat the oven to gas mark 4, 350°F (180°C).

Begin this by making the sauce, which can be done using the all-in-one method. This means placing the milk, butter, flour and bay leaf together in a saucepan, giving it a good seasoning, then, over a medium heat, whisking the whole lot together continually until it comes to simmering point and has thickened. Now turn the heat down to its lowest possible setting and allow the sauce to cook gently for 5 minutes. After that, stir in 2 oz (50 g) of the Parmesan, then remove it from the heat, discard the bay leaf and place some clingfilm over the surface to prevent a skin from forming.

Now you need to deal with the spinach. First of all remove and discard the stalks, then wash the leaves really thoroughly in two or three changes of cold water and shake them dry. Next, take your largest saucepan, pop the knob of butter in it, then pile the spinach leaves in on top, sprinkling them with a little salt as you go. Now place the pan over a medium heat, put a lid on and cook the spinach for about 2 minutes, turning the leaves over halfway through. After that, the leaves will have collapsed down and become tender.

Next drain the spinach in a colander and, when it's cool enough to handle, squeeze it in your hands to get rid of every last drop of liquid. Then place it on a chopping board and chop it finely. Now put it into a bowl, add the Ricotta, then approximately 5 fl oz (150 ml) of the sauce. Give it a good seasoning of salt and pepper and add the grated nutmeg. Then mix everything together really thoroughly and, finally, fold in the crumbled Gorgonzola.

Now you need to place a small frying pan over a medium heat, add the pine nuts and dry-fry them for about 1 minute, tossing them around to get them nicely toasted but being careful that they don't burn. Then remove the pan from the heat and assemble the lasagne. To do this, spread a quarter of the sauce into the bottom of the dish and, on top of that, a third of the spinach mixture, followed by a scattering of toasted pine nuts. Now place sheets of pasta on top of this – you may need to tear some of them in half with your hands to make them fit. Now repeat the whole process, this time adding a third of the grated Mozzarella along with the pine nuts, then the lasagne sheets. Repeat again, finishing with a layer of pasta, the rest of the sauce and the remaining Parmesan and Mozzarella. When you are ready to cook the lasagne, place it on the middle shelf of the pre-heated oven and bake for 50-60 minutes, until the top is golden and bubbling. Then remove it from the oven and let it settle for about 10 minutes before serving.

Sicilian Pasta with Roasted Tomatoes and Aubergines

Aubergines, tomatoes and Mozzarella are the classic ingredients of any classic Sicilian sauce for pasta, and roasting the tomatoes and aubergines to get them slightly charred adds an extra flavour dimension.

Serves 2

8 oz (225 g) spaghetti

12 large tomatoes (roughly 2 lb/900 g)

1 large aubergine, cut into 1 inch (2.5 cm) cubes

2 large cloves garlic, peeled and finely chopped

about 4 tablespoons olive oil

12 large basil leaves, torn in half, plus a few extra for garnish

5 oz (150 g) Mozzarella, cut into ½ inch (1 cm) cubes

salt and freshly milled black pepper

You will also need two baking trays measuring 14 x 10 inches (35 x 25.5 cm).

Pre-heat the oven to gas mark 6, 400°F (200°C).

First of all place the aubergine cubes in a colander, sprinkle them with salt and leave them to stand for half an hour, weighed down with something heavy to squeeze out the excess juices.

Meanwhile, skin the tomatoes by pouring boiling water over them and leaving them for 1 minute, then drain off the water and, as soon as they are cool enough to handle, slip off the skins. Cut each tomato in half and place the halves on one of the baking trays (cut-side uppermost), then season with salt and freshly milled black pepper. Sprinkle over the chopped garlic, distributing it evenly between the tomatoes, and follow this with a few drops of olive oil in each one. Top each tomato half with half a basil leaf, turning each piece of leaf over to give it a good coating of oil. Now place the baking tray on the middle shelf of the oven and roast the tomatoes for 50-60 minutes or until the edges are slightly blackened.

Meanwhile, drain the aubergines and squeeze out as much excess juice as possible, then dry them thoroughly with a clean cloth and place them in the other baking tray. Then drizzle 1 tablespoon of the olive oil all over them and place them on the top shelf of the oven, above the tomatoes, giving them half an hour.

Towards the end of the cooking time, cook the pasta. When the tomatoes and aubergines are ready, scrape them, along with all their lovely cooking juices, into a saucepan and place it over a low heat, then add the cubed Mozzarella and stir gently. Now drain the pasta, pile it into a warm bowl, spoon the tomato and aubergine mixture over the top and scatter over a few basil leaves.

Souffléd Macaroni Cheese

I've made many a macaroni cheese in my time, but this, I promise you, is the best ever.

Begin by having all your ingredients weighed out and the cheeses grated. Fill a large saucepan with 4 pints (2.25 litres) of water containing a dessertspoon of salt and put it on the heat to bring it up to the boil. Then, in a small saucepan, melt the butter over a gentle heat, add the onions and let them soften, without browning and uncovered, for 5 minutes. Then add the flour to the pan, stir it in to make a smooth paste, then gradually add the milk, a little at a time, stirring vigorously with a wooden spoon. Then switch to a balloon whisk and keep whisking so you have a smooth sauce. Then add some salt and freshly milled black pepper, as well as the nutmeg, and leave the sauce to cook gently for 5 minutes. After that, turn off the heat and whisk in the Mascarpone and egg yolks, followed by the Gruyère and half the Parmesan.

Next place the baking dish in the oven to heat through, then drop the macaroni into the boiling water and, as soon as the water returns to a simmer, give it 4-6 minutes, until *al dente* (it's going to get a second cooking in the oven). When it has about 1 minute's cooking time left, whisk the egg whites to soft peaks. Drain the pasta in a colander, give it a quick shake to get rid of the water, then tip it back into the pan and stir in the cheese sauce, turning the pasta over in it so it is evenly coated. Then lightly fold in the egg whites, using a cutting and folding movement so as to retain as much air as possible.

Remove the warm dish from the oven, pour the pasta mixture into it, give it a gentle shake to even the top, then scatter the reserved Parmesan over and return the dish to the oven on a high shelf for 12 minutes or until the top is puffy and lightly browned. Serve it, as they say in Italy, *presto pronto*. Note: To make this for four people, just double the ingredients and use a 10 x 8 x 2 inch (25.5 x 20 x 5 cm) dish, increasing the cooking time by 3-5 minutes.

Serves 2 generously

6 oz (175 g) macaroni
1 oz (25 g) butter
1 medium onion (about 4 oz/110 g), peeled and finely chopped
1 oz (25 g) plain flour
10 fl oz (275 ml) milk
¼ whole nutmeg, freshly grated
3 oz (75 g) Mascarpone
2 large egg yolks, lightly beaten
2 oz (50 g) Gruyère, finely grated
2 oz (50 g) Parmesan (Parmigiano Reggiano), finely grated
2 large egg whites
salt and freshly milled black pepper

You will also need a shallow ovenproof baking dish with a base measurement of 8 x 6 inches (20 x 15 cm), 2 inches (5 cm) deep, lightly buttered.

Pre-heat the oven to gas mark 6, 400°F (200°C).

Baked Cannelloni

I have discovered that the best way to make this excellent supper dish is to buy fresh sheets of lasagne that don't need pre-cooking, which are now quite widely available. The filling, conveniently, is the meatball mixture on page 224.

Serves 4

For the filling:
8 fresh lasagne sheets (weighing about 6 oz/175 g)
1 quantity meatball mixture (see page 224)
5 oz (150 g) Mozzarella, diced
1½ oz (40 g) finely grated Parmesan (Parmigiano Reggiano), plus a little extra to serve

For the béchamel sauce:
1 pint (570 ml) milk
2 oz (50 g) butter
1¼ oz (35 g) plain flour
1 bay leaf
good grating of whole nutmeg
2½ fl oz (65 ml) double cream
salt and freshly milled black pepper

You will also need a baking dish with a base measurement of 7 x 9 inches (18 x 23 cm), 2 inches (5 cm) deep, buttered.

Make the sauce first by placing the milk, butter, flour, bay leaf, nutmeg and seasonings into a medium-sized saucepan over a medium heat, then, whisking all the time, slowly bring it up to simmering point until the sauce has thickened. Then turn the heat down to its lowest setting and let the sauce simmer for about 5 minutes, then remove the bay leaf, stir in the cream, taste to check the seasoning, cover and leave aside.

Now pre-heat the oven to gas mark 4, 350°F (180°C), then cut the lasagne sheets in half so that you have 16 pieces. Next divide the meatball mixture in half and then each half into eight, then lightly roll each of these into a sausage shape about 3 inches (7.5 cm) long. Place each one on to a piece of lasagne and roll it up, starting from one of the shorter edges. As you do this, arrange them in the baking dish with the join underneath – what you should have is two rows neatly fitting together lengthways in the dish. Now pour the sauce over and scatter the Mozzarella cubes here and there. Finally, scatter the Parmesan over the top and place the dish on the centre shelf of the oven to bake for 40 minutes, by which time it should be golden brown and bubbling. Then remove it from the oven and let it settle for about 10 minutes before serving. Finally, sprinkle a little extra Parmesan over.

Suppliers and stockists

Mail-order kitchen suppliers in the country are as follows:

Lakeland Ltd
Alexandra Buildings
Windermere
Cumbria
LA23 1BQ

Telephone 015394 88100

David Mellor
4 Sloane Square
London
SW1W 8EE

Telephone 0171-730 4259

Divertimenti
45-47 Wigmore Street
London
W1H 9LE

Telephone 0171-935 0689

Mail-order telephone number
0181-246 4300 (mail-order
catalogue operation is seasonal)

For quality pasta and other Italian ingredients, contact:

Fratelli Camisa Ltd, 53 Charlotte Street, London W1P 1LA, telephone
0171-255 1240, or their mail-order service: Fratelli Camisa Ltd, Unit 3,
Lismirrane Industrial Park, Elstree Road, Elstree, Hertfordshire WD6 3EE,
telephone 0181-207 5919, fax 0181-905 1238.

For information on the availability of equipment or ingredients in this book,
send an sae to: *How To Cook*, 20 Upper Ground, London SE1 9PD.

Index